THE BOOK OF

TOY
MAKING
PAMELA PEAKE

THE BOOK OF
TOY
MAKING

PAMELA PEAKE

DAVID WELLINGS & PAUL COLLINS

EBURY PRESS
LONDON

Published by Ebury Press
Division of The National Magazine Company Ltd
Colquhoun House
27-37 Broadwick St
London W1V 1FR

First impression 1986
Copyright © 1986 The Paul Press Ltd

ISBN 0 85223 580 1 (hardback)
ISBN 0 85223 543 7 (paperback – export only)

Typeset by Wordsmiths, Street, Somerset
Origination by Adroit Photolitho, Birmingham
Printed and bound in Italy by New Interlitho, SpA, Milan

This book was designed and produced by The Paul Press
Ltd, 22 Bruton Street, London W1X 7DA

Contributors Pamela Peake (Consultant, Soft Toys), Paul
Collins (Wooden Toys), David and Frøydis Wellings (Doll's
House), Ann Trudgill (Wooden Toys Paint Finishes), and
W.A. Hinckley (Paddle Boat).

Art Editor Tony Paine
Project Editor Susanne Haines
Editorial Sally MacEachern
Emma Warlow, Moira Taylor
Designer David Ayres
Art Assistant Sarah McDonald
Illustrations Hayward and Martin Ltd
Photography Don Wood

Art Director Stephen McCurdy
Editorial Director Jeremy Harwood
Publishing Director Nigel Perryman

CONTENTS

FOREWORD

Toys are an essential part of growing up; from babyhood onwards, children need toys – not just as things to play with, but as tools to help them to learn more about the world and to aid in their physical and mental development. The next two pages tell you why play is such an important part of child development, so read these through before you start on the chapters devoted to practical toy-making, which form the core of this book.

Project by project, toy by toy, here you will find something to suit the needs of children of all ages. You will also find projects to match your growing toy-making skills. So that you can tackle each and every one of these with confidence in the end result, each of the main chapters – Making Soft Toys, Making Wooden Toys, Making Mixed Media Toys and Making Advanced Toys – starts with an introductory section, outlining the basic principles involved and telling you exactly what items of equipment you will need. When it comes to the toys themselves, you will find specific materials and equipment checklists, together with patterns and templates – all designed to make the task of toy-making really enjoyable.

For, above all, toy-making should be fun. Our hope is that you will find the projects as exciting and stimulating to make as they are to play with. You have a wide variety from which to choose – from cuddly elephants and kangaroos to rag dolls and jigsaws, from swings and a lunar space station to glove and string puppets and a home for a unqiue family of dolls – together with their furniture – whose design will fulfill every child's dreams. There is also a careful balance between indoor and outdoor toys.

Remember, though, that safety is of key importance. All the designs in this book have been devised with this in mind, so it is important that you are equally aware of potential danger, especially when it comes to the business of sewing on eyes, as in the case of some of the soft toys, or painting on decoration. If you are in any doubt at all about the suitability of a material you plan to use, check with your supplier before purchasing it.

INTRODUCTION

Play is a vital aspect of childhood, since it is through this that children learn about themselves and the world around them. It is an essential preparation for life, so you should appreciate its very real importance and provide your youngsters with every opportunity to express themselves in as many different ways as possible through it.

Children need to be able to play quietly as well as exuberantly; inside the home as well as outdoors; to combine freedom with organized games and other such activities; and to play with unstructured materials, such as paints, sand and water, as well as with purpose-built toys. As a parent, you must recognize when it is time to join in, so helping your children to enjoy new experiences and activities to the full, but also when to stand back and simply keep a watchful eye on the proceedings.

Stages of play
Children pass through clearly recognizable stages of play; these stages are related to their physical and mental development. Specific toys are similarly appropriate to these various stages. But, though you will find that toy manufacturers often recommend certain toys as suitable for particular age groups, you should realize that not all children develop at the same rate. One child, for instance, may be in advance of his or her years; another may be mentally developed, but have poor physical co-ordination; and a few children may never be able to develop beyond a certain point at all.

A good toy is one that suits a particular child at a particular time. It should take into account the age, temperament and sex of the child, as well as the stage of mental and physical development. It should be fun to play with and, above all, safe.

The tools of play
Toys are the tools of play. To a youngster, a toy may be something as transient as a paper dart, or an empty shoe box; it could be an improvised drum set, consisting of a pot and a wooden spoon; or it could be a craftsman-designed and made Noah's Ark or fully furnished doll's house. Each of these will give a child pleasure in its own way, for it is a fact that children are seemingly unconcerned as to whether their toys are the best that money can buy, or designed by experts and recommended by educationalists and psychologists! As far as children are concerned, toys work if they fulfill a purpose and are enjoyable. Consequently, such toys encourage children to learn through play; undoubtedly, children learn best when learning is fun.

Your child's first toys
During the first months of life, all learning comes through stimulation of the senses – sight, hearing, touch, taste and smell. Babies need to be played with, cuddled and talked to; it is as yet too early for the majority of toys. As they grow older and become more aware of their surroundings, however, they should be given new experiences, which is where toys have a vital part to play.

Take something as simple as a mobile for instance. Babies can derive hours of pleasure from simply looking at one of these as they lie on their backs in a cot. You can tie a string of toys across the cot as well, so encouraging little fingers to reach out and touch. Then there are rattles to grasp and shake, too. This is the time to introduce your child to small clutch toys. Not only do clutch toys have interesting surfaces and textures to explore – they will undoubtedly find their way to the mouth, so they must be washable and super-safe.

When movement begins
Once babies are sitting up and crawling around, they are ready for a whole new range of toys. Now, you can introduce them to lightweight balls, which help them to develop hand and eye co-ordination. Push-and-pull toys that move across the floor also encourage a child to learn how to use its limbs, while a baby walker provides invaluable body support during these early walking days – that is, before it becomes a trolley, or pretend wheelbarrow!

In broad terms, toys at this stage of life are generally designed to help your child control bodily movement and thus aid physical development. At the same time, stacking toys, building bricks, musical toys, and simple jigsaws will aid the development of intellectual skills by stimulating the brain and encouraging the child to experiment and think. Toys your child can play with in the bath will help to overcome any fear of water and promote a sense of security, so aiding the development of stable emotions. Likewise, encouraging a child to cuddle up with a soft toy at night is helpful if your child is afraid of the dark, or of being left alone. Soft toys are friends – in some cases, this means for life. After all, there are adults who still retain an attachment to their childhood teddy bear!

Group play
Once children are fully mobile, they will be in a position to play with others and starting to share their

experiences. This kind of play aids the development of social skills, which are so important when it comes to understanding and relating to others. However, having said this, in reality it is still not easy for two-year-olds to share either their parents or their toys. In both instances, they are fiercely possessive. They need to be really emotionally secure to understand that toys can be loaned, will be returned and that parents can talk to other children and be shared.

It is important to realize that physical, intellectual, emotional and social skills are all closely linked. They simply do not develop separately, and playing, almost by definition, involves more than one of them. Here, time is on your side. So-called 'difficult' children need more time to develop, so you should not be in a hurry to rush children ahead of their natural development rate.

Stretching the imagination

From about three years and onwards children mix together more amicably and enjoy learning together. This is the great play period, when all the basic skills are being mastered and much exploration and experimentation is going on. Language and the ability to communicate are both improving quickly as well.

This is the time for make-believe and pretend, when children will spend endless hours imitating the activities that they see happening around them. It is a time of role playing, when toys will be used to represent objects and situations in the adult world. Above all, it is a time for imagination – to make a cardboard carton become a boat, house, castle or bed, for instance.

Playing with dolls and pretending to be mother is a typical make-believe game, while dressing a doll provides a child with a less obvious way of practising finger dexterity. Soon, children will want to dress up themselves and act out their chosen roles completely.

From home to school

At school, work and play gradually merge, until play becomes a recreational activity, something done in a child's spare time. Games become more important – they are generally structured with rules, as well as being competitive. Children are thus required to learn how to win and lose graciously.

Many of these games are centred around balls, thus bringing the story full circle. A ball, one of a baby's first toys, follows a child through life. Who knows, that child may become a star football or golf player!

Safety first!

Ensuring children's safety while they are playing should be of paramount importance to caring adults. Between them, toys and the play environment can present all manner of potential hazards. Consequently, all the obvious precautions and safeguards must be taken. Fortunately, outrightly dangerous toys are rare today, given the legal crack-down on toy safety.

Some hazards are obvious and therefore more easily overcome. Toys your child may chew or suck must not use any poisonous elements in their manufacture. Paints must be lead-free. There should be no sharp edges or points on, or in, toys. Surfaces should be smooth and free from splinters, nail heads or screws standing proud.

Attachments such as eyes and noses on cuddly dolls and animals must be securely fixed, so that they cannot be pulled out in normal play conditions. Otherwise the danger is that they could be swallowed, or, even worse, pushed up a nostril or into an ear.

Toys that can be sat upon must be stable, as well as strong enough to support a child's weight. Houses, tents, wigwams and suchlike should also stand securely; they must open from the inside as well as the outside and they must be ventilated.

Watch out for long strings that could become entangled around a youngster; equally, make sure that kites are flown well away from overhead wires.

Toy abuse

Despite all these safeguards, there are still accidents every year that involve toys. Some are caused by badly made toys and are the result of carelessness on the part of the maker. But undoubtedly most accidents are caused by toy misuse – that is, toys being played with by children for whom they were not intended, or being played with in the wrong way. Here, the responsibility lies with the person supervising.

The message is quite clear. It is essential for adults to choose toys carefully, making sure that they match the individual child's level of physical and mental development. This vigilance must be continuous, for toys must be maintained, kept clean and in a good state of repair. It also follows that toys must not fall into the wrong hands.

Children, toys and play are thus an inseparable mix. The early years of growing up are so important that we owe it to our children to enrich this period of their lives by providing them with a wide variety of carefully chosen toys with which they can play. The following sections of this book provide all the classics you will need to start you on your way.

MAKING
SOFT TOYS

No special skills are required to make soft toys – even knowledge of simple sewing procedures, though helpful, is unnecessary if you read the general instructions given here. Indeed you will discover that with little more than scissors, needle, thread and a handful of colourful fabrics you can make a simple, hand sewn ball for a baby. The projects are graded – beginning with the simple clutch toys, they gradually increase in complexity, culminating in instructions to make a fully jointed teddy bear.

Tools and equipment

1. Scissors *A selection of sharp scissors is essential: dressmaking shears for cutting fabrics, embroidery scissors for working with threads and trimming fur, a pair for cutting paper and card.* **2. Quick unpick-it** *Useful for removing wrongly positioned seams and embroidered facial features.* **3. Pins** *Avoid using pins whenever possible to lessen the danger of leaving any behind in a toy. Coloured glass-headed pins are easier to see.* **Awl** *Used for making holes in fur fabrics for eye*

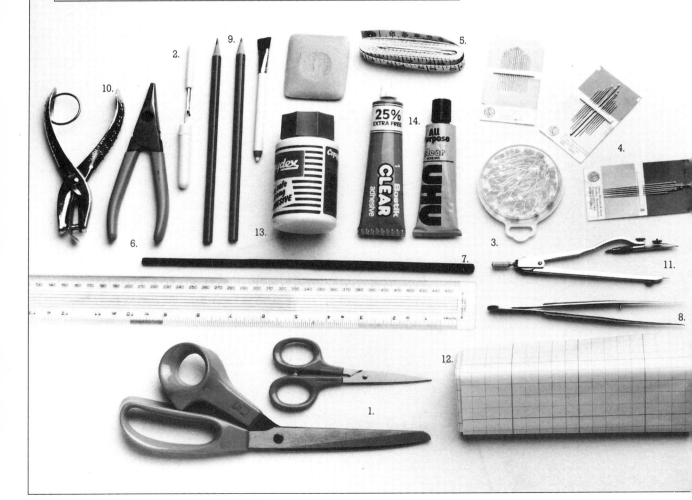

shanks and joints. A knitting needle or the closed points of embroidery scissors can also be used. **4. Needles** *A selection of hand sewing needles for seaming, embroidery and tacking. Darning needles are used for needle modelling and when sewing on ears and tails with strong thread. Darning needles are also used when embroidering with tapestry thread or six-stranded embroidery cotton.* **Sewing machine** *Useful for speedy sewing but not essential. Use a strong needle when sewing thick fabrics.* **5. Measures** *Either tape measures or rulers can be used for measuring fabric. Use a ruler to copy patterns.* **6. Pliers** *Long-nosed electrician's pliers are used for bending cotter pins when making crown joints.* **Wire cutters** *Useful for cutting the metal washers when removing wrongly positioned safety eyes.* **7. Chopsticks** *Used for packing the stuffing into limbs. There are many alternatives, such as dowel rod, pencils, and rulers.* **8. Forceps and pincers** *Invaluable for inserting wisps of stuffing into extremities.* **9. Pencils** *Soft lead pencils (2B) are needed for preparing patterns and for transferring them to the wrong side of the fabric. Use yellow or white crayons or chalk on dark coloured furs. Avoid using felt tip pens and ball point pens as these bleed into the fabric.* **10. Paper punch** *A single-hole paper punch can be used to punch holes for eye shanks in interfacing and felt.* **Card** *Use thin card to make full-size patterns, or templates. These can then be drawn around, so that pins do not have to be used with paper patterns.* **11. Compasses** *Essential for drawing circles accurately. There are many alternatives to be found in the kitchen, such as egg cups and plates.* **12. Dressmaker's graph paper** *These ready-prepared grids are usually ruled with 5cm (2in) squares. To adapt one for use with the soft toy patterns you will have to rule in lines to make 25mm (1in) squares (see p.12).* **13. Rubber latex glue** *Used for sticking tracing paper onto card and for glueing felt and wool to fabrics.* **14. Fabric glue** *Use a brand that bonds felt to fabric and dries clear.*

Threads

A variety of threads are needed for soft toymaking. Choose the correct quality and match the colour carefully.

Sewing threads In general a natural cotton thread should be used with natural fabrics when seaming and an artificial thread should be used with man-made fabrics. Tacking can be done with a weaker thread, since it is usually temporary sewing. If an overcasting tacking stitch is to be left in place in fur fabric toys, use the same thread as that used for seaming.

Strong thread Strong threads, such as carpet thread, button thread, upholstery thread or even crochet cotton must be used to attach the parts of the toy that are sewn onto the outside of the body, so that these parts can withstand the pulling and tugging that they will receive during play. General sewing thread is not strong enough. Strong thread should be used to close all stuffing openings with ladder stitch. Bracing stitches (such as those used for the elephant, see p.27), are worked with strong thread, as are the stitches used for knee hinges for the rag doll. Choose a natural coloured thread.

Embroidery threads Six-stranded embroidery cottons are used to work facial features on the animals and the rag doll. Any number of threads can be used. For instance, a nose will require all six strands, an eye three strands. Interesting effects can be obtained by mixing strands of different shades, particularly effective for areas such as the iris of the eye.

Tapestry thread Dark brown and black tapestry thread can be used for working satin stitch noses on large bears. Persian yarn can be used as an alternative.

Invisible nylon thread This is ideal for working fine whiskers on animals.

Thicker whiskers can be worked using different grades of nylon fishing line.

Fabrics

All the animals have been made of fur fabrics, while the body of the rag doll is made from a firm woven fabric. The clothes for the doll and the animals are all made from dress-weight cottons. Other fabrics are needed in smaller quantities.

Fur fabrics These man-made furs offer a wonderful choice of colour, pattern and quality for the toymaker. They are usually made in widths of 140cm (54in) although shops will often precut the roll (or bolt) into smaller pieces that are easier to handle. The amount that you need to make each toy has been carefully calculated and is given in the list of materials. The most important measurement is the length, along which the pile of the fabric lies.

A good quality fur has a thick pile that covers the knitted backing. The backing should not be visible when the pile is flattened. A toy made from poor fabric will have bald seams, thus spoiling the appearance. Pile varies in length and in density. Thus a dense, short pile has the texture of a rich velvet, while a long, medium-dense pile makes wonderful fur for teddy bears. The fabric can be polished to give the fur a lovely sheen. Each toy has been designed with a specific fur in mind, consequently the finished appearance will not be the same if a different choice is made.

Interfacing This is a useful sewing aid for adding weight to lightweight fabrics, for strengthening weak felt and for protecting the edges of holes made for safety eyes and joints in fur fabrics. There are two basic interfacings: a sew-in variety and a fusible, iron-on variety. Follow carefully the manufacturer's instructions. Always test iron-on interfacings on a scrap of fabric first, particularly if using fur fabric. Press lightly through a damp cloth rather than using a back and forth ironing action to avoid flattening the pile.

It is advisable to use interfacing to back pieces made of felt, such as paws and beaks. It helps to protect the felt from splitting when the toy is stuffed and it also bonds the felt, which will protect it if the toy must be washed.

Calico This is a firm, woven cotton fabric that is ideally suited to making rag dolls. It is readily available in different qualities. Choose lighter weights for small dolls and firm weights for very large dolls. Alternative fabrics are any skin-coloured firm woven cottons such as denim, poplin or lawn. Some curtain linings are also very useful for dollmaking.

Dress-weight cottons When making clothes for your toys, choose fabrics that drape well, are not too stiff and have attractive, small prints, such as cotton lawn or poplin. The fabrics should be easy to wash and iron.

Velvet, Velveteen and Velours
These short-pile fabrics are good alternatives to felt when making paws and feet. These fabrics have the advantage of not needing to be strengthened with interfacing, and they are easy to wash. Knitted velours is a stretch fabric, which makes it ideal for combining with fur fabrics.

Felt A very popular craft material much used by toymakers to make small animals. Its attractions are the great variety of colour, ready availability all year round (velvet can be hard to find in the shops in the summer), and non-fraying edges. Felt is a non-woven fabric made from

MAKING A PATTERN

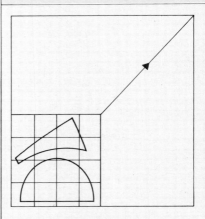
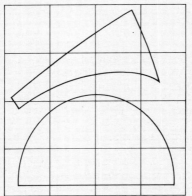

Pattern-making equipment
You will need: large sheet of paper (or dressmaker's graph paper), tracing paper, card, glue, paper scissors, ruler and a pencil.

Enlarging a pattern grid
The patterns are given at half size, with each square of the grid representing a 25mm (1in) square at full size. The basic grid should be enlarged as a reusable master grid. To do this, rule up a large sheet of paper accurately with ruler and set square into a grid of 25mm (1in) squares. Check that you have the correct number of squares. Dressmaker's graph paper (see p.11) makes the job easier.
Transferring the pattern *Lay a piece of tracing paper over the master grid, place*

the book next to it and transfer the outline of the pattern, square by square. Care at this stage will pay off with pattern pieces that fit together comfortably. Cut out the pattern pieces and glue the tracing to the card. When dry cut out the card. For some symmetrical pattern pieces only one half is shown. This is indicated by a note to 'place on fold'. To make a full-size template of this piece, simply transfer the enlarged pattern to a folded piece of paper, cut out, and you will have your full-size pattern pieces, ready to glue onto card.
Photocopying *If you have access to a photocopying machine that enlarges, then your work is over. Simply have the grid or pattern enlarged to twice its size.*

fibres either matted together by heat, moisture and pressure, or by artificial means such as an adhesive. There are different qualities, slipper felt being far too thick for general toymaking. Remember that felt can tear apart because it is not a woven fabric, and that washing can destroy the bonding of weaker felts.

Muslin An open weave muslin used in toymaking to wrap noise units in so that they can be stitched to the inside skin of a toy.

Stuffing materials
Materials used for stuffing toys should be clean and hygenic, free from dirt and any foreign particles. There are several to choose from that meet these requirements,

including polyester fibre, kapok, acrylic fibre, foam chips and waste fabric.

Polyester fibre is the most popular of all present day stuffing materials and is used for all the toys in the book. It is readily available, lightweight and meets all the other requirements of a good stuffing material. It comes in various qualities, all of which are white, making it especially useful for fur animals and rag dolls made from pale fabrics.

Making pattern templates
No special skills are needed for making the patterns for these soft toys. However, it is important to measure and copy very accurately.

Whilst dressmakers use ready-printed patterns on tissue paper, toymakers generally make a copy of a pattern on card so that it can be used several times. In addition, a card pattern can be used as a template, eliminating the need to use pins.

You will find pattern instructions given in two different ways:
1. Some very simple shapes, such as the petticoat for the rag doll are given as measurements in the text. These should be ruled directly onto a piece of card.
2. All of the patterns for the animals, the rag doll and for some of the clothes have been reduced to half size for reasons of space. You will have to enlarge them in order to make a toy that fits the measurements and materials given in the instructions. Note also that many of the pattern pieces overlap each other or are superimposed one on top of another on the grid. Make sure that you follow the correct outline for each piece when enlarging and transfer the matching set of markings for each.

Pattern layouts

The amount of fabric required is given in the list of materials for each toy. Always lay out the pieces first, finding the best arrangement before you mark the fabric and cut.

Layouts are done on the wrong side of the fabric and are determined by the nap of fur fabrics (the direction in which the fur lies), and the straight grain of cotton fabrics (parallel to the selvage edge) which is marked on the pattern with an arrow.

To determine the nap of fur fabric, stroke the fur and mark the direction in which it lies with an arrow on the wrong side of the fabric. Arrange the fur on the cutting surface so that the

wrong side is uppermost and the nap runs towards you from top to bottom. Arrange the pattern templates, matching the arrows with the direction of the nap.

Use the selvage edge as the guide for the direction of the arrows when cutting cotton fabrics. Felt does not have a grain, therefore pattern pieces are not marked with an arrow.

Lay out the longest pieces first, followed by the largest and lastly the smallest. Check that you allow for the correct total number of pattern pieces.

Take care to differ between cutting two and cutting a pair. Cut two means cut two exactly the same. Cut a pair means cut a right and a left sided piece. To cut a pair, draw around the pattern template, then turn it over and draw around it again for the second piece. You may wish to cut a separate template for every piece that you need to cut, which will help you to plan your cutting layout.

Cutting out

When you are satisfied with your layout you can mark around the edge of the template. Use a soft pencil held vertically and close in to the edge. Use a light coloured crayon or chalk for dark fabrics, and do not use biro or felt tip pens. Keep the pencil sharpened or it will affect the thickness of your line and thus the size of your pattern. It is more accurate to cut just inside the line. Correct any mistakes in a different coloured pencil to show up the correct outline.

Use your sharp dressmaking shears for cutting out and always cut on a firm surface so that your scissors rest against the surface. Fur fabric needs care if you are not to destroy the pile. To avoid bare seams, slide the scissors between the pile and

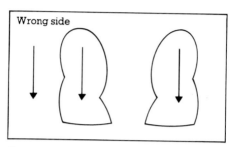

Pattern pieces arranged to cut a pair (ie a left and a right).

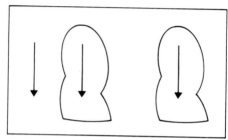

Pattern pieces arranged to cut two pieces the same.

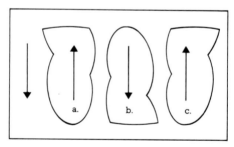

Example of an incorrect layout – a and c are a pair, but the nap lies in the wrong direction; b is placed correctly.

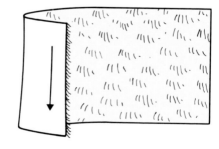

The arrow indicates the direction of the nap on fur fabric.

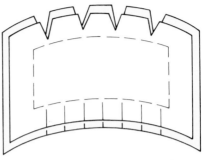

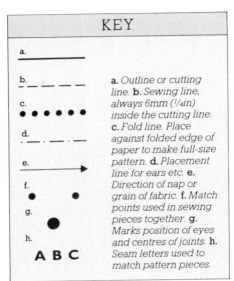

KEY	
a. ————	**a.** *Outline or cutting line.* **b.** *Sewing line, always 6mm (¼in) inside the cutting line.* **c.** *Fold line. Place against folded edge of paper to make full-size pattern.* **d.** *Placement line for ears etc.* **e.** *Direction of nap or grain of fabric.* **f.** *Match points used in sewing pieces together.* **g.** *Marks position of eyes and centres of joints.* **h.** *Seam letters used to match pattern pieces.*
b. – – – –	
c. ● ● ● ● ●	
d. – · – · –	
e. ——→	
f. ● ●	
g. ●	
h.	
A B C	

To ease curved seams, clip the inside curves and remove notches from the outside curves.

only cut through the backing.

Now transfer the instructions from the pattern template onto the fabric. There are several ways that this can be done:

1. Insert dressmaker's carbon paper between the template and the fabric, then trace over the placement lines with a tracing wheel and press firmly on the pattern with a pencil to mark the dots.

2. Make small holes in your pattern template and then use a pointed pencil to spot the marks onto the wrong side of the fabric. These same pencil marks can then be made more visible by sewing a tailor's tack on the spot, using coloured thread.

It is not necessary to transfer the sewing line if you can sew accurately 6mm (¼in) in from the edge.

Sewing

The sequence of sewing a toy together is given in detail with each particular set of instructions, but it is important to know the basic methods of working that are common to all the toys.

In general, pieces are sewn on the wrong side, with the right sides together. Tacking, or basting, is used to hold fabric together temporarily,

preparatory to sewing. When instructions tell you to tack it will usually mean overcast for a fur fabric and running stitch for non-pile fabrics. Sewing of seams may be by hand, using backstitch, or by machine, using straight stitch.

Darts are made first and then the parts of the body are assembled.

Openings for stuffing are left in inconspicuous seams wherever possible or in places that will be covered by another part of the body.

Before stuffing, the completed skin should be checked for seam strength and clipped at the corners and along the curves as shown.

Construction stitches

1. Running stitch The simplest of all the stitches. It is generally a small, regular stitch used for seams or joining edges when strength is not important. It is also used for gathering in fullness and in this instance is usually worked as two rows. A long running stitch is used for tacking to hold edges together ready for sewing firmly by machine or hand, and it is always removed once the seaming is finished.

2. Overcasting This is a slanting stitch used by dressmakers when neatening the raw edges of darts and seams. Soft toymakers use overcasting for a different purpose and always work it from left to right. It is used as a tacking stitch in place of running stitch when holding two or more fur fabric pieces together prior to seaming. The stitch enables the

fur pile to be tucked in as the stitches are made. It can be left in place permanently as it is not in the way of the seam.

Take the needle over the edge of the fabric and insert beneath the edge, about 6mm (¼in) to the right. Pull through and repeat. Continue working along the edge in this way, tucking in the pile as you go.

3. Backstitch Used for sewing seams by hand, worked from right to left. Bring the needle up 3mm (⅛in) beyond the start of the seam. Go back to insert the needle at the start of the seam, taking a stitch that emerges 3mm (⅛in) beyond the start at which it emerged. Take the needle back to meet the first stitch and continue. Backstitches worked one on top of another are also used to secure a row of stitching.

4. Stab stitch Similar to running stitch in appearance, but worked in an up and down movement, one stitch at a time.

5. Hemming There are several stitches that can be used for hemming. The most useful is slipstitch. It is worked from right to left, taking a small stitch from the main part of the fabric and passing into the hem and along the fold for 6mm (¼in) before taking another small stitch.

6. Ladder stitch An ideal stitch for closing openings, attaching parts and bracing limbs because it is invisible. It is simply a running stitch worked on the surface. Always use strong thread. Secure the thread with backstitches in the seam allowance, then take the needle across the opening to the seam line on the other side; take a small running stitch, then pass it directly across the opening to the seam line on the opposite side, and repeat. Make several stitches and then pull up the thread, encouraging the raw

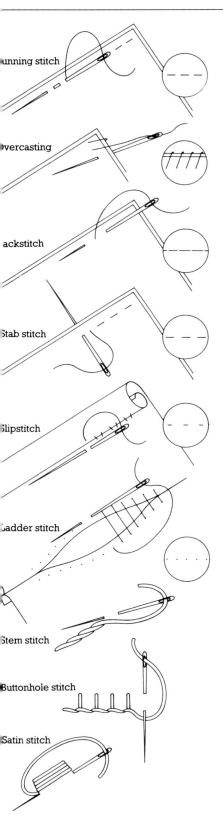

Running stitch

Overcasting

Backstitch

Stab stitch

Slipstitch

Ladder stitch

Stem stitch

Buttonhole stitch

Satin stitch

edges of the opening to roll in, out of sight. For extra strength, work another row of ladder stitch along the seam line in between the existing stitches.

Decorative stitches

1. Stem stitch An outline stitch ideal for facial features. Bring the needle up at a starting point on the left side. Insert the needle a short distance ahead and emerge halfway between the two points. Continue in this way, always making stitches of the same length and keeping the thread either above or below the needle when working.

2. Satin stitch Straight stitches, worked closely side by side with no fabric visible between them.

3. Buttonhole stitch This stitch has the appearance of straight stitches with a rope edge connecting them all together. It is ideal for embroidering the irises of the rag doll, where it radiates from the centre to form a circle. Bring the needle up on the outline of the eye then insert it into the inside of circle and take a small straight stitch to emerge on the line again with the thread looped under the needle as in the diagram. Continue in this way until the circle is completely covered with buttonhole stitch.

Facial features

Treatment of the facial features will determine the character of the toy. Use the markings on the pattern as a guideline only. All the features can be embroidered.

Safety eyes These commercially made bright plastic eyes are designed so that children are not able to pull them out of the toy. They are attached before the toy is stuffed. Make a hole in the fur with an awl, then push the shank through from the right side to the inside of the toy.

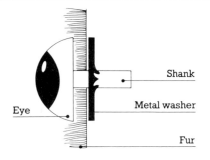

Safety eye in place. The shank is pushed through the fur fabric and held in place with a washer.

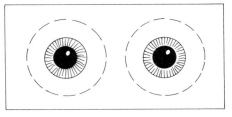

Eyes embroidered on interfacing. They are cut out along the dotted line. Gathering stitches are worked around the edge and pulled tight behind the eye.

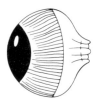

Now level the washer on the shank and using finger pressure only, push the washer in place. Make sure that the teeth on the washer are facing away from the back of the eye when you position it. Wrongly inserted washers can only be removed by cutting them away with wire cutters.

Embroidered eyes for animals

These eyes are perfect for toys for very young children where safety is of paramount importance. Draw circles of the required size onto a piece of firm interfacing. Embroider the irises with satin stitch first, then the pupils. Lastly work a few stitches in white to represent the highlights. Now cut out the eyes from interfacing, leaving a border as shown. Gather around the edge of the interfacing and pull up a thread

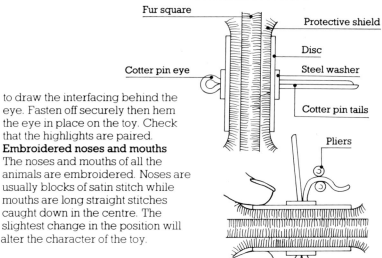

Assembling a crown joint

Fur square

Protective shield

Disc

Cotter pin eye

Steel washer

Cotter pin tails

Pliers

Use the pliers to bend the tail over so that it forms a loop and comes to rest on the disc.

A finished crown joint.

to draw the interfacing behind the eye. Fasten off securely then hem the eye in place on the toy. Check that the highlights are paired.

Embroidered noses and mouths
The noses and mouths of all the animals are embroidered. Noses are usually blocks of satin stitch while mouths are long straight stitches caught down in the centre. The slightest change in the position will alter the character of the toy.

Jointing
Joints allow parts of a body, like the head and limbs, to pivot around a central axis, and for selected positions to be held. They are quite unlike the stitched-hinge joints where limbs only move backwards and forwards and always return to a set position. To be successful, joints must be really tight – in fact so tight to begin with that they are difficult to move. The components for the joints are sold in sets. There are plastic safety joints available which are easy to assemble, but the size range is restricted, and they are not of such good quality as those made with hardboard or wooden discs, the type used for the jointed teddy described in this book.

Assembling a crown joint
Joints are available in several sizes, ranging from 12mm (½in) to 15cm (6in) in diameter. They are always referred to by imperial measurements. They consist of two steel washers. two discs and a split cotter pin. The whole joint is locked in place by the cotter pin.

There is an art in making a firm joint, so it is worth practising before working on the toy. You will need a 2in joint, an awl, long-nosed pliers and a piece of fur.
1. Cut the fur fabric into four pieces – two 15cm- (6in)-squares (to represent the skin of the limb and

the body wall) and two 7.5cm- (3in)-diameter circles. The circles will act as shields to protect the skin from the abrasive action of the discs turning.
2. Use the awl to pierce a hole through the centre of each square and circle. The hole should be just large enough to take the cotter pin. Protect or strengthen the hole with buttonhole stitch, a felt patch glued in place or a piece of iron-on interfacing.
3. Dismantle the joint into separate pieces and reassemble it with the fur fabric positioned between the discs. Do this by holding the eye of the cotter pin in your left hand and load on first a steel washer then a disc with the smooth side upwards, a protective shield and a fur square with the pile facing upwards, the second fur square and the second

protective shield with the pile facing downwards, the second disc with smooth side downwards, and lastly a steel washer.
4. Press the discs together between the forefinger and thumb of the left hand. Spread the pins of the cotter apart, getting ready for the joining action.
5. Slide the tips of the pliers down the longest tail of the pin until they rest 12mm (½in) above the disc and grip firmly. Whilst maintaining the pressure of your left hand, holding all the parts together, use the pliers to bend the tail over so that it forms a loop and comes to rest on the disc.
6. Turn the sample around and form a loop in the same way with the second cotter tail. While bending the tails, you should be holding the joint firmly together as well as pulling up hard on the cotter tails.
7. Test the firmness of the joint by pulling on the fur squares. If the joint is not tight enough for your liking there are two things that you might try. Firstly, insert the pliers back in each loop, in turn, and twist down closer towards the disc. Secondly pull each loop in turn, out and away from its mate. If both these efforts fail, remove the cotter pin and start again. The cotter pin will have to be replaced when reusing the joint for a toy.

Squeaks and growls
Most of the devices used to produce sound effects are inserted into the body when the stuffing is nearly complete. They are held in place with a few stitches worked at the same time as you close the stuffing opening. In order to do this you must first wrap the chime or growler in muslin, or make a close-fitting muslin bag to fit over it. Push the unit into the body, with the unit positioned so

that the holes of the cylinder or the hole for a winding key lies against the fur skin. Pack the stuffing closely around the unit then close the opening, catching the muslin cover into the seam.

Most music boxes have a protruding shank into which a key fits. Remove the key, cover the box and push the shank through a hole in the muslin. The shank will protrude through the body wall as you close the opening. Screw on the winding key.

Bells can be tied on ribbons around the neck of a toy. However, if the toy is intended for a very young child it is much safer to insert the bell in an empty ear. In this way the bell can be heard without being muffled by the stuffing and the chance of the bell being torn off and swallowed is removed.

Finishing touches
Grooming Check over all the seam lines to see that no fur is trapped. Use a suede brush or a needle held horizontally in your fingers to tease out any trapped fur. Particular care is needed at the tip of ears and around curved seams. If longer pile furs have been used you may want to trim fur away from the eyes. Trimming is best done with small embroidery scissors, snipping little bits at a time, cutting with the pile, rather than against it.
Bracing Occasionally limbs tend to splay out, and upset the balance of a toy. Push the offending limbs into the desired position and hold them there by working a row of ladder stitch between the limb and the body.
Tying a bow There is an art in tying an attractive bow and for this reason it is well worth practising. Do a trial run by holding a milk bottle between your knees and pretending that it is a neck!

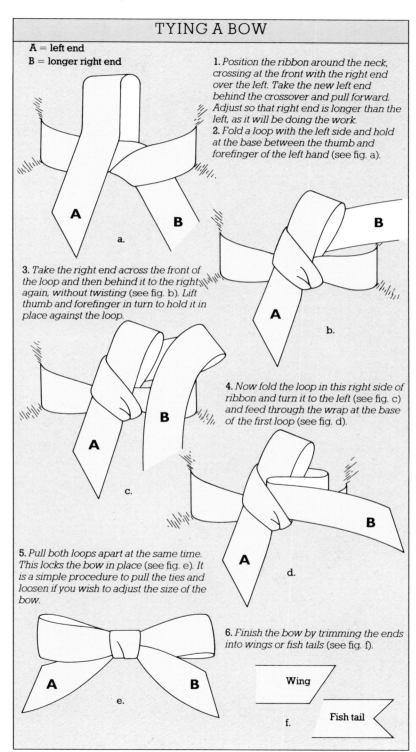

TYING A BOW

A = left end
B = longer right end

1. *Position the ribbon around the neck, crossing at the front with the right end over the left. Take the new left end behind the crossover and pull forward. Adjust so that right end is longer than the left, as it will be doing the work.*
2. *Fold a loop with the left side and hold at the base between the thumb and forefinger of the left hand (see fig. a).*

3. *Take the right end across the front of the loop and then behind it to the right again, without twisting (see fig. b). Lift thumb and forefinger in turn to hold it in place against the loop.*

4. *Now fold the loop in this right side of ribbon and turn it to the left (see fig. c) and feed through the wrap at the base of the first loop (see fig. d).*

5. *Pull both loops apart at the same time. This locks the bow in place (see fig. e). It is a simple procedure to pull the ties and loosen if you wish to adjust the size of the bow.*

6. *Finish the bow by trimming the ends into wings or fish tails (see fig. f).*

Wing

Fish tail

MAKING
SIMPLE CLUTCH TOYS

Feel and touch are among the first senses that very young children develop, so a set of clutch toys is an ideal introduction to the world of play. All such toys should have the following qualities in common; they should be small, lightweight, soft, easy to grasp, washable and safe. Whenever possible, they should also contain an element of surprise – a squeaker is hidden in the teddy bear's tummy, for instance.

Balls are always firm favourites, as they stimulate children in many different ways. Here, there are patterns for balls of different sizes, weights, textures and colour – balls which your child can knock and roll to hear chimes, balls to reach out for in basic catch games, balls to kick and a puzzle ball for young fingers to explore. All the patterns are easy to follow and require a minimum of equipment and materials.

SOFT BALL
Preparing the pattern
This is a simple ball, consisting of just two segments. Its circumference is 32cm (12½in). Make a full-size pattern from the grid on a piece of card and transfer the markings (see p.12). Cut two pieces; one in each colour.

Making the ball
1. Pin the segments together, matching the centres of the outside curves (A), of one segment to the centres of the inside curves (B), of the other segment (see fig. a). Continue pinning between these centres.

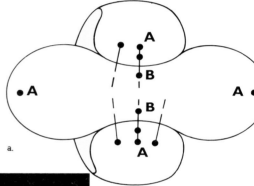

a.

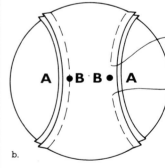

b.

2. Stitch all around to make a continuous seam, leaving a small opening on one side (see fig. b). Remove the pins.
3. Turn the ball right side out and stuff lightly, but using enough material to hold the shape. Close the opening with ladder stitch.

From left to right: the chime ball, soft ball, puzzle ball, nursery teddy and the patchwork ball.

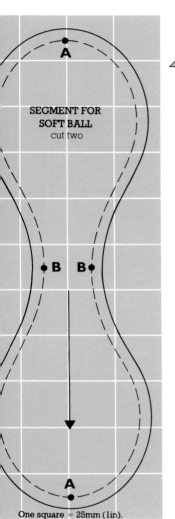

SEGMENT FOR
SOFT BALL
cut two

A

B B

A

One square = 25mm (1in).

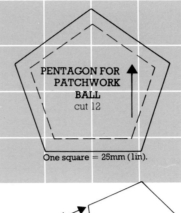

PENTAGON FOR
PATCHWORK
BALL
cut 12

One square = 25mm (1in).

The different patterning on the pentagon pieces represents different coloured fabrics. Arrange the pieces following this plan. The arrows indicate the edges to be joined.

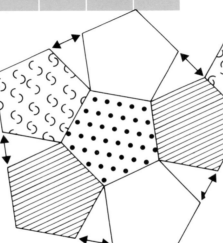

MATERIALS

Soft ball
2   15 x 30.5cm (6 x 12in) pieces of short-pile fur fabric in different colours
56g (2oz) stuffing

Patchwork ball
12   10cm (4in) square pieces of short-pile fur fabric in 4 different colours
84g (3oz) stuffing

EQUIPMENT

Dressmaking shears, pins, needles, thread, tape measure or ruler, pencil, pattern-making equipment.

PATCHWORK BALL
Preparing the pattern
Make a full-size pattern of the pentagon shape on card (see p.12). Use the pattern to cut three pentagons in each colour, making a total of 12 pieces. The finished ball measures 38cm (15in) in circumference.

Making the ball
Join all pieces with right sides together by hand sewing with a firm backstitch along the seam line.
1. Take one of the pieces and sew one edge of five other pieces to each of the five sides as shown. Now sew the adjacent edges of the pentagons together to complete one half of the ball.
2. Repeat this process with the remaining six pentagons to make the other half of the ball. By following the diagram, which shows all the pentagons laid out flat, you will be able to arrange the different colour patches so that they are evenly distributed over the ball.
3. Slip one half of the ball inside the other, with right sides together, making sure that they are correctly positioned. Sew together around the midline leaving two edges free. Turn right side out through this opening and stuff, taking care to form a firm, rounded shape. Close the opening with ladder stitch and remove any trapped fur from the seams.

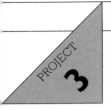

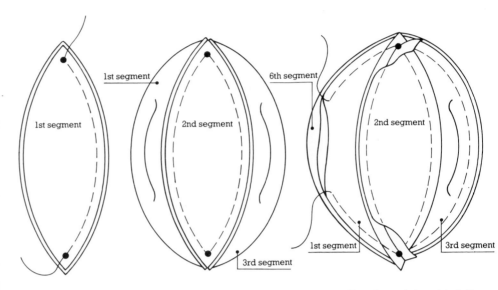

CHIME BALL
Preparing the pattern
The ball consists of six segments and is 34cm (13½in) in circumference when completed. Make a full-size pattern *(see p.12)* of the segment shape on card and use this as the cutting guide – you will need two segments in each colour.

Making the ball
You can make this ball on a sewing machine – this is the quickest method – or by hand. When sewing the various segments together, make sure that the pile runs in the same direction, so that the textures match.
1. With right sides facing, sew two segments of different colours together between the dots *(see fig. a)*.
2. Sew a third different coloured segment to the first two *(see fig. b)*. This completes one half of the ball.
3. Sew the remaining three segments together in the same way and following the same colour sequence. This completes the other half of the ball.
4. Place the two halves together with dots matching top and bottom and sew around the edge, leaving an opening on one side *(see fig. c)*.
5. Turn the ball right side out and start to stuff it firmly. Insert the chime in the middle of the ball and pack the stuffing around it to hold it in place. Close the opening with ladder stitch.

a. Sew together two segments of different colours along one side between the dots.

b. Sew a third segment of a different colour to the first two, making half the ball.

c. Place the two halves of the ball right sides together, and sew around the edge, leaving a small opening.

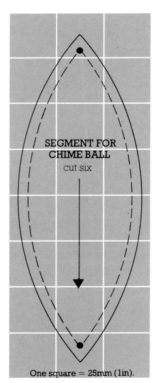

SEGMENT FOR CHIME BALL
cut six

One square = 25mm (1in).

PUZZLE BALL
Preparing the pattern
Make full-size patterns of the two shapes *(see p.12)* and use these to cut 12 of each from the fabrics. Mix the colours to make an attractive design. The red and blue ball illustrated here uses six different fabrics – each colour having a dark and light patterned piece, as well as a plain, unpatterned one. The finished ball has a circumference of 48cm (19in).

Making the ball
The geometrical symmetry of this ball makes it appear something of a puzzle at first

glance. However, it can be made quite easily, using a sewing machine.
1. Clip the seam allowance at B on a semicircular piece of fabric. Then take a gusset of a different colour and lay it right sides together on the semicircle along a curved edge from A to B. Sew between the dots *(see fig. a)*. Leave the machine needle through the material at B.
2. Lift the machine foot and swing the fabrics around until

a. Sew together a semicircle and a gusset of a different colour, from A to B.

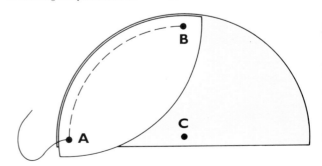

PROJECT 4

the unstitched curved edge of the semicircle lies along the other side of the gusset. Lower machine foot and continue sewing from B back to A *(see fig. b.)*. Take care not to trap any seams at the points of the gusset.

3. Carefully fold the gusset in half lengthways and sew the straight sides of the semicircle together, making a short seam down from A. Leave the lower half open *(see fig. c)*.

4. Trim and cut the gusset seams then turn the triangular bag right side out, stuff and close the opening. Make 11 more bags in the same way taking care to mix the fabrics.

5. Take three stuffed bags and stitch them together securely at the gusset corners *(see fig.d)*. Use strong thread and make inconspicuous stitches..

6. Turn the unit upside down (continued on p.22)

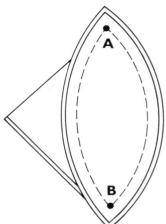

b. *Sew the second side of the gusset to the remaining curve of the semicircle from A to B.*

c. *Fold the gusset in half and sew a short seam down from A along the straight edge. Leave the lower half open.*

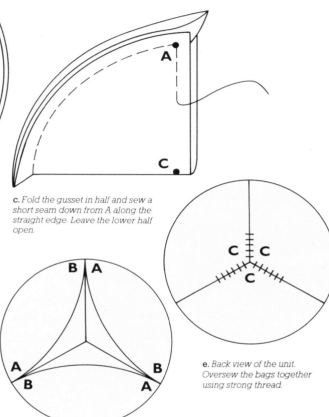

d. *Front view of the unit. Stitch three stuffed bags together at the gusset corners, using strong thread.*

e. *Back view of the unit. Oversew the bags together using strong thread.*

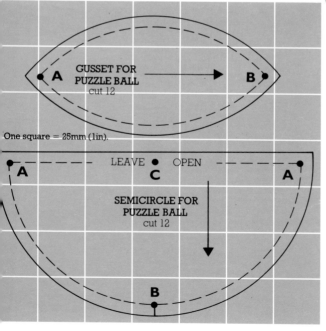

GUSSET FOR PUZZLE BALL
cut 12

One square = 25mm (1in).

LEAVE ● OPEN

SEMICIRCLE FOR PUZZLE BALL
cut 12

MATERIALS

Chime ball
6   20 x 7.5cm (8 x 3in) pieces of short-pile fur fabric in 3 different colours
    56g (2oz) stuffing
    cylindrical chime

Puzzle ball
    remnants of colourful cotton fabrics: 12 pieces 18 x 10cm (7 x 4in), 12 pieces 18 x 7.5cm (7 x 3in)
    227g (8oz) stuffing
6   guipure daisies

EQUIPMENT

Dressmaking shears, pins, needles, thread, tape measure or ruler, pencil, pattern-making equipment.

and oversew the bags together at C *(see fig. e)*. Again use strong thread. This time, however, the stitches need not be concealed, as they will be hidden within the ball.

7. Make three more units in the same way, so that all 12 bags are stitched together into four units of three.

8. Now join two of these units together, stitching four gusset points together on the front and at C on the back. Join the remaining two units in the same way *(see fig. f)*. You now have the two halves of the ball.

9. Place the two halves together crossways, so that all the Cs are in the centre of the ball and all the gussets face outwards. Stitch the gusset points together at the Xs marked *(see fig. g)*. Cover the outside joining stitches with the daisies.

f. Join two units together, stitching four gusset points together on the front, and at C on the back. This makes up half of the ball.

g. Match all the Cs of both halves, so that all the gussets face outwards and stitch together at the Xs marked.

NURSERY TED
Preparing the pattern

Make a full-size pattern from the grid *(see p.12)*. Note that only half a back is drawn, so you will need to complete this. Transfer all the markings. Cut one each head back, head front, snout and body back. Cut two body fronts, reversing the pattern to get a left and right front. The bear is 20cm (8in) tall.

Making the bear

Because of its size, this toy is best made by hand sewing with a firm backstitch. The result is softer to cuddle than a machine-made bear would be.

1. Start by folding over the arm to sew the shoulder dart on the body front. Fold over the foot likewise to sew the ankle dart *(see fig. a)*. Make the darts on the other half of the front body. Trim the darts to release tension.

2. With right sides together sew both fronts down the centre front seam.

3. Make the small seating darts on the body as well back as the two heel darts on each leg.

4. Place the body front and back together and oversew around the edge, leaving the neck and the slit in the centre back open. Take particular care to tuck in the fur when working along the underside of the arms and around the feet. You will also need to ease the fullness between the toes and the soles. Seam together.

5. Match A of the snout to A of the head with right sides together. Then, working each side in turn, ease the snout to fit the opening, pin and sew in place *(see fig. b)*. Complete the snout by sewing the two small darts.

6. Sew the dart on the head back then place the front and back heads together and sew all round the edge, leaving the neck open. Turn right side out and fix the safety eyes in place.

7. Carefully remove any trapped fur from the seams, especially around the ears. Stab stitch across base of each ear to seal them off from stuffing.

8. Place the completed head inside neck of body and with

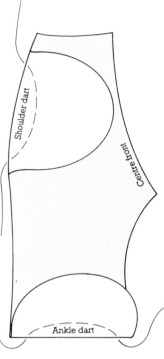

a. Sew the shoulder and ankle darts and clip the seams to release tension.

right sides together and side seams matching sew in place. Some easing will be necessary to get a good fit. Turn the completed skin right side out through the back opening.

9. Stuff the head, arms, feet and legs in that order. Stuff the body cavity last, inserting the squeaker into the tummy area and making sure that it is surrounded by stuffing *(see p.16)*. Crease the top of the legs where they join the body, so that they flex.

10. Embroider a block of satin stitch for the nose with two straight stitches for the mouth *(see fig. c)*. Finally, tie a gaily coloured bow around the neck.

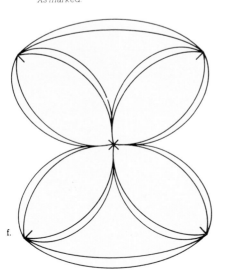

f.

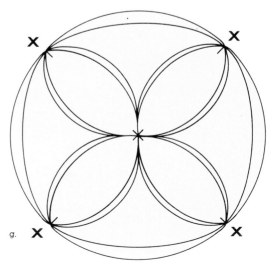

g.

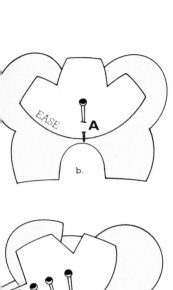

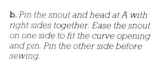

b. Pin the snout and head at A with right sides together. Ease the snout on one side to fit the curve opening and pin. Pin the other side before sewing.

c. The safety eyes are fixed in place before the head is attached to the body. The nose and mouth are embroidered when the teddy has been assembled.

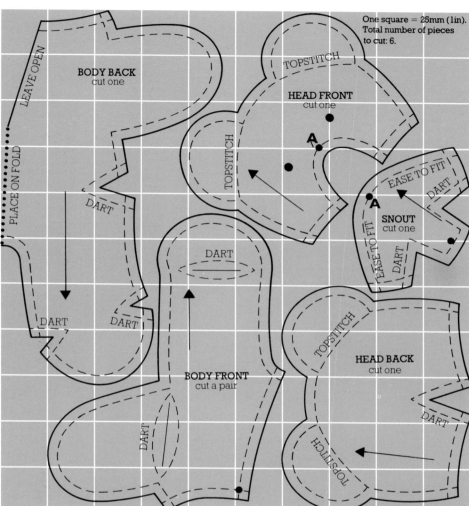

One square = 25mm (1in).
Total number of pieces to cut: 6.

LEAVE OPEN

PLACE ON FOLD

BODY BACK
cut one

TOPSTITCH

HEAD FRONT
cut one

TOPSTITCH

A

DART

A

EASE TO FIT

DART

EASE TO FIT

EASE TO FIT

DART

SNOUT
cut one

DART

DART

DART

DART

BODY FRONT
cut a pair

DART

TOPSTITCH

HEAD BACK
cut one

DART

TOPSTITCH

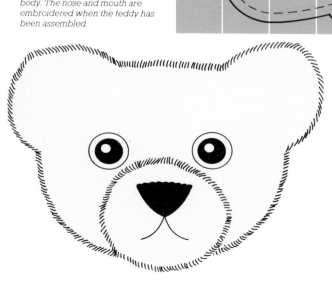

MATERIALS
45.5cm (18in) square of short-pile fur
pair of 12mm amber safety eyes
84g (3oz) stuffing
brown embroidery thread for nose
squeaker
length of ribbon for bow

EQUIPMENT
Dressmaking shears, embroidery scissors, pins, needles, thread, tape measure or ruler, pencil, pattern-making equipment.

MAKING AN
ELEPHANT

The design of this elephant continues a tradition that started just over 100 years ago when Margarete Steiff made her first small grey felt elephant to sell in her shop in Giengen, West Germany. She gave one of these elephants to her young nephew Richard who later joined his aunt in her toymaking business and designed the first European jointed teddy bear.

Preparing the pattern
Make a full-size pattern from the pattern grid and transfer all the markings onto your copy *(see p.12)*. Cut all the pieces from the main colour, except for one pair of ears, which should be cut from the white fur to make the ear linings. The

finished elephant stands 25cm (10in) tall.

Making the body
1. Start by sewing an ear lining to an ear piece around the curved edge. Turn the ear right side out and carefully release any fur trapped in the

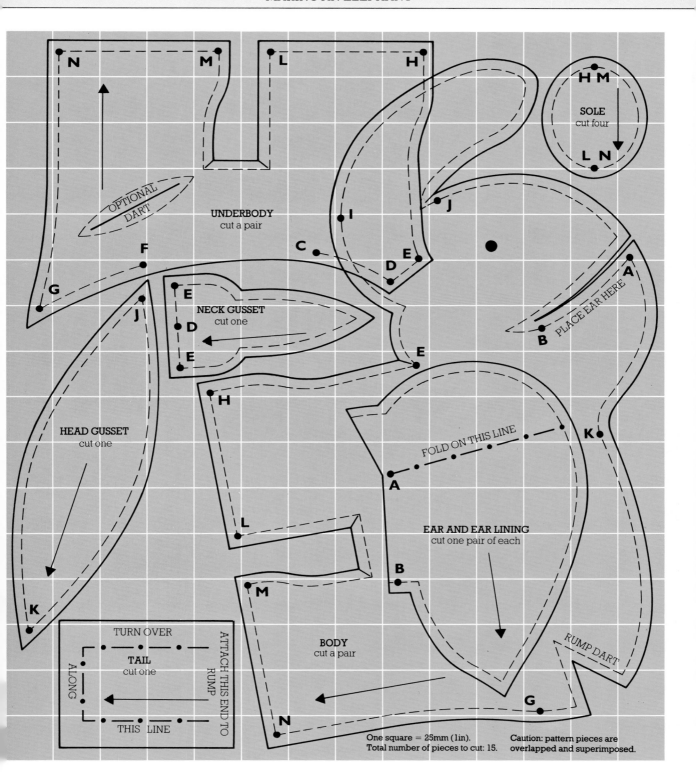

N **M**

L **H**

H M

SOLE
cut four

L N

OPTIONAL DART

UNDERBODY
cut a pair

I

J

C

E

D

F

G

E

D

NECK GUSSET
cut one

E

J

E

A

B PLACE EAR HERE

H

HEAD GUSSET
cut one

E

FOLD ON THIS LINE

A

K

L

EAR AND EAR LINING
cut one pair of each

K

B

M

RUMP DART

TURN OVER

TAIL
cut one

ALONG

THIS LINE

ATTACH THIS END TO RUMP

BODY
cut a pair

N

G

One square = 25mm (1in).
Total number of pieces to cut: 15.

Caution: pattern pieces are
overlapped and superimposed.

25

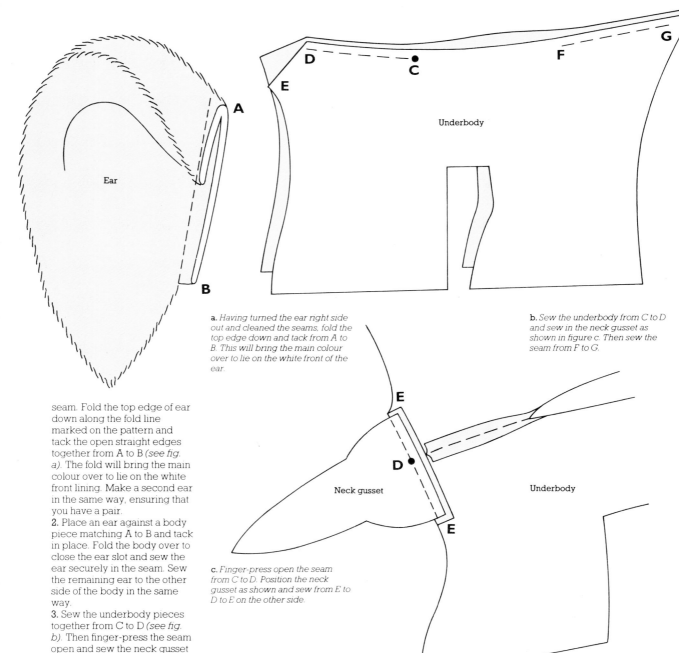

Ear

Underbody

a. *Having turned the ear right side out and cleaned the seams, fold the top edge down and tack from A to B. This will bring the main colour over to lie on the white front of the ear.*

b. *Sew the underbody from C to D and sew in the neck gusset as shown in figure c. Then sew the seam from F to G.*

Neck gusset

Underbody

c. *Finger-press open the seam from C to D. Position the neck gusset as shown and sew from E to D to E on the other side.*

seam. Fold the top edge of ear down along the fold line marked on the pattern and tack the open straight edges together from A to B (see fig. a). The fold will bring the main colour over to lie on the white front lining. Make a second ear in the same way, ensuring that you have a pair.

2. Place an ear against a body piece matching A to B and tack in place. Fold the body over to close the ear slot and sew the ear securely in the seam. Sew the remaining ear to the other side of the body in the same way.

3. Sew the underbody pieces together from C to D (see fig. b). Then finger-press the seam open and sew the neck gusset in place from E through D to E on the other side (see fig. c).

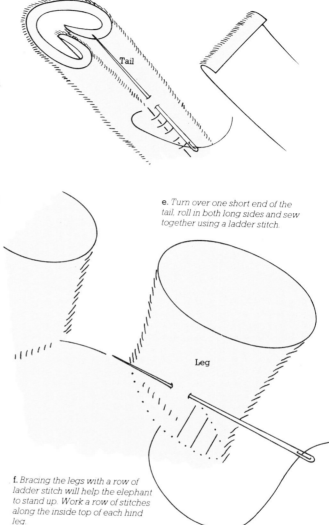

Continue sewing the underbody pieces together from F to G.

4. Now place the underbody against a body piece and with right sides together sew up the front leg from H, through E to the end of the neck gusset at I. Sew the remaining body to the other side of the underbody in same way.

5. Seam the trunk pieces together from I to J then insert the head gusset. After pinning and tacking by overcasting, sew from J to K on each side in turn.

6. Make the darts on the rump of each body, then seam together from K back to G.

7. Finish joining the underbody by seaming from L to M on each side and then from N to G, again on each side in turn.

8. Insert the soles in turn, making sure that the fur lies in the same direction on each one. Pin, tack by overcasting, then sew, pressing open the leg seams as you work around the sole (see fig. d).

9. Turn the completed skin right side out and fix the eyes in place.

10. Stuff the elephant, working on the legs first, followed by the trunk, head and body

proper. Close the opening with ladder stitch.

Finishing touches

11. Catch the back of each ear to the head gusset seam with ladder stitch for about 2.5cm (1in)

12. Turn in one short edge of the tail piece. Then roll in both long sides and ladder stitch the folded edges together (see fig. e). This makes a thin tail that is self-stuffed. Check that the pile runs down the tail before sewing it in place at G.

13. Finally, work a row of ladder stitch along the inside top of each hind leg (see fig. f). This should pull the legs inwards on to the underbody, so bracing them to help the elephant stand securely. Without this bracing, the legs will tend to splay apart. Another way of achieving the same effect is to sew the optional dart marked on the underbody pattern piece, although this will mean predetermining the exact amount of bracing needed, which is not easy to judge.

14. Groom the elephant carefully, especially the soles, which are sure to have fur trapped in the seams.

e. Turn over one short end of the tail, roll in both long sides and sew together using a ladder stitch.

f. Bracing the legs with a row of ladder stitch will help the elephant to stand up. Work a row of stitches along the inside top of each hind leg.

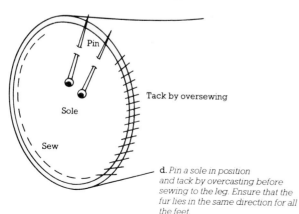

Tack by oversewing

d. Pin a sole in position and tack by overcasting before sewing to the leg. Ensure that the fur lies in the same direction for all the feet.

MATERIALS

69cm (27in) wide by 61cm (24in) long piece of pink short-pile fur
25cm (10in) square of white, short-pile fur for ear linings
280g (10oz) stuffing
pair 16mm brown eyes

EQUIPMENT

Dressmaking shears, embroidery scissors, pins, needles, thread, tape measure or ruler, pencil, pattern-making equipment.

PROJECT
1

── MAKING A ──
RABBIT

Rabbits, especially fluffy baby bunnies, are firm favourites in the nursery. Many of the best loved characters in nursery rhymes and stories are rabbits – the White Rabbit, Brer Rabbit, Little Grey Rabbit, Peter Rabbit, Flopsy, Mopsy and Cottontail are just a few of the most celebrated. As a result, rabbits are extremely popular soft toys. This pattern is for a simple sitting rabbit which can be dressed easily by young children.

Preparing the pattern
Make a full-size pattern and transfer all markings to the pattern *(see p.12)*. Cut out the body sides, base, ears, arms and feet from the short pile fur and the tail from the fluffier white fur. The finished rabbit will stand 30cm (11¾in) tall. The pattern for the dress is a rectangle with a neck frill. Simply cut the cotton into two strips, one piece measuring 18 x 61cm (7 x 24in) and the other 7.5 x 61cm (3 x 24in).

Making the body
It will be quicker to sew the body on the machine, but you must be careful not to trap fur in the centre front seam that runs down the head and through the tummy.
1. Fold an arm in half and, with the right sides together, seam round the paw to the shoulder *(see fig. a)*. Turn the arm right side out and stuff it almost to the top. Keep the stuffing away from the opening with a pin. Make a second arm, using the same method.
2. Place one arm on a body side, matching A to A and B to B in the lower half of the dart and tack it in place *(see fig. b)*. Fold the body over to bring all the As together and then sew from C through A to B *(see fig. c)*. Check that the arm is

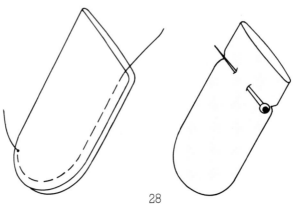

a. *Fold each arm in half and sew around the paw to the shoulder, using backstitch. Turn the arms right side out and stuff them, keeping the stuffing in place with pins.*

28

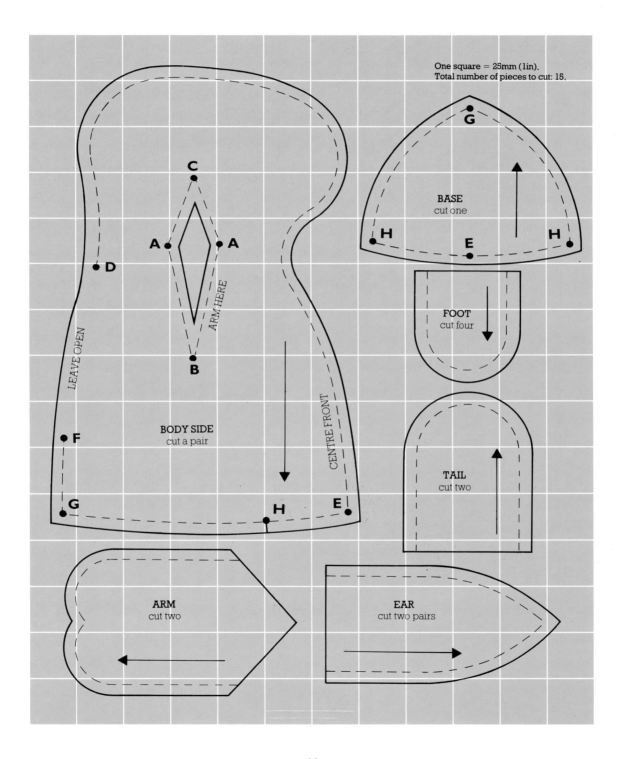

One square = 25mm (1in).
Total number of pieces to cut: 15.

G

BASE
cut one

H   E   H

FOOT
cut four

TAIL
cut two

C

A   A

ARM HERE

B

LEAVE OPEN

D

CENTRE FRONT

F

BODY SIDE
cut a pair

G   H   E

ARM
cut two

EAR
cut two pairs

PROJECT 7

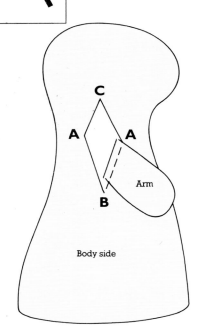

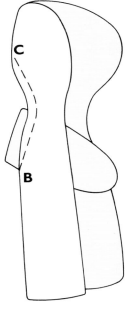

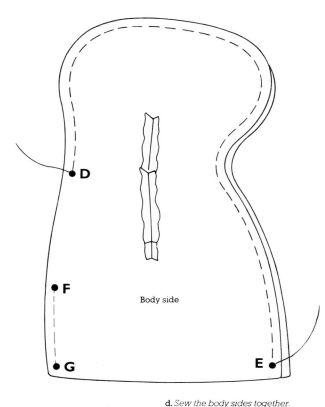

b. *Match As and Bs of one arm with one body side. Tack in place.*

c. *Fold the body over, match up all the As and sew from C through A to B. Repeat with the other arm and body side. Make sure that the arms are firmly sewn in to the seams and remember to remove the pins.*

d. *Sew the body sides together. First sew around the head from D, then continue down the centre front seam to E. Sew from F to G and leave an opening in the back for stuffing.*

securely attached. Sew the rabbit's second arm to the remaining body side in the same way. Then remove the pins from the arms.
3. Place both of the body sides, so that their right sides are together, and sew from D around the head and down the centre front to E. Leave an opening in the centre back by sewing a short seam from F to G. Reinforce the stitching at the front of the neck by sewing a second row on top of the original seam line.
4. Place the feet pieces together in pairs and sew around the curved edges. Turn them right side out and stuff lightly, so that they will flop forwards when sewn in place. Position the feet on the right side of the base, so that the straight edges of the feet align with the straight edge of the

base. Sew the feet in place from H through E to H.
5. Position the base against the lower edge of the body and sew it in place from E to H to G on each side in turn. Do not forget to cut the seam allowance at H so that you can change direction without making puckers.
6. Turn the completed skin right side out and stuff, paying particular attention to shaping the cheeks and neck. The body must be firmly stuffed if the head is not to wobble. When you are satisfied with its appearance, close the opening with ladder stitch.
7. Sew the tail pieces around the curved edge then turn it right side out. Turn in the raw edges and insert a small amount of stuffing to give the tail some bulk. Ladder stitch it in place against the body.

e. *Having stuffed the feet, position them on the base, aligning the straight edges, and sew from H, through E to H.*

f. *Turn in the edges of the tail and attach it firmly to the body with ladder stitch.*

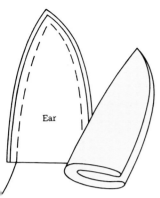

Ear

g. *Sew the curved edges of the ears together in pairs. Turn right side out, turn in the edges and shape the ears by folding in half and oversewing the lower edges together.*

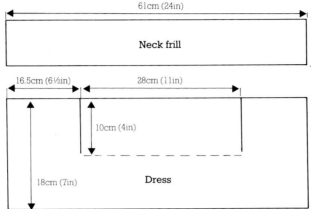

61cm (24in)

Neck frill

7.5cm (3in)

16.5cm (6½in) 28cm (11in)

10cm (4in)

18cm (7in) Dress

8. Sew the ears together in pairs, leaving the straight edges open. Turn right side out. Turn under the raw edges, then fold each ear in half and oversew the open base edges together.

9. Position the ear on the head and ladder stitch in place, with the fold next to centre top seam. Use the same method to sew on the second ear.

10. Embroider a pair of brown eyes on interfacing with a diameter of 18mm (¾in). Sew them in place on the head.

11. Work a block of satin stitches for the nose and use straight stitches for the mouth.

The dress Make two slits for the arms on the larger piece (left) and tidy up all the edges. Hem three edges of the neck frill and match up the right side of the unhemmed edge to the wrong side of the dress neck edge. Sew together, turn the frill up and press the seam towards the frill (below left). Turn the frill over, press, sew two rows of stitching along the neckline leaving a channel between them (below).

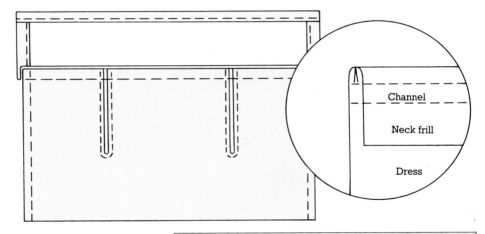

Channel

Neck frill

Dress

Making the dress
12. Cut two slits for the arms in the large rectangle of cotton print, as shown.
13. Make a narrow hem on both sides of the arm slits, as well as on both short sides of the dress. Trim the neck frill to the same measure as the neck of the dress, allowing for hems on both sides.
14. Now make a narrow hem along one edge and both short sides of the neck frill. Place the unhemmed edge of the neck frill right side to wrong side of the dress with neck edges level. Sew along the length of

the neckline, then turn the frill up and press the seam towards the frill.
15. Turn the frill over and press. Sew two rows along the length of the neckline, making a channel for the ribbon as shown.
16. Thread the ribbon through the channel, pull it up and fit the dress on the rabbit. Finish by measuring the length required for the dress and hemming. Additional bows can be stitched to the front of the dress for decoration or, if you wish, tied around the ears.

MATERIALS

45.5cm (18in) square of short-pile fur
small piece of medium-pile white fur
112g (4oz) stuffing
pair embroidered eyes
embroidery thread for the nose
61 x 25.5cm (24 x 10in) piece of cotton print
61cm (24in) length of narrow ribbon

EQUIPMENT

Dressmaking shears, embroidery scissors, pins, needles, thread, tape measure or ruler, pencil, pattern-making equipment.

PROJECT **8**

MAKING A
DUCKLING

For a really cuddly duckling, choose a soft fur with medium-length pile to give the feel of real downy feathers. The thickness of the pile makes it necessary to tack by overcasting all the curved edges together before sewing, as otherwise they will slip and stretch. This method of working will give a professional finish to the toy and ensures that the duckling maintains its original shape.

Preparing the pattern
Make a full-size pattern and transfer all the markings on to your copy *(see p.12)*. Remember to cut the slits for the wings and feet. Cut the beak and feet from velvet and all the other pieces from fur. The finished duckling will stand 30.5cm (12in) tall.

Making the body
1. With right sides together sew the feet, leaving an opening between A and B. Clip to the corners between the feet and turn right side out. Lightly stuff the toes of each foot. Tack the open edges on to the matching curve (A-B) of the right side of the body gusset, with the toes pointing towards the neck edge *(see fig. a)*. Fold the gusset right sides together and bring all the raw edges together; seam from A to B to enclose the feet.
2. Place the wings right sides together in pairs and sew round the edges, leaving an opening between C and D. Take care to tuck in the fur on the tip of the wings, so that it is not trapped in the seams, as this would spoil the fluffy appearance. Turn the completed wings right side out and clean the seams.
3. Place a wing in position on a body side, matching points C and D *(see fig. b)*. Fold over the top portion of the body side

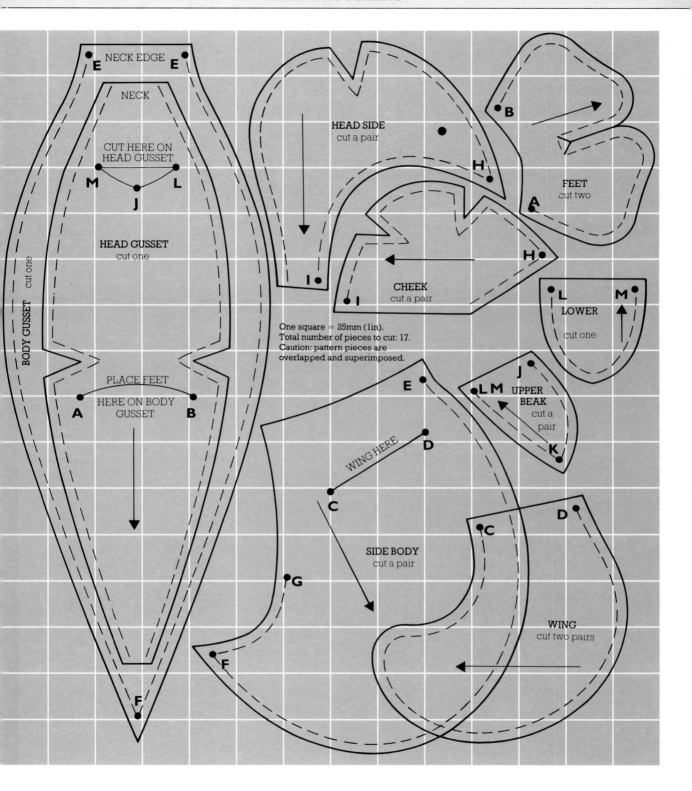

NECK EDGE

E   E

NECK

CUT HERE ON
HEAD GUSSET

M   L

J

HEAD GUSSET
cut one

BODY GUSSET   cut one

PLACE FEET

HERE ON BODY
GUSSET

A   B

F

F

HEAD SIDE
cut a pair

B

H

I

CHEEK
cut a pair

H

I

One square = 25mm (1in).
Total number of pieces to cut: 17.
Caution: pattern pieces are
overlapped and superimposed.

FEET
cut two

A

L   M

LOWER

cut one

E

D

WING HERE

C

SIDE BODY
cut a pair

G

F

J

L M   UPPER
BEAK

cut a
pair

K

D

C

WING
cut two pairs

PROJECT **8**

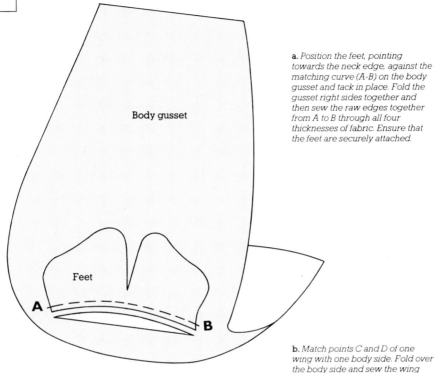

Body gusset

Feet

A   **B**

a. Position the feet, pointing towards the neck edge, against the matching curve (A-B) on the body gusset and tack in place. Fold the gusset right sides together and then sew the raw edges together from A to B through all four thicknesses of fabric. Ensure that the feet are securely attached.

head side at H and I and halfway between *(see fig. c)*. The pins must lie at right angles to the edges and the darts should be finger-pressed open to reduce bulk. Now pin again at intervals, gently easing in the fullness. Tack by overcasting and sew. Attach the second cheek and sew in the same way.

6. Sew the two upper beaks together (right sides together) from J to K then sew them on to the lower beak from L through K to M *(see fig. d)*. Turn right side out and place in position in the head gusset. Tack in place before sewing. This is easier to do by hand with a small, firm backstitch.

7. Using all six strands of the black embroidery thread, work two straight stitches for nostrils on the upper beak. End the threads off on the seam allowance.

8. Sew the head gusset to both side pieces, working from the front neck edge to the back of the head on each piece.

9. Turn the head right side out; stuff the beak firmly to help you check the positioning of the eyes. When happy with your choice, fix the eyes in place.

b. Match points C and D of one wing with one body side. Fold over the body side and sew the wing securely in position.

(near E), bring all the edges together and then sew across. Tug the wing to make sure that it is firmly attached. Sew the second wing to the other body side in the same way.

4. Now attach the body gusset to the body sides. Match up point E of the right and left sides with E on the body gusset; with right sides together, tack by overcasting from E to F, working a little on each side in turn. Take care not to stretch the curved edges and so distort the shape. Sew the short centre back seam from G to F. Turn the body skin right side out and check appearance. Put to one side.

Making the head

5. Start by sewing the darts on the head pieces. There are eight in all. With right sides together, pin one cheek to a

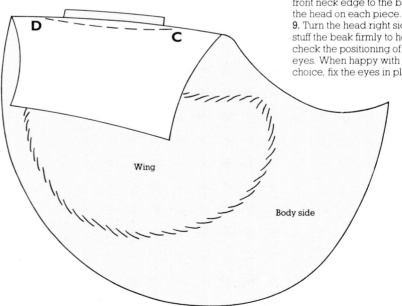

D   **C**

Wing

Body side

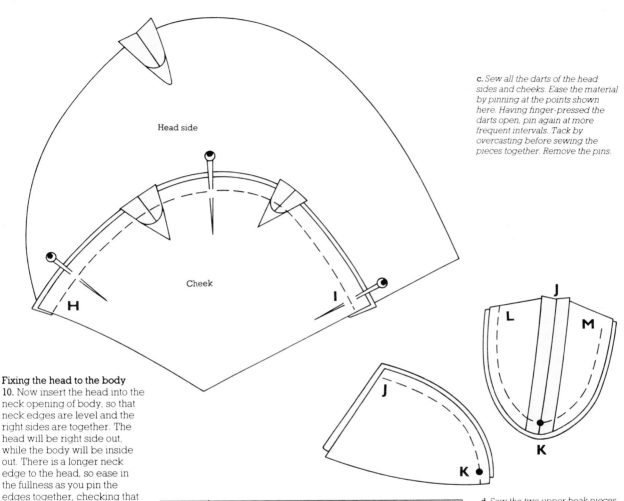

Head side

Cheek

H

I

J

L

M

K

J

K

c. *Sew all the darts of the head sides and cheeks. Ease the material by pinning at the points shown here. Having finger-pressed the darts open, pin again at more frequent intervals. Tack by overcasting before sewing the pieces together. Remove the pins.*

d. *Sew the two upper beak pieces together, first from J to K and then sew these two pieces to the lower beak (from K to M through J).*

Fixing the head to the body
10. Now insert the head into the neck opening of body, so that neck edges are level and the right sides are together. The head will be right side out, while the body will be inside out. There is a longer neck edge to the head, so ease in the fullness as you pin the edges together, checking that the centre fronts and backs are matching. If you are not happy with pinning, run a strong gathering thread around the neck edge and pull up until it fits the body neck edge. In both instances, tack before sewing either on machine or by hand sewing a backstitch with doubled, strong thread.
11. Turn the completed skin right side out. Stuff the head first, then the body. Make sure that the duckling stands easily and does not topple over. Close the opening with ladder stitch. As a finishing touch, tie a blue bow around the neck *(see p.17)*.

MATERIALS

61cm (24in) long x 69cm (27in) wide length of white medium-pile fur
23cm (9in) square of old gold velvet or felt for beak and feet
240g (8oz) stuffing
1m (1yd) blue satin ribbon
pair 22mm blue eyes
black embroidery thread for nostrils

EQUIPMENT

Dressmaking shears, embroidery scissors, pins, needles, thread, tape measure or ruler, pencil, pattern-making equipment.

PROJECT **9**

MAKING A
KANGAROO

Kangaroos make lovable and amusing toys – this one has the added attraction of a baby in its pouch. The mother kangaroo can be made by machine or by hand, but it is easier to sew the baby by hand, as he is so small. To complete the family, make up father kangaroo – without a pouch, of course!

Preparing the pattern
Make a full-size grid and mark out the pattern pieces on it *(see p12)*. Cut out both kangaroos and keep the pieces separate. The mother kangaroo stands 38cm (15in) tall to the tip of her ears. The baby kangaroo is only 15cm (6in) tall.

Making the mother
1. Fold the pouch lengthways to make a dart by bringing Ys together, right sides together. Sew from X to Y *(see fig. a)*. Sew the dart in the pouch lining in the same way. Press both darts open.
2. Place the pouch and the pouch lining right sides together, matching the top and bottom edges. Sew across the top from A to A and across the

bottom from B to B. Then turn the faced pouch right side out.
3. Tack each open side of the pouch.
4. Make the centre front dart in the body gusset by folding it lengthways and bringing Ys together. Sew from X to Y. This leaves the lower part of the dart open so that the lower part

of the body can be stuffed later.
5. Position the pouch against the body gusset by matching As to As and Bs to Bs on each side, with the lining of the pocket against the right side of the body *(see fig. b)*. Tack in place down each side.
6. Position one inside leg to the

matching side of the body gusset and sew from C to D. Check this seam to see that the edge of the pouch has been caught in place securely. Sew the inside leg on the other side in the same way.
7. Place the gusset between the body sides and tack by overcasting on each side from

a. Sew a dart in the pouch flap from X to Y. Sew the lining in the same way. Press the darts open before sewing the pieces together.

b. With the pouch lining against the right side of the body gusset match up points A and B and tack down the sides of the pouch before attaching the inner leg pieces.

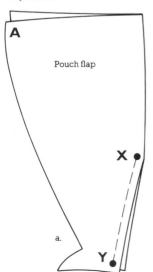

A

Pouch flap

X

a.

Y

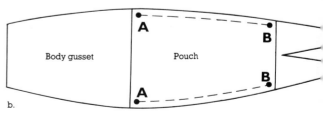

A

B

Body gusset

Pouch

A

B

b.

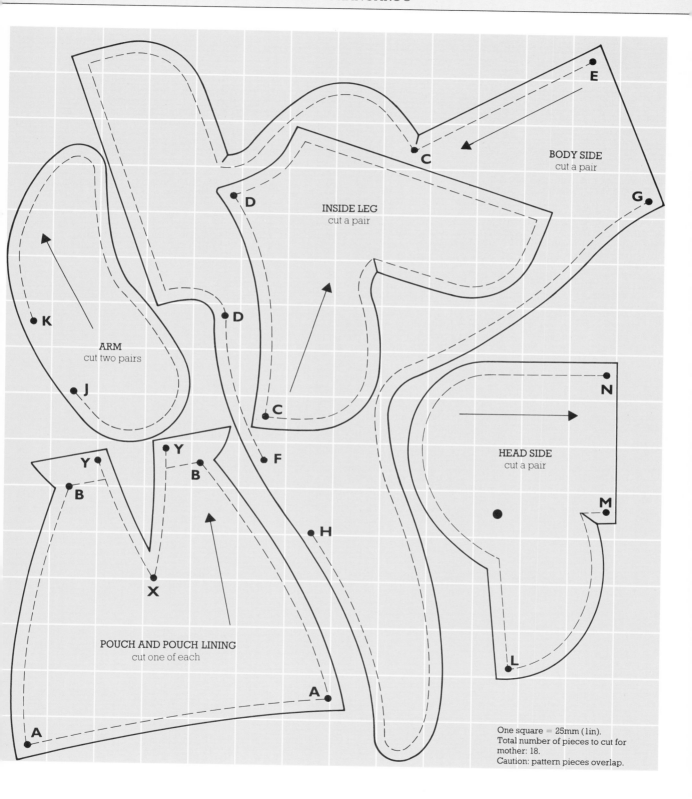

BODY SIDE
cut a pair

INSIDE LEG
cut a pair

ARM
cut two pairs

HEAD SIDE
cut a pair

POUCH AND POUCH LINING
cut one of each

One square = 25mm (1in).
Total number of pieces to cut for
mother: 18.
Caution: pattern pieces overlap.

PROJECT **9**

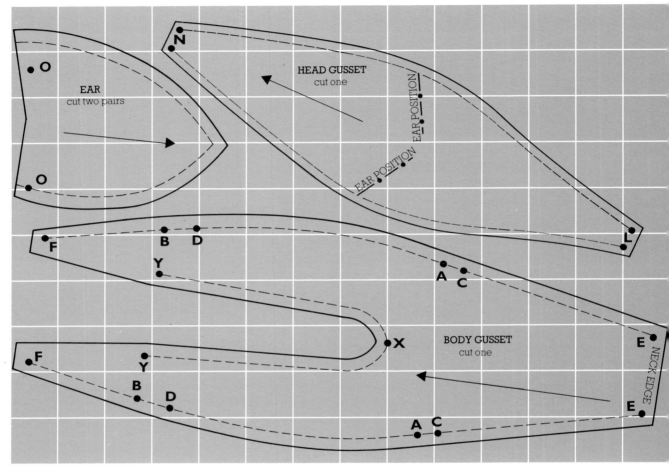

 O

EAR
cut two pairs

O

N

HEAD GUSSET
cut one

EAR POSITION

EAR POSITION

L

F

B D

Y

A C

X

BODY GUSSET
cut one

E

NECK EDGE

E

F

Y

B D

A C

E through C, around the leg and through D to F. Check on the right side for appearance, then sew in place.

8. Complete sewing the body sides together. Tack by overcasting and then sew from the neck edge at G, down the back and around the tail to H.

9. Turn the completed body skin right side out and commence stuffing. Push small pieces of stuffing into each leg and into the tip of the tail through the opening on the underside of the tail. Pack the stuffing in really firmly, as

these points provide the base on which the kangaroo stands. Stuff the haunches and then the rest of the body through the open neck.

10. Run a gathering thread around the neck edge and pull up sufficiently to turn the raw edges inwards. Close the undertail opening and the lower edge of the pouch with ladder stitch.

11. Place the arm pieces together in pairs and sew round the edges, leaving an opening between J and K. Turn each completed arm right side

out, stuff firmly then close the opening with ladder stitch.

12. Position the arms against the side of the body and ladder stitch to secure. Be careful not to have them outstretched, as otherwise they might get in the way of the baby while the inbalance could also throw the mother forward *(see fig. c)*.

13. Sew the under chin seam of the two head sides from L to M, with right sides together. Clip the corner.

14. Position the head gusset between the head sides and tack by overcasting. Then sew

in place from L to N on both sides.

15. Turn the head right side out and insert the safety eyes *(see p.15)*. Now stuff the head, rounding it into a pleasing shape. Run a strong gathering thread around the neck edge, pull up and fasten off. Place both neck edges together and ladder stitch the head to the body. Work around the neck several times to make sure that the head is securely attached.

16. Place the ears together in pairs and sew the curved sides. Turn right side out and

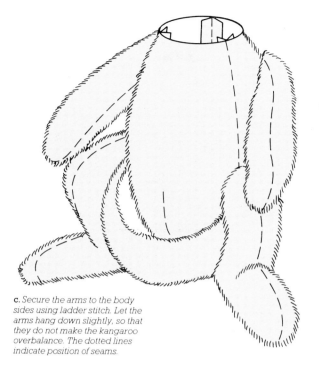

c. *Secure the arms to the body sides using ladder stitch. Let the arms hang down slightly, so that they do not make the kangaroo overbalance. The dotted lines indicate position of seams.*

free any trapped fur from the seams, especially the tips. Fold one ear in half, so that the Os meet, and tack by overcasting the open edges together. Fold and sew the second ear in the same way to make up a pair.
17. Position the ears on the head gusset. Ladder stitch in place along the front sides first, then sew the back side so that they are pulled back.
18. Embroider the nose by working a block of satin stitch (see p.15 and fig. d).

Making the baby
1. Sew the inside legs together from A to B.
2. Position the inside legs between the body sides and sew in place from A through B to C on each side in turn.
3. Match the head gusset at D on each side in turn and baste in place before sewing back to E and just beyond.
4. Fold the head gusset at F

One square = 25mm (1in).
Total number of pieces to cut for baby : 13.

and sew under the nose from F through D to A.
5. Turn the completed skin right side out and insert the safety eyes (see p.15).
6. Stuff the body through the opening on the back, then close it with ladder stitch, working back from C towards E. Pull slightly on the working thread to curl the tail upwards.
7. Place the ear pieces together in pairs and tack by overcasting the curved edges together before sewing. Turn each completed ear right side out and tack the straight edges of each ear together. Ladder stitch in place across the head gusset seam on each side.
8. Embroider the nose on the tip of the snout by working a small block of satin stitch.

d. *Use satin stitch to embroider the nose and mouth.*

Finishing touches
Groom mother and baby carefully. Pinch the legs of baby together and sit him sideways in the pouch.

MATERIALS

61cm (24in) of 136cm- (54in)-wide short-pile grey or beige fur
280g (10oz) stuffing
pair 18mm safety eyes for mother
pair 8mm safety eyes for baby
six-stranded embroidery thread in black

EQUIPMENT

Dressmaking shears, embroidery scissors, pins, needles, thread, tape measure or ruler, pencil, pattern-making equipment.

MAKING A
RAG DOLL

Children the world over have delighted in rag dolls of all shapes and sizes for literally thousands of years. This pattern is a popular twentieth century version worked with familiar everyday materials. The clothes themselves can be changed, making the doll even more attractive for young children.

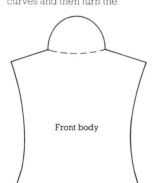

Preparing the pattern
Make a full-size pattern and transfer all the markings onto it (see p.12). Notice that the pieces for the front and back of the body are very similar, so they are given together. The difference between them is that the front is shorter and lacks darts, while the back is longer with a pair of seating darts. Cut out all the pieces from calico, except for the face panel, which you should leave until the features have been embroidered. The finished doll stands 61cm (24in) tall.

Making the body
1. Fold the lower section of the back body so that the Ys on each side come together. Then sew each dart from X to Y and finger-press the seam open.
2. Sew the front and back bodies together from A on one side up to B at the top of the neck and down to A on the other side. Clip the neck curves and then turn the completed body right side out.
3. Sew a row of stay stitching around the ankle curve of each foot from C to D to strenghten the curve (see fig. a). Now clip the inside curve so that you can stretch the foot piece to fit between C and D on the ankle

Notice that the pattern pieces for the front body and the back body are very similar and are given together. The front is shorter and lacks darts while the back is longer and has a pair of seating darts.

edge of the leg. Sew together and repeat for the other foot.
4. Press open the ankle seam as much as possible and fold the leg right sides together to sew the centre back and under foot seam from E through C/D to F (see fig. b).

Back body

Front body

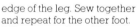

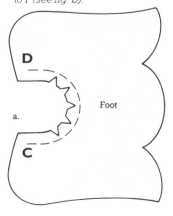

D

Foot

a.

C

a. A row of stay stitching will strengthen the ankle curve of the foot. Clip the inside curve, so that it can be fitted onto the leg.

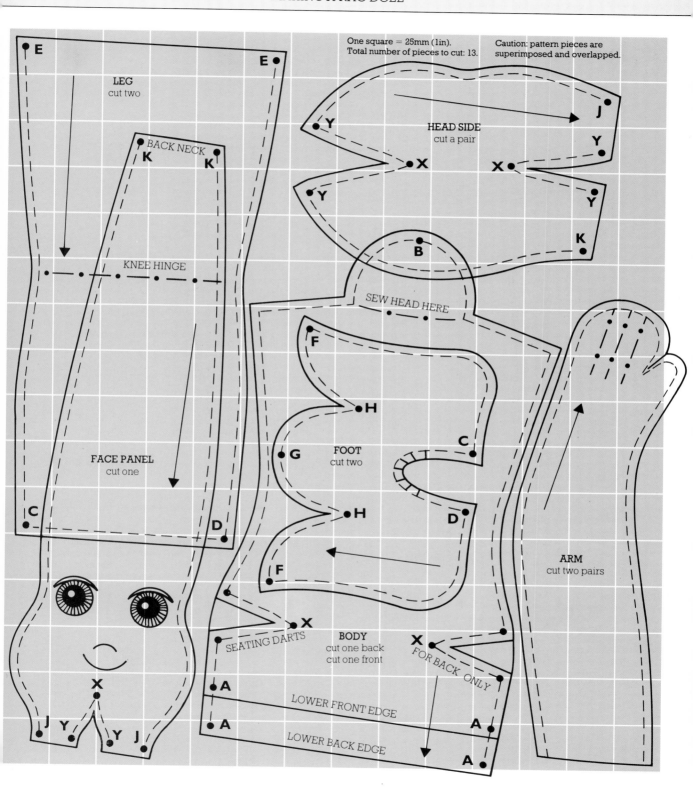

One square = 25mm (1in).
Total number of pieces to cut: 13.

Caution: pattern pieces are
superimposed and overlapped.

LEG
cut two

E   E   E

HEAD SIDE
cut a pair

Y   J
Y   X   X   Y   K

BACK NECK
K   K

B

KNEE HINGE

SEW HEAD HERE

F

FACE PANEL
cut one

H

G   FOOT
cut two   C

H   D

F

C   D

ARM
cut two pairs

SEATING DARTS

X

BODY
cut one back
cut one front

X
FOR BACK ONLY

A

LOWER FRONT EDGE

A   A

LOWER BACK EDGE

A

J Y   Y J
X

41

b. *Press open the ankle seam and sew from E down the centre back seam of the leg, under the foot to F.*

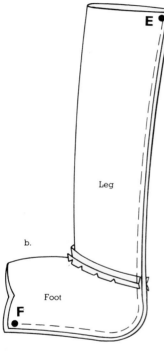

Leg

b.

Foot

F

E

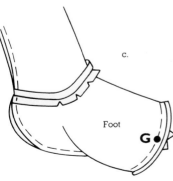

c.

Foot

G

c. *Press open the edge of the foot flap to bring G and F together, then sew across from H to H, forming the toes.*

5. Press open the edge of the foot flap to bring G and F together *(see fig. c)*. Then sew across from H to H, forming the toes. Complete the second leg in the same way.

6. Turn the completed leg right side out and stuff the foot firmly before stuffing the leg up to the knee line. Hold the stuffing in place with a pin *(see fig. d)* and then work across the knee line with stab stitches using strong thread. Pull up slightly on the thread before fastening. Continue stuffing the leg to the top, but not as firmly as the lower leg. Hold the stuffing away from the top of the leg with a pin. Complete the second leg to this stage.

7. With raw edges level, tack each leg in place against the lower edge of the front body. The legs should meet in the middle; toes should lie over the shoulders, so that when they drop down the toes point forwards. Sew across from one side to the other to attach the legs securely. Remove all the pins from the legs.

8. Stuff the body firmly, then turn under the lower back edge and ladder stitch the front to the back. Make a small pleat on each side at A to take in the fullness as you do this.

9. Sew the arm pieces together in pairs leaving the top edges open. Clip between the thumb and forefinger, then turn right sides out. To make the fingers simply insert a small amount of stuffing into each hand and hold it in place with a pin before stitching.

10. Top stitch the finger divisions using strong thread. Work the fingers of both hands at the same time, so that you consciously make a pair. Remove the pins and stuff each arm firmly up to the top. Hold the stuffing in place with a pin while you turn under the raw

edges of the opening, pleat each side *(see fig. e)*, then oversew the edges together.

11. Lay the top of the arms over the shoulders, checking that the thumbs face forwards before sewing in place. Remove the holding pins. If the arms do not hang down beside the body, you will have to take them off and remove a little stuffing from the top before re-attaching them.

Making the head

12. Make a tracing of the facial features on tissue paper and transfer your design to the face panel by rubbing the outline through the paper onto the fabric. Pull the tissue paper away extremely gently.

2. Start by embroidering the

d.

Leg

d. *Make sure that the foot is firmly stuffed before filling the lower leg up to the knee joint. Pin at the knee and sew with stab stitch to indicate the joint.*

e.

Arm

e. *Form pleats on each side of the top of the arms to tuck in the excess fabric before oversewing the edges together.*

irises and then the pupils in buttonhole stitch, using three strands of embroidery thread *(see p 15)*. Use black for the pupils and green or blue for the irises. The highlights are made with a few white straight stitches worked as a small 'v' to cover the area marked out by the hands of a clock at 10 o'clock. The upper eyelids are worked in brown stem stitch; the mouth is worked with the same stitch but with a pink or rosy coloured thread. Now cut out the face panel.

14. Sew both darts on each head side piece and at the chin on the face panel by folding to bring Ys together then sewing from X to Y for each dart in turn.

15. Position the face panel

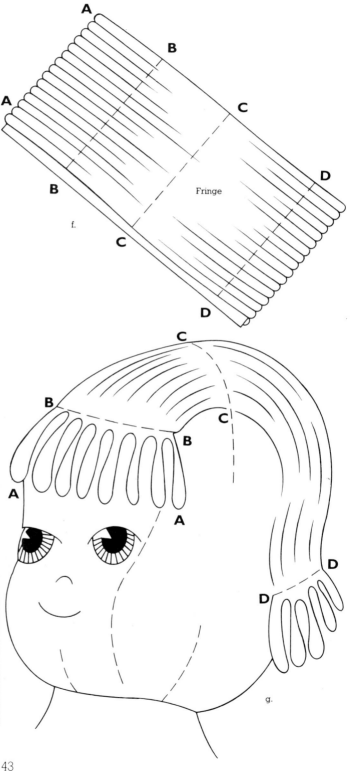

between the head sides and tack carefully before sewing from J at the front to K at the back neck edge on each side in turn. Turn the head right side out and check that the cheeks are level.

16. Turn under a narrow hem around the neck edge and tack in place. Now stuff the head firmly, carefully rounding out the fullness of the cheeks. Leave a hollow just large enough to fit the neck stalk into the body. Push the body and head together, screwing the neck stalk into position. Ladder stitch in place carefully, so that the head does not twist off centre. Remove the tacking stitches from the neck edge.

17. Now make the hair. Cut approximately 80 strands of wool, each 61cm (24in) long. Machine these lengths together through the middle, so that you make a wig about 15cm (6in) wide from front to back.

18. Cut a piece of card 20cm (8in) long by 10cm (4in) wide. Wind the wool over this card template, covering it evenly. Slip the loops off and without disturbing them stitch across three times (see fig. f). This part of the wig forms the fringe

at the front and back and is the first part to be positioned.

19. Lay the fringe over the top of the head and backstitch in place at the front, then on the crown and finally at the back, making sure that it is pulled tight into place before sewing.

20. Now lay the long strands across the head so that it hangs down the sides with the machine parting positioned centrally. Backstitch the central parting to the doll's head.

21. Catch the long hair down on each side of the head where the ears would be, and sew in place. Again pull the strands taut before stitching so that little fingers cannot pull the hair off. Cover the stitches with bows as a final finishing touch.

22. The hair may be left in bunches or plaited as you wish.

f. *Wind wool around a piece of card, then remove the card without disturbing the wool. Sew across by machine in the order given here.*

g. *Attach the fringe first. Sew in position at the front, on the crown, and finally at the back.*

MATERIALS

61cm (24in) of 92cm (36in) wide calico
340g (12oz) white stuffing
selection of six-stranded embroidery threads for facial features
blushing powder for cheeks
approx 50g (2oz) brushed acrylic wool or mohair for hair

EQUIPMENT

Dressmaking shears, embroidery scissors, pins, needles, bodkin, thread, tape measure or ruler, pencil, tissue paper, pattern-making equipment.

PROJECT 11

DRESSING A
RAG DOLL

For many children, dolls are truly members of the family, taking their place as a make believe sister, brother, baby or best friend. Half the fun comes from dressing such dolls and tending to all their needs. The removable clothes for this doll are all made from pure cotton, so that they may be easily laundered and maintained.

Preparing the patterns

Prepare a full-size pattern of the drawers *(see p12)*, with a higher back waist edge and a lower front. The petticoat is a simple rectangle of cotton measuring 92cm (36in) wide by 29cm (11½in) deep, which can be cut without a pattern.

Prepare card patterns for the back and front bodice and sleeves. The dress skirt measures 92cm (36in) wide by 25.5cm (10in) long and the frill is made from two strips, each measuring 14cm (5½in) by 92cm (36in). Cut a bias strip (a thin strip of material cut on the cross of the fabric) to neaten the neck edge.

The pinafore pattern can be made by cutting card copies of the following sizes or by ruling directly onto the fabric. The skirt measures 92cm (36in) wide by 23cm (9in) long, the waistband measures 6.5cm (2½in) by 33cm (13in) while the straps are two pieces each measuring 25.5cm (10in) by 4.5cm (1¾in) and the two frills are each 46cm (18in) long by 7.6cm (3in) wide.

Prepare a card pattern of the shoe pieces from the pattern grid. Remember to transfer all the markings.

Making the underwear

1. Turn over a narrow hem to the right side at the lower end of each leg of the drawers, then cover the raw edges by sewing lace around the hem on

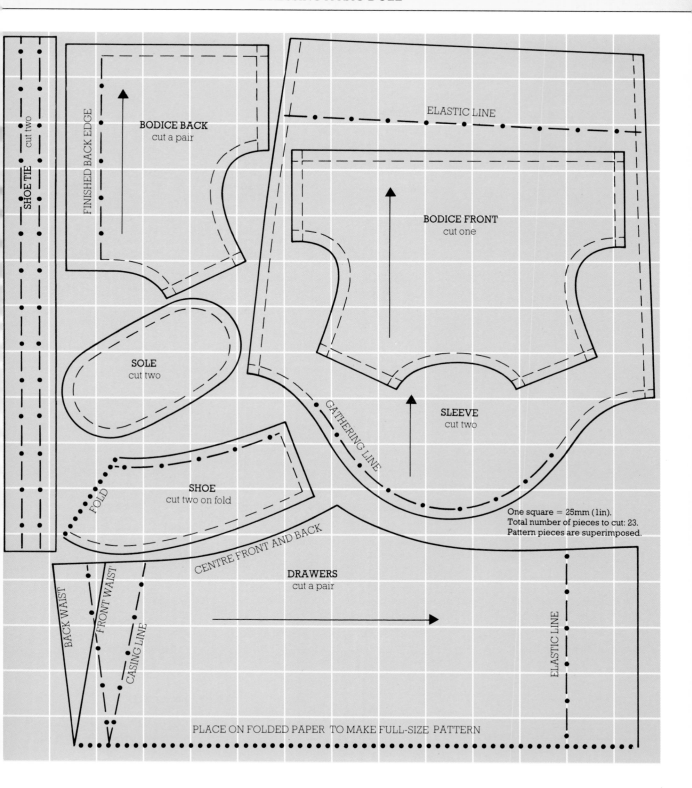

SHOE TIE cut two

BODICE BACK cut a pair

FINISHED BACK EDGE

ELASTIC LINE

BODICE FRONT cut one

SOLE cut two

GATHERING LINE

SLEEVE cut two

SHOE cut two on fold

FOLD

One square = 25mm (1in).
Total number of pieces to cut: 23.
Pattern pieces are superimposed.

CENTRE FRONT AND BACK

BACK WAIST

FRONT WAIST

CASING LINE

DRAWERS cut a pair

ELASTIC LINE

PLACE ON FOLDED PAPER TO MAKE FULL-SIZE PATTERN

45

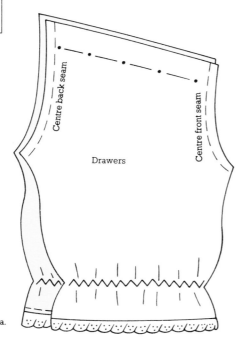

Drawers

Centre back seam

Centre front seam

a.

raw edges will now be enclosed in a French seam.

8. Make a narrow double hem along one long edge then attach a row of lace to this edge on the right side.

9. Turn under a narrow fold to the wrong side along the waist edge and press. Now turn under again to make a casing for the elastic. This casing should be about 12mm (½in) deep. Sew all around the edge of the casing, leaving a small opening.

10. Cut a length of elastic to fit the waist, again allowing for an overlap.

11 Thread the elastic through the waist casing and draw up to fit the doll. Overlap the ends and fasten off securely. Close the opening of the casing.

Making the dress

12. Sew the back bodice to the front bodice on both shoulder seams.

13. Run a row of gathering stitches along the head of each sleeve. Pull up to fit the armhole opening and then sew in place.

14. Make a narrow double hem at the wrist edge of each sleeve.

15. Stretch a row of elastic across each sleeve, as marked on the pattern, and sew in place either with zig-zag or straight stitching.

16. Fold the bodice to bring the

edges of the sleeves together then sew each underarm seam and side bodice seam in turn.

17. Gather the waist edge of the skirt and draw it up until it fits the waist edge of the bodice. Distribute the gathers evenly, tack in place and then sew.

18. Make a narrow double hem down both edges of the dress from the neck to the lower edge. Now turn a narrow, single hem to the front along the lower edge of the dress and sew to hold.

19. Prepare the dress frill by sewing the long strips together across one short end. Press the seam open. Fold the strip in half and sew all along the long edge. Turn right side out and press. Turn in both short ends and ladder stitch or top stitch the edges together in turn.

20. Run a double gathering thread along the folded edge of the frill – not the seaming edge. Pull up to fit the lower edge of the skirt.

21. Position the frill along the lower edge of the dress and sew in place through the gathering stitches.

22. Cover the lines of sewing with a row of ric rac. Finish the wrist edges with a row of ric rac, too.

23. Fit the dress on the doll and check the fit. Make any necessary adjustments at the neck.

a. Sew the lace and elastic on the drawers and then sew together the right side.

2. Stretch a piece of elastic across the line marked on each leg and sew in place either with zig-zag or straight stitching.

3. Join each half of the drawers together by sewing both the centre front and centre back seams (see fig. a).

4. Fold the drawers right sides together and sew up one inside leg and down the other one.

5. Turn under a narrow single hem at the waist edge, then fold again to make a casing for

b. Make a casing for the elastic in the waist band of the drawers. Leave a small opening at the centre back.

c. Sew the bias strip to the right side of the neck edge, turn over the wrong side of the bodice and hem in place.

along the centre front and centre back seams.

the elastic. Sew, leaving a small opening at the centre back (see fig. b).

6. Cut a length of elastic to fit the waist, allowing for overlap. Thread through the casing, sew ends together and then close opening.

7. The petticoat is a simple half slip. Fold the cotton in half with wrong sides together and sew a narrow seam along the short end. Turn to wrong side and sew another narrow seam, enclosing the first seam. All the

b.

c.

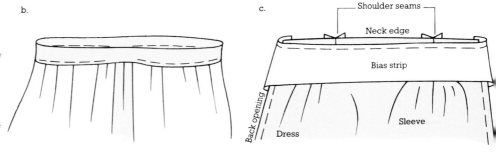

Shoulder seams

Neck edge

Bias strip

Back opening

Dress

Sleeve

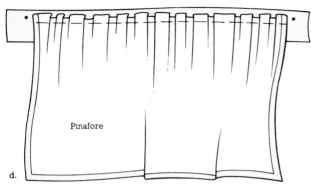

d.

d. Gather up the waist edge of the pinafore and pull up to fit the waist band between the dots. Sew in place.

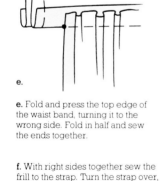

e.

e. Fold and press the top edge of the waist band, turning it to the wrong side. Fold in half and sew the ends together.

f. With right sides together sew the frill to the strap. Turn the strap over, fold the edge under and hem it to the back of the frill.

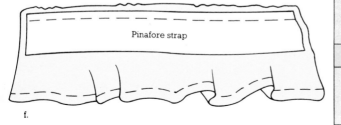

f.

24. Finish the neck edge by attaching a bias strip *(see fig.c)*.
25. Sew press studs on the back opening.

Making the pinafore
26. Make the skirt of the pinafore first by hemming both the short sides and the longer lower edge.
27. Run a gathering thread along the waist edge and pull up to fit the waist band between the dots *(see fig. d.)*. With raw edges level and right sides together, sew in place.
28. Fold and press, turning in to the wrong side of the waistband on the unsewn edge. Then fold the waistband in half and sew the ends together *(see fig. e)* with straight stitches.
29. Turn the waistband right side out and slip stitch the pressed edge in place.
30. Hem one long edge of each frill piece. Run a gathering thread along each unhemmed long edge and pull up to fit the length of the strap.
31. Sew a frill to a strap with right sides together and raw edges level *(see fig. f)*. Turn

the strap over, fold the edge under and hem it to the back of the frill. Attach the frill to the other strap.
32. Position both straps behind the front and back of the waist band and sew in place.
33. Sew a hook and eye on the back waist opening.
34. Cut the daisies into separate units and arrange them over the apron, sewing in place with yellow thread using straight stitches.

Making the shoes
35. Fold under a narrow hem to the wrong side on the ankle edge of each shoe and sew in place in order to give the edge extra strength.
36. Sew a 3mm (⅛in) seam at the heel.
37. Tack and sew the shoe to the sole, easing in the fullness around the toes.
38. Fold the shoe tie in thirds lengthways and sew along its

length in the centre to hold the fold in place.
39. Sew the tie to the back of the shoe on the heel seam.
40. Make a small pleat at the front of the shoe and cover with a bow or daisy.
41. Finish the second shoe in the same way.

Finishing touches
42. The clothes should all be pressed before dressing.
43. Put on the socks first, re-shaping the toes if they are too big.
44. Follow with the drawers and petticoat.
45. The dress goes on next (with a full back opening this should prove easy for any young child). The pinafore follows; lastly the shoes are tied in place.
46. Finally, brush the cheeks lightly with blusher to bring some warmth and colour to the face of the doll.

MATERIALS

For the dress:
1m (1yd) of 92cm (36in) wide cotton print
1.5m (1½yds) ric rac
4 press studs for back fastening
30.5cm (12in) narrow elastic
For the pinafore:
46cm (18in) of 92cm (36in) wide, white spotted cotton
12 guipure daisies
1 hook and eye
For the underwear:
61cm (24in) of 92cm (36in) wide, white lawn or cotton
2m (2yds) cotton lace
76cm (30in) narrow elastic
For the shoes and socks:
30.5 (12in) square of felt
pair of first-size baby socks

EQUIPMENT

Dressmaking shears, embroidery scissors, pins, needles, thread, tape measure or ruler, pencil, tissue paper, pattern-making equipment.

PROJECT 12

— MAKING A —
CLASSIC TEDDY

Teddy bears have only been made since the beginning of the twentieth century, and yet in that time they have become firmly established as one of the world's classic toys. A fully jointed teddy is extra special and often becomes a lifelong companion and a family heirloom.

Preparing the pattern
Make a full-size pattern and transfer all the markings on to it *(see p.12)*. Cut the body pieces out of the fur and cut protective shields for the joints from the remnants. Dismantle the joint *(see p.16)*. The soles and paws are cut from velvet. Mark the joint positions with a soft pencil dot on the wrong side of the fur, then draw a cross through each dot, so that it can be easily located. The teddy stands 46cm (18in) tall when finished.

Making the arms and legs
1. Sew the shoulder dart on an outside arm and finger-press open *(see fig. a)*. Repeat for the other arm.
2. Sew a velvet paw in place on an inside arm, matching As and Bs and finger-press the seam open *(see fig. b)*. Make a hole for the joint with an awl and then protect the edges of the hole. You can do this by working a row of buttonhole stitching around the edge, by pressing on an iron-on interfacing patch, or by glueing a felt disc over the

a. *Sew the shoulder darts on the outside arms and finger-press them open.*

b. *Sew the paws to the inner arms. Match As and Bs, sew the seam and finger-press the seam open. Make holes for the joints and reinforce the openings.*

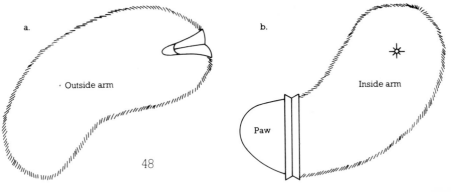

a.

· Outside arm

b.

Inside arm

Paw

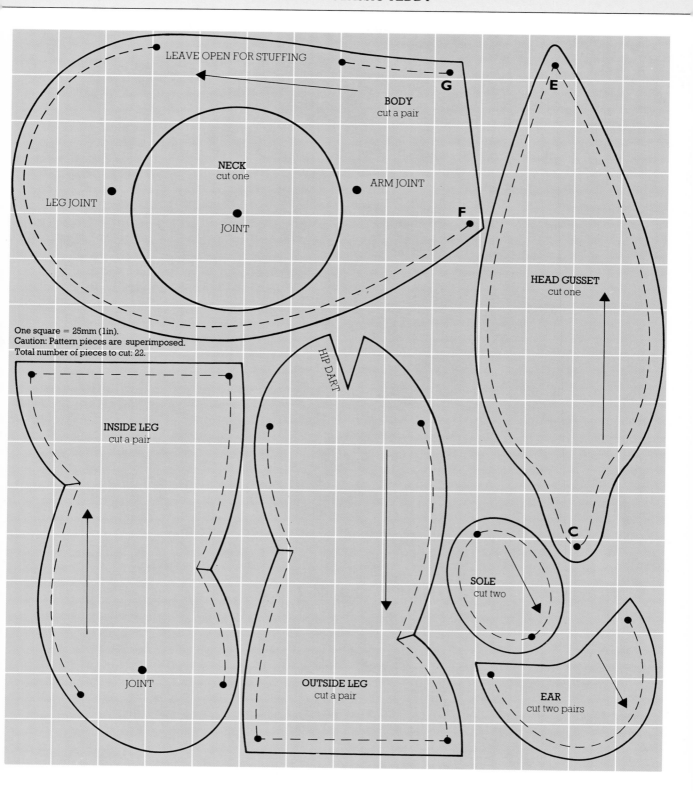

LEAVE OPEN FOR STUFFING

G

BODY
cut a pair

E

NECK
cut one

ARM JOINT

LEG JOINT

JOINT

F

HEAD GUSSET
cut one

One square = 25mm (1in).
Caution: Pattern pieces are superimposed.
Total number of pieces to cut: 22.

HIP DART

INSIDE LEG
cut a pair

C

SOLE
cut two

JOINT

OUTSIDE LEG
cut a pair

EAR
cut two pairs

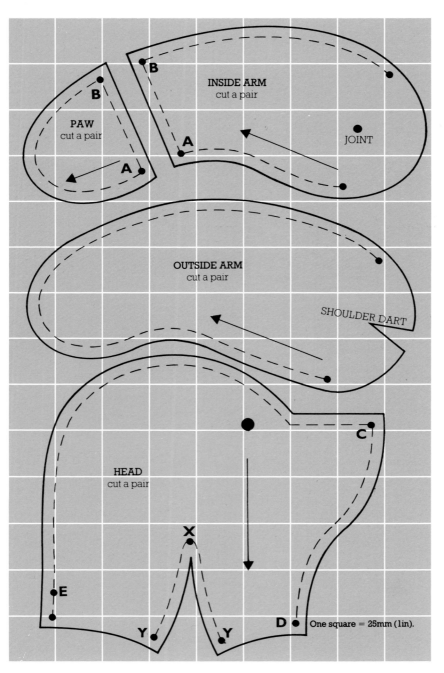

PAW
cut a pair

INSIDE ARM
cut a pair

JOINT

OUTSIDE ARM
cut a pair

SHOULDER DART

HEAD
cut a pair

One square = 25mm (1in).

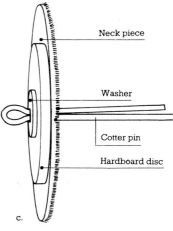

Neck piece

Washer

Cotter pin

Hardboard disc

c.

c. Assemble the neck joint. Hold the cotter pin in your left hand and thread a steel washer and a hardboard disc on to it. Push the pin through the neck piece from the wrong side. This piece will act as the protective shield for the joint.

area (having first made a hole in the centre of the felt). Repeat for the other arm.
3. Place one pair of outside and inside arm pieces right sides together and tack by overcasting the edges before sewing. Leave an opening at the shoulder. Repeat for the other arm.
4. Turn the arms right side out and stuff each firmly up to the joint mark. Load a cotter pin for each arm with a washer, hardboard disc and a protective shield *(see fig. b)*.
5. Insert a loaded cotter pin into an arm and push it through the hole for the joint. Turn the protective shield over the disc edge and hold in place with stuffing as you finish stuffing the shoulder area.
6. Close the shoulders with ladder stitch and then remove any trapped fur from the seams. Put to one side while you work on the legs.
7. Make the hip darts on each outside leg piece and then

make a hole for the joint on the inside legs, protecting the openings in the same way as you did for the arms *(see step 2)*.

8. Match up the pairs of inside and outside leg pieces (check that you have a left and a right one). Tack by overcasting the edges together for each leg, leaving the hip curve and the sole edge open. Sew together and clip the seam allowance at the corner at the top of the foot and behind the knees.

9. Pin and then tack by overcasting each sole in place, opening out the back and front seam allowances of the legs, so that they lie flat *(see fig. d)*. Remove the pins. Sew the soles to the leg and turn right side out. Check that the two soles match in size and that the pile of the velvet lies in the same direction.

10. Stuff the legs firmly up to the jointing position. Insert the loaded cotter pins into each

d. *Pin the sole in position on the leg and flatten out the seam allowances of the leg pieces before tacking. Remove the pins and sew together with backstitch. Turn right side out.*

d.

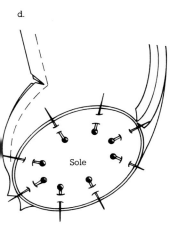

Sole

Inside leg

e.

leg, finish stuffing and close in the same way as described for the arms in steps 4-6. *(see fig.e.)*.

Making the head and body
11. Start by making the cheek darts in each head piece. Bring Y to Y and sew from X to Y. Sew left and right head pieces together from C at the nose down to the neck edge at D.
12. Now insert the head gusset matching C to C and pinning back to E on one side first and then to E on the other side. Check that the gusset is level and has not twisted the head. Tack by overcasting, remove the pins and then sew in place. Close the remainder of the head seam from E down to the back neck edge. Turn the completed head right side out.
13. Make holes for the eyes and then fix in place *(see p.15)*.

e. *The cotter pin is inserted through the joint hole in the inside leg after the leg has been stuffed to the level of the joint mark. The edge of the disc should be protected by turning the fabric shield over it before the hip area is stuffed. Close the limb with ladder stitch.*

f. *When attaching the neck piece to the neck edge of the head, make sure that it does not stand proud of the head.*

Stuff the head firmly, shaping the cheeks and moulding the head. Run a gathering stitch around the neck edge with strong double thread, pull in to gather up the opening and fasten off securely. The neck piece will be fitted into this opening, so do not close too tightly.

14. Make a hole in the centre of the neck piece. Strengthen the opening with buttonhole stitch. Take the cotter pin for the head joint and thread on a washer and a hardboard disc. Then push the pin through the neck piece from the wrong side *(see fig. c)*. Using strong thread, gather around the

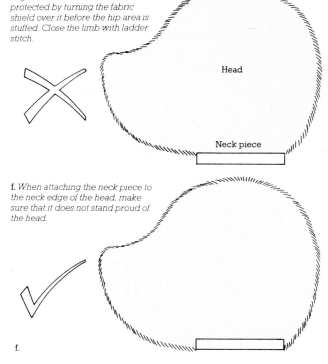

Head

Neck piece

f.

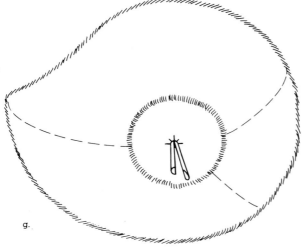

g.

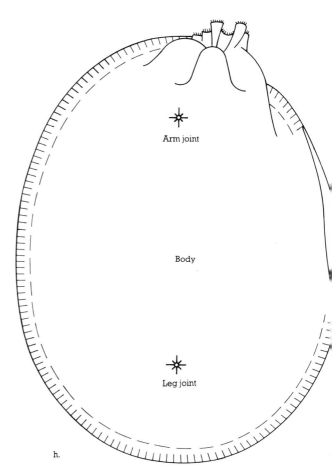

Arm joint

Body

Leg joint

h.

g. Neck piece with cotter pin protruding, sewn in position on the neck edge of the head.

edge of the neck piece and pull up, so that it encloses the hardboard disc. Fasten off.
15. Place the prepared neck piece against the gathers of the head neck edge and ladder stitch it in place. Make sure that the neck disc nestles into the head; it must not be left proud, as this would spoil the final appearance of the teddy *(see figs. f and g).*
16. Make and protect the holes for jointing the limbs on the two body pieces. Tack by overcasting and then sew the body together from F down the tummy to G, leaving an opening on the back seam and at the neck edge for stuffing. Run a strong gathering thread around the neck edge and pull as tightly as possible and fasten off securely *(see fig. h).* Turn the completed body skin right side out.
17. Carefully thread the cotter pin of the head through the neck edge of the body between the gathers. From the inside of the body, thread a protective shield on to the

cotter pin, followed by a hardboard disc and finally a washer. Spread the pins open and pull really tight with the pliers as you make a crown joint *(see p. 16).* This is the hardest joint you will have to work. There are two points to watch out for in particular: do not allow the neck disc to sink into the head and do not let the body neck gathers become too bulky, as this would force the head and body apart.

Attaching the arms and legs
18. All four limbs are attached in the same way, but it is easier to do the arms first, followed by the legs. Take up an arm and push the cotter pin through the body wall. Check that the paw faces forward and upwards – in other words, the right arm is on the right side of the body and the left arm matches the left side of the body. Thread a protective shield on to the cotter pin, followed by the hardboard disc and washer. Bend the pins into a crown joint *(see p. 16).* Attach the other arm and then the legs in the same way. Check that all the joints are secure before proceeding.
19. Stuff the body, taking care

to pack the stuffing around the joints, particularly at the shoulders and neck. Round out the tummy and the buttocks. Take time over the stuffing. It must be firm if all the joints are to work properly.
20. Close the opening with ladder stitch, using strong doubled thread. Clean the seam and tease out the pile.
21. Now you can embroider claw marks on the teddy's paws and soles if you wish. Use all six strands of embroidery

h. After reinforcing the arm and leg joint holes with buttonhole stitching, sew the two body pieces together. Tack by overcasting and then sew from F to G, leaving an opening at the back. Gather the neck edge, avoiding bulkiness at this point, so that the head can be attached closely and firmly.

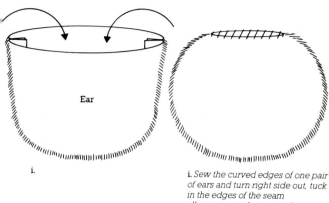

Ear

i.

i. *Sew the curved edges of one pair of ears and turn right side out, tuck in the edges of the seam allowances and oversew the opening.*

thread to work long straight stitches in each claw position.

Finishing touches
22. Pin and tack by overcasting the ears together in pairs before seaming.
23. Turn the ears right side out and tease any pile away from the seams. Turn in the edges of the seam allowances on both sides of each ear and oversew the open edges together *(see fig. i.)*.

24. Position one ear on the head behind the eye and just reaching up on to the head gusset seam. Ladder stitch in place on the front side first, taking care not to catch the fur on the back of the ear. Then ladder stitch along the back of the ear. By keeping the stitches 6mm (¼in) above the base you will spread the bottom of the ear, making a shorter ear that is really securely attached. Sew the

other ear in position in the same way.
25. Use all six strands of embroidery thread in a long darning needle to work a block of satin stitches for the nose.
26. The mouth is worked at the same time as the nose. Take a straight stitch down the centre front from the nose for about 2cm (¾in), then pass the needle into the head and out on the lower left side to define one corner of the mouth. Thread the needle behind the base of the straight stitch and pass it back into the head on the lower right side, level with its emergence on the other side. This completes the mouth. If you are not satisfied with its appearance, simply unthread the needle, hook out the stitches and start again. Mouths are very expressive and will determine whether the teddy is happy or sad, serious or mean.
27. As a final finishing touch, tie a lovely bow around your teddy's neck. If you like, you can follow the current fashion of tying a small bow around each ear for a girl teddy.

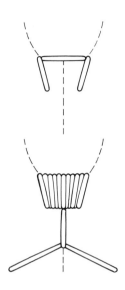

k.　Nose and mouth

k. *The nose is worked in satin stitch, using six-stranded embroidery thread. Define the outline and then fill it in. Continue to work on the mouth with the same thread.*

j.

j. *The ears are positioned behind the eye, with the inside edges touching the gusset seam. Make sure that the features are arranged symmetrically. The slightest change in placements will alter the teddy's character.*

MATERIALS

46cm (18in) of 137cm- (54in)-wide medium-pile honey-coloured fur
23cm (9in) square of velvet for paws and soles
pair 18mm amber safety eyes
dark brown embroidery thread of tapestry wool for nose
2½in joint for head
2　1¾in joints for arms
2　2in joints for legs
500g (1lb 2oz) stuffing
1m (1yd) ribbon for bow

EQUIPMENT

Dressmaking shears, embroidery scissors, pins, needles, thread, tape measure or ruler, pencil, long-nosed pliers, awl, pattern-making equipment.

──MAKING──
WOODEN TOYS

To make the wooden toys in this section, you do not have to be an expert woodworker. The basic information in this introduction will prepare you with all the skills you need to follow the simple methods given for the projects.

The appeal of hand made wooden toys will always outlast that of their more modern metal and plastic counterparts. The natural beauty of the wood itself enhances the look of any toy and its durability makes shaping, construction and repair relatively easy.

The tools required for building the projects in this section are all familiar to the home D.I.Y. enthusiast, as are the techniques needed for construction.

Wood Types

Wood falls into two categories: softwood and hardwood. There is also a wide range of manmade boards available.

Softwood

Broadly, this is wood produced from evergreen, coniferous trees. It is easier to work, more readily available and generally cheaper than hardwood. Its quality varies, but if you ask for 'good quality knotfree softwood', it is unnecessary to specify a particular type (which could include yellow pine, yellow or red deal and white deal, or whitewood). The disadvantage of softwood is that it tends to deteriorate if exposed to the weather, unless it is well protected with paint or varnish. The exceptions are western red cedar and redwood, which weather very well.

Hardwood

Hardwood comes from deciduous trees, such as ash, beech, lime, oak and elm, the most suitable for toymaking being beech. However,

Hand tools and equipment
1. **Panel saw** *For straight cuts along and across the grain.* 2. **Tenon saw** *For cross cutting small sections and cutting joints.* 3. **Fretsaw** *For cutting curves.* 4. **Coping saw** *Similar to the fretsaw but with a more robust blade.* 5. **Padsaw** or **keyhole saw** *For cutting internal shapes.* 6. **Smoothing plane** 7. **Wheelbrace** *Drill which takes bits to 6mm (1/4in) in diameter.* 8. **Brace and bit** *Drills larger holes than the wheelbrace.* 9. **Screwdrivers** *Flat-bladed and cross head.* 10. **Claw hammer** *450g (16oz) For driving and withdrawing nails.* 11. **Cross pein** or **Pin hammer** *The tapered end is used for working in confined areas.* 12. **Chisels** *Available in a range of widths.* 13. **Pliers** 14. **Mallet** 15. **Bradawl** *Used to make starter holes before drilling.* 16. **G-cramps** *Used to hold two surfaces together.* **Sash cramps** *Used for cramping larger pieces* 17. **Try square** *To measure right angles.* 18. **Tape measure** and **Metal rule** 19. **Craft knife** 20. **Dowelling jig** *Used to prepare holes for dowelling joints.* **Sandpaper** *Three grades required. A cork sandpaper block is useful.* **Nails** and **Screws** *Panel pins, round head, and countersink woodscrews are used.* **Workbench,** *preferably with a built-in vice.*

Power tools
21. **Power drill** *A general purpose two-speed drill with a 10mm (3/8in) chuck is quite adequate.* 22. **Jigsaw** *Used to saw straight and curved cuts.* 23. **Circular saw** *For straight cuts across and along the grain.* 24. **Holesaw** *A specialized drill attachment for cutting circles.* 25. **Countersink bit** *Fits in standard wheelbrace or power drill.*

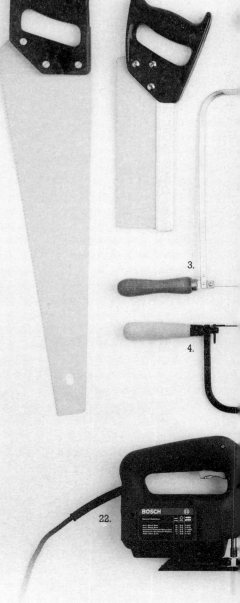

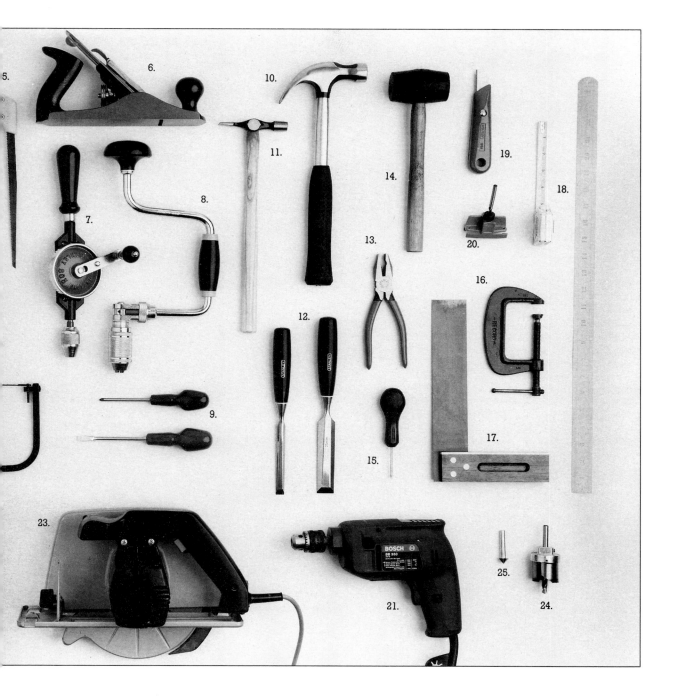

hardwood is expensive and also hard to work, so it is not recommended for toymaking unless a particularly hard-wearing finish is required.

Choosing the wood

It is important to find a reliable timberyard where you can rely on the quality of the wood. This depends chiefly on three factors: the way it has been dried, cut and stored. If wood has been well seasoned (either kiln-dried or air dried) its moisture content will have stabilized and been reduced. Check before buying that the wood is not warped and that there are no knots in it. Timberyards classify softwood according to quality – selected, or unselected. Hardwood is not given a general classification.

Wood sizes

Softwood is stocked in a wide range of standard sizes and is available 'rough sawn' (timber sawn into

Wood is officially sized in metric measurements, but it continues to be more popularly referred to in imperial sizes. Always specify the thickness first when ordering.

Standard thickness		Standard width	
in	mm	in	mm
⅜	10	¾	19
½	12	1	25
¾	19	1½	38
⅞	22	2	50
1	25	3	75
1¼	32	4	100
1½	38	5	125
1¾	44	6	150
2	50	7	175
2½	63	8	200
3	75	9	225
		10	250

planks) or 'prepared' (sawn and planed on all four sides to give a smooth finish, and ready for use). Hardwoods are normally cut and planed to the required size. The standard width measurements refer to the nominal size of the 'rough sawn' wood, which is obviously reduced with planing.

Manmade boards

A variety of boards, all based on reconstituted wood, are very useful to the toymaker. Their advantages over natural timber are that they are generally cheaper, more stable and less likely to warp. They are available in a range of thicknesses, and a standard size of 2440 x 1220mm (8 x 4ft). Most of them are also available with special finishes, suitable for indoor or outdoor use. They are essential for large panels.

Plywood This sheet material is made from thin layers, or veneers, of wood which have been glued together in such a way that the direction of the grain alternates in order to give the board strength and stability.

Hardboard Made from softwood pulp which has been compressed under high pressure. Tempered hardboard is suitable for outdoor use as it has been impregnated with oil to make it relatively water resistant.

Blockboard A sheet material made from rectangular strips of softwood glued together side by side and sandwiched between single or doubled veneers of wood.

Chipboard Made from small wood chips which have been coated with resin and compressed into sheets.

Marking out wood from the template

The easier projects recommend that you have wood cut to size by your timber merchant, but remember to accommodate the 'prepared size' in your order *(above)*. Templates are

given as a guide to the pieces you will require, and these should be used as a pattern for the more complicated shapes. Where detail is required, as for the dog's head *(see p.72)*, enlarge the pattern by squaring it up *(see p.120)* as a paper template and transfer it to the wood. Use a steel rule and a try square to mark accurate 90° angles. If there are several similar pieces identify each by labelling. Be sure to follow either the metric, or the imperial measurements, but you cannot mix them.

Cutting the wood

You can ask your timber merchant to cut the wood into manageable pieces, and tackle the rest yourself with a hand or power saw.

Straight saw cuts Cross-cutting (across the grain) and rip-sawing (along the grain) are done with a panel saw, powered circular saw or jigsaw. To help maintain a straight cut when using a panel saw, hold the wood steady and level and as you cut, look down, with one eye closed, at the top edge of the blade. If either side of the blade can be seen it means that you are cutting at an angle and you will have to plane the wood square.

A tenon saw is used for smaller straight cuts. To ensure a clean saw cut, first scribe the grain on the surface by marking it with a sharp craft knife.

Curved cuts A fretsaw or power jigsaw will cut very tight curves and gives a fine, neat cut. A coping saw is useful for cutting curves in thicker timber. The blade can be set at any angle to cut curves more easily. The wood should be held steady by hand, or in a vice. The trick is to cut slowly, constantly checking that a smooth curve is being achieved.

Cutting internal shapes A padsaw,

fretsaw or coping saw can be used. A pilot hole must first be drilled so that the blade can be inserted. One end of the blade of the fretsaw and coping saw must be unscrewed, pushed through the hole and then reconnected before sawing can begin.

Planing
Prepared wood should not require further planing. However, if it does, ensure that the blade of the plane is set correctly and that it is very sharp. Fix the wood in a vice, protecting the gripped surfaces with offcut scraps of wood. When you plane it is essential to keep the blade flat; use a smooth gliding action.

Drilling holes
A wheelbrace hand drill, a brace and bit, or a two-speed power drill with a 10mm (⅜in) chuck are all suitable for toymaking.

Make a small starter hole with a bradawl before drilling. If the drill binds, ease it out of the hole to relieve the pressure, remove the waste sawdust, and try again.

If drilling to a specific depth, stick a piece of masking tape around the drill bit to mark the required depth.

Screwing
Steel woodscrews should be countersunk so that the top of the screw is flush with the surface of the wood. A countersink drill bit will prepare a tapered opening for the screw. If you do not have a countersink bit, use a hand-held countersink tool to make the tapered opening by twisting it around in the pre-drilled holes. Make sure that the holes you drill are small enough to allow the thread of the screw to bite firmly into the wood. Always screw into the cross grain, never into end grain as the thread has to cut into the

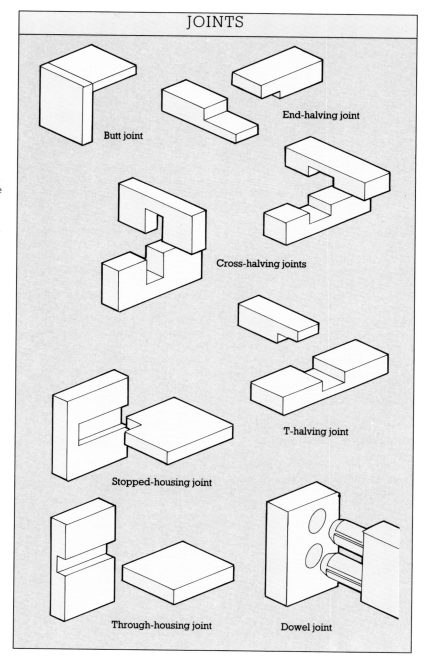

JOINTS

Butt joint

End-halving joint

Cross-halving joints

T-halving joint

Stopped-housing joint

Through-housing joint

Dowel joint

grain for a good fixing. It will be easier to drive the screws into the wood if you first rub a little soap on the threads to lubricate them.

Nailing

Nails and pins should always be dovetailed (hammered in at alternating angles), giving a much more secure fixing than nailing at right angles. Never drive nails in along the same line of grain as this will tend to split the wood.

When using small nails or pins protect your fingers from injury by using a piece of thin cardboard to hold the nail in position while hammering. Use the tapered end of the cross pein hammer to start tapping in the nail and then drive it home with the large end.

Never nail directly into hardwood – always drill a pilot hole first.

Glueing

Polyvinyl acetate (PVA) glue is suitable for both indoor and outdoor toys, as it becomes waterproof when dry. The glue should usually be applied to both surfaces and the wood then clamped together under pressure. However, there is no need to clamp joints that have been glued together if they are screwed or nailed.

Epoxy resin, or adhesive should be used to fix nuts tightly over axles when fixing wheels. Wallpaper paste can be used to glue paper to wood.

Joints

All the joints used for making the toys are easy to achieve. Accurate marking, scoring and sawing will ensure a good finish.

Butt joint The simplest joint used, it is made by nailing or screwing the end of one piece of wood to another. The edges can also be glued for additional strength.

Halving joints The end-halving joint is useful for constructing frames. Mark and score the cutting lines and saw through half the depth of each corresponding piece of wood, both along and across the grain. Smooth the sawn edges with a chisel, glue the area and fix with woodscrews. For cross-halving, and T-halving joints, saw across the grain and chisel out the wood from side to centre.

Through-housing joint A strong joint where the end of a cross piece is recessed into the side of an upright. Mark and score the position of the channel, or housing, and saw across the width of the wood to a depth of one third of its thickness. Chisel out the wood, working from both edges. Glue the cross piece in position. Fix in nails at an angle to hold the joint.

Dowel joint Accuracy in aligning the holes for the dowels, in drilling the holes vertically and to the exact diameter and half the length of the dowel is ensured by using a dowelling jig. Shape the ends of the dowel and saw a groove along its length to allow the excess glue to escape. Clamp it in position until set.

Fitting wheels

There are several types of wheels suitable for toymaking.

Proprietary wheel systems

Many cycle accessory shops stock wheel systems that come complete with axles, wheels and connecting bushes. All you need do is to specify the length of axle and size of wheel required, and simply buy them over the counter. In most cases they will come with fittings, including brackets and screws for attaching them to the toy.

Re-cycled wheels

Make use of existing wheels and convert them to a new use. Pram wheels, which come complete with axles, need only be removed from, say, a pram and refitted to the new vehicle, such as the go-cart (see pp. 128-31).

Castors

Castors are made in a wide variety of shapes and sizes. The smaller sizes are suitable only for indoor use, but the larger castors, particularly those with foam-filled tyres, can be used outdoors. Wheel sizes up to 20cm (8in) in diameter are available. Unlike the large universal castors, the smaller roller castors come in sets containing both right and left castors (see pp. 72-5).

Wooden wheels

Wooden wheels for smaller toys such as the train and the truck (see pp. 76-9 and 84-7) can be purchased or cut from thick dowelling, or from a section of handrail. However, you must be able to saw with sufficient accuracy to produce straight edges. Sandpaper all the surfaces. Mark the centre of each wheel by drawing two bisecting lines across it, then drill the fixing hole – large enough to allow the wheel to rotate freely, but not so large that it wobbles. Attach the wheel with two washers and a round head screw.

Plywood wheels

You can draw circles on a piece of plywood with a pair of compasses and then cut them out with a fretsaw, coping saw or jigsaw as for the hobby horse (see pp. 80-1). The most accurate results, however, are obtained with a holesaw, attached to a power drill and a pillar drill stand. The holesaw not only cuts perfect rounds, but also drills a hole through the exact centre of the wheel. It can be used for circles up to 7.6cm (3in) in diameter.

Wood finishes

Brightly painted toys have great appeal for children, but a good finish is not purely decorative. Its practical function is to make the toy durable, and, when necessary, weatherproof. It is essential that all paints and varnishes are non-toxic.

Preparing the wood
For both appearance and safety it is essential to give the toy a smooth finish. Sand all the surfaces, particularly edges that are cut across the grain, and fill countersunk holes with a proprietary filler.

Gloss paint
There are stringent regulations regarding the lead content of paint used for children's toys. Gloss paints that meet these requirements are now being produced. First seal the wood with a primer (white emulsion paint does this job). It will disguise any repairs that may have been done. Follow with an undercoat, and a final top coat of gloss. Gloss is too thick for fine detailed work but it covers large areas well and has a good depth of colour.

Water-based acrylic paint
A wide range of ready-mixed, quick-drying colours available in small quantities make this a popular paint for toymakers. The paint covers well, and will also give a very delicate line when used with a fine sable brush.

First clean the surface of the wood with white spirit. Next, seal the surface of the wood with white emulsion, or to retain the grain of the wood, use a light varnish (made by diluting polyurethane varnish with an equal quantity of white spirit). When dry, apply the acrylic paint. The paint will dry to a matt finish, so for a shiny protective coating, seal it with a full strength polyurethane varnish. This will darken the colour slightly and give it a richer quality.

Enamel paint
Enamel paint gives a hard-wearing, high gloss finish. It is available in small quantities and in a good range

of strong colours. However, it has a fairly long drying time. For finer, more detailed work, thin down the paint with enamel thinners.

Polyurethane varnish
This synthetic varnish can be used to give a clear gloss finish to toys painted with water-based paint, or used directly on unpainted wood to enhance and protect its natural features. When diluted it can be used as a primer before painting.

The varnish can be applied by brush or by spraying. When using a brush apply the first coat across the grain, allow it to dry overnight and rub down with a fine grain sandpaper before applying the second coat, working along the direction of the grain. Clean brushes with white spirit. If you use a spraycan, you will have to touch up areas with a fine brush, especially on the end grain.

Coloured varnishes are available, which leave the grain visible, while still giving colour to the toy.

Painting techniques
Attractive decorative effects can be achieved with a few simple techniques.

Masking
For a candy-stripe effect, stick strips of masking tape at regular intervals on a painted surface. Apply a coat of a second colour and when dry, unpeel the tape to reveal perfect, crisp stripes of colour.

Any shapes can be cut from adhesive film and treated in the same way.

Stencilling
Numbers, letters and decorative motifs can be stencilled onto toys. Cut your own stencil from special oil-coated stencil card, or buy one ready made. Use unthinned paint. Position the stencil carefully, and stipple the paint onto the design with

a short-bristled stencil brush. Work out the positions and spacing of your lettering before you begin stencilling.

Ruling fine lines
A ruling pen will produce fine lines for more detailed work. Mix up paint until it is sufficiently fluid to flow from the pen and adjust the blades of the pen to give the required thickness of line. Practise before working on the finished toy – this technique requires confidence.

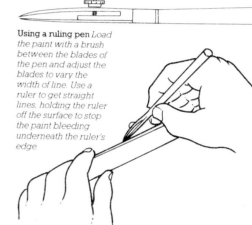

Using a ruling pen *Load the paint with a brush between the blades of the pen and adjust the blades to vary the width of line. Use a ruler to get straight lines, holding the ruler off the surface to stop the paint bleeding underneath the ruler's edge.*

Applied decoration
Instant transfer lettering and self-adhesive or gummed stickers can be used to add interest to toys. Give the toy a final top coat of varnish to seal the decoration.

Safety tips
Be aware of the hazards of working with wood – keep your workspace well organized and make sure that all wiring is safe. Keep saws, planes, chisels and drills sharp so that they do their job efficiently. Most importantly, keep all tools out of the reach of children, and remember that the finished toy must be safe for them to play with.

MAKING
BUILDING BRICKS

The easiest of toys to make, these building bricks will give hours of pleasure to your young child, while at the same time teaching skills in hand and eye co-ordination. Play value and learning potential can also be increased by adding pictures, numbers or letters, by using dry transfers, or by sticking pictures on the six sides of the bricks. The more elaborate building bricks, shaped as arches and columns, require curved saw cuts, but they are also easy to make.

Making simple building bricks

1. It is important that the bricks can be stacked, so use a try square and ruler to check that the sides are square and of equal size before cutting. You can ask your timber yard to cut the cubes for you if you want to make the job easier.

2. Use a try square to help you mark out the cubes with a pencil at 5cm (2in) intervals, on all sides of the wood. Now go back over the lines on one side, line up the try square and score with a craft knife. This will sever the grain and ensure a clean cut.

3. The wood can be held steady by hand, but it is preferable to use a vice. Sandwich the wood between two offcuts so that the grip of the vice does not mark the surface of the wood. Use a tenon saw to cut the cubes. Ensure that the cut is accurate by looking down at the blade from directly above. The sides of the blade should not be visible – if they are, it means that you are cutting at an angle.

4. When you have cut the 12 bricks, smooth the sawn edges. Start with coarse sandpaper, then use the medium grade; finish with fine sandpaper. The

Add interest and educational value to the building blocks by choosing a theme for each cube. For instance, have a picture of an animal and the first letter of its name on one brick, a number and the corresponding number of dots on another.

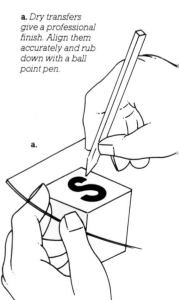

a. Dry transfers give a professional finish. Align them accurately and rub down with a ball point pen.

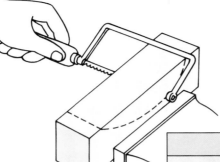

b. Cut the curve carefully with a coping saw so that both parts of the wood can be used.

best method for sanding is to lay the sandpaper on a smooth surface and to hold it steady while you rub the block of wood against it.

Decorating the bricks
5. Use a non-toxic varnish for a natural finish, or use brightly coloured non-toxic paint *(see p.59)*.
6. Cut out colourful pictures and glue them onto the cube with wallpaper paste; apply transfer lettering or numbers *(see fig. a)*; or stick on self-adhesive spots or shapes.
7. Give the bricks a final coat of varnish to seal the wood and decoration. If you have applied dry transfers, test first to see that the varnish does not make them blister.

Making columns and arches
1. Have the wood cut to the lengths specified by your timber merchant, or cut them to size yourself, using a tenon saw.
2. Smooth the sawn ends and any sharp edges with sandpaper.
3. Make a template for the curve of the arch on the two large pieces. The curve should begin at least 3.2cm (1¼in) from the end of the wood to allow the arch to be supported by the columns. Draw around a plate to get a smooth curve, or use a section of a circle drawn with compasses. Transfer the curve onto both sides of each piece of wood, making sure that they align.
4. Fix the wood in a vice and cut out the arch carefully, using a coping saw *(see fig. b)* or a power jigsaw.
5. Sand the curves smooth.

Painting and finishing
Use brightly coloured non-toxic paint *(see p.59)*.
6. Make sure that all the surfaces of the bricks are sanded smooth.
7. Apply one coat of water-based paint and allow to dry.
8. Sand the surface lightly, wipe away the dust and give a second coat of paint.
9. For a glossy finish apply a coat of non-toxic varnish.

TEMPLATES

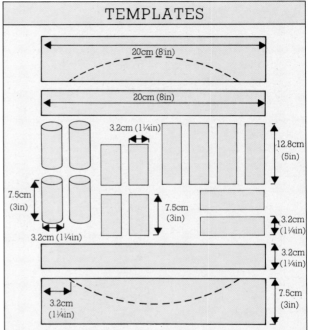

MATERIALS

For the cubes:
1 piece 50 x 50 x 610mm (2 x 2 x 24in) of knotfree prepared softwood, or hardwood (such as beech)

For the arches and columns:
Knotfree prepared softwood or hardwood:
2 pieces 32 x 75 x 200mm (1¼ x 3 x 8in)
2 pieces 32 x 32 x 200mm (1¼ x 1¼ x 8in)
6 pieces 32 x 32 x 128mm (1¼ x 1¼ x 5in)
4 pieces 32 x 32 x 75mm (1¼ x 1¼ x 3in)
Dowelling:
4 pieces 32 x 75mm (1¼ x 3in)

TOOLS

Ruler, sharp pencil, craft knife, try square, tenon saw, smoothing plane, sandpaper (coarse, medium and fine), coping saw or jigsaw (for cutting arches).

MAKING A
JIGSAW

Jigsaw puzzles were first invented in the middle of the 18th century, when they were illustrated with maps and used to teach geography. Today they are popular with adults and children alike. The puzzles that are most popular with very young children are those that incorporate a base, or tray in their design. These can be simply made – use a favourite character as a basis for the painted design and cut around the contours to make large pieces that are easy to handle. A pattern is also given for traditional jigsaw shapes.

Making a tray jigsaw
1. Enlarge one of the designs given here by squaring up on a grid *(see p.120)* or by photocopy enlargement. Trace the outline onto a sheet of plywood and mark where the cuts will be made with a heavier line. (If you choose a design that is more complex you will have to simplify it into large shapes.)
2. Trace the design onto one sheet, leaving a border of at least 19mm (¾in).
3. Drill a small pilot hole at an intersection on the outline *(see fig. a)*. Unscrew the blade of a fretsaw, insert it through the hole and then reconnect it. Saw carefully around the outline *(see fig. b)* and then make all the other cuts.
4. Use fine-grade sandpaper to smooth all the edges of the jigsaw pieces, the border and the second piece of plywood (which will form the base).
5. Apply a thin coat of PVA

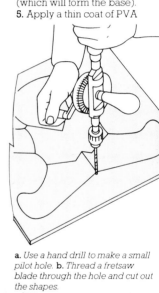

a. *Use a hand drill to make a small pilot hole.* **b.** *Thread a fretsaw blade through the hole and cut out the shapes.*

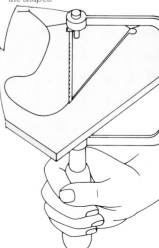

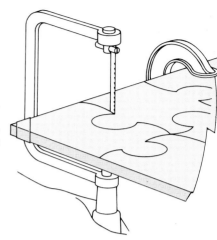

glue to the underside of the border and place it in position on the base board. Weight it down and allow to dry.
6. Paint the base and the jigsaw pieces and allow to dry. Use a non-toxic sealant if required.

Traditional jigsaw shapes
Use the pattern for the interlocking pieces of a traditional jigsaw to make a simple six-piece puzzle.
1. Cut out a picture from a magazine.
2. Enlarge the jigsaw pattern to the size you require and trace it onto a sheet of plywood.
3. Cut out the pieces with a fretsaw *(see fig. c)*.
4. Assemble the pieces on a flat surface and glue the picture onto the wood, using wallpaper paste.
5. When dry, cut through the paper from the back, using a craft knife.

c. *The tight curves of the traditional jigsaw shapes can be cut with a fretsaw, or with a power jigsaw fitted with a scroll-cutting blade.*

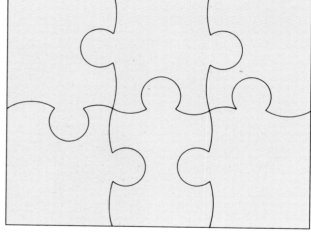

Left: *cutting patterns for the simple teddy bear and clown jigsaws.* Above: *pattern for the traditional jigsaw shapes. Use these as templates and enlarge to the size you require (see p.120).*

MATERIALS

For the tray jigsaw:
2 pieces 3 x 255 x 305mm (⅛ x 10 x 12in) plywood
  tracing paper, PVA glue, non-toxic paint

For the traditional jigsaw:
1 piece of plywood or hardboard
  picture, tracing paper, wallpaper paste

TOOLS

Fretsaw or power jigsaw, wheelbrace, craft knife, ruler, soft pencil, paint brush.

MAKING A
DRUM, PIPE AND RATTLE

Making a drum, pipe and rattle for your children will help you to open up two related worlds for them – the worlds of sound and music. Here, you can utilize old sweet- or biscuit-tin lids for the striking surface of the drum, while the rattle can be made from odd scraps of wood. When it comes to the traditional whistle, you can use bamboo cane, PVC or aluminium tubing – the former is the more traditional material, but the other two are readily available. You will find the tubing you require in most good hardware stores.

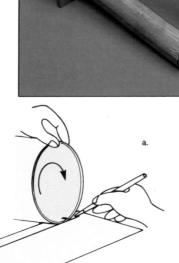

DRUM

Before you start, remember that the length of the cardboard is determined by the internal circumference of the lids you are using. You will need two of these; both must be of the same size. You will also need one of the tins, which will be used as a mould for the drum cylinder.

1. The easiest and most accurate way of measuring the required lengths of cardboard is to mark a point on the rim of the tin and then roll it along the cardboard until you come to the marked spot again (see fig. a). This will give you the tin's circumference; the cardboard should be cut about 3mm (⅛in) shorter so that it will fit inside the tin. Each successive sheet should be slightly shorter than the previous sheet, so that it will fit inside.

2. To make the cylinder of the drum, curl the first sheet of cardboard into the tin (see fig. b). If necessary, carefully trim

a. Use the tin to measure the required lengths of cardboard.

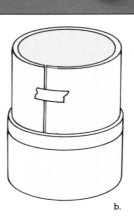

b. Next, use the tin as a mould to form the cylinder of the drum, making sure that the three joins are staggered.

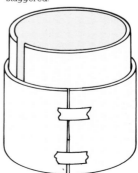

b.

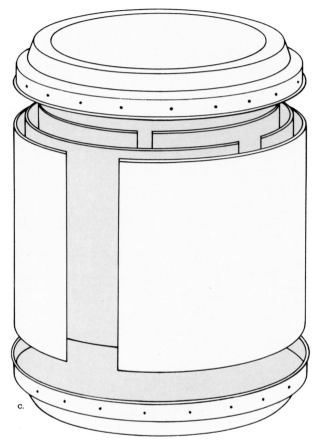

around the circumference of each lid.

5. The size of the holes required will depend on the thickness of the cord you plan to use. The holes should be large enough to allow the cord to pass through easily. To prevent the drill from slipping, make starting indentations with a bradawl, centre punch or a large nail *(see fig. d)*. The masking tape will also help to prevent the drill from slipping.

6. Glue the third sheet of cardboard in place and, when all the surfaces are completely dry, remove the cylinder from the tin.

7. All three components of the drum should be painted before assembly, although the cylinder can be covered with a soft decorative vinyl, if preferred. Cut the vinyl to the correct length and glue it to the cardboard cylinder.

8. Lace the three components together with cord *(see fig. e)*. Finally, make a loop so that the drum can be carried.

9. Shape the ends of the dowelling with a craft knife and sandpaper to form drumsticks *(see fig. f)*.

e.

e. Lace the three components together with decorative cord.

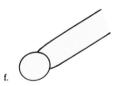

f.

f. Using a craft knife and sandpaper, shape the ends of the dowelling to form drumsticks.

the edges until they meet exactly. Hold them together with a strip of masking tape.

3. Apply generous amounts of PVA glue to the internal surface of the cardboard sheet and insert the second cylinder of cardboard. Make sure that the joins are staggered for extra strength *(see fig. c)*. Press the two cylinders together and leave to dry.

4. It is important to mark the holes around the lids accurately before they are drilled. Apply two strips of masking tape to a suitable clean surface. Mark points for holes every 7.5cm (3in). Peel the tape off and stick one strip

d. Make a pilot indentation for the drill holes with a sharp point, such as a centre punch, bradawl or nail.

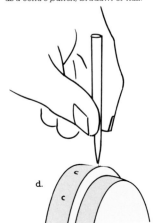

d.

MATERIALS

Drum

2 metal lids from similar sized biscuit or sweet tins
3 pieces of flexible cardboard, approx. 254 x 737mm (10 x 29in)
1 piece soft vinyl, approx 254 x 737mm (10 x 29in)
4 metres (4yd) decorative cord
2 piece dowelling 10 x 305mm (⅜ x 12in)
   PVA glue, non-toxic paint

TOOLS

Tape measure, pencil, craft knife, bradawl, wheelbrace and bit or power drill and bits, paint brushes, masking tape.

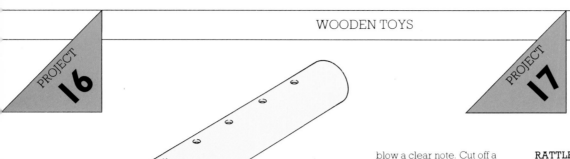

PIPE

Whether you make a pipe from plastic, or from aluminium, you will use much the same methods of construction. The only real difference is in the internal diameter and, therefore, in the size of the cork needed.

1. Cut the uPVC pipe to 28cm (11in) in length with a hacksaw.

2. Drill a hole 6mm (¼in) in diameter approximately 3.5cm (1⅜in) from one end of the tube. Square one side of the hole with a craft knife and file the flat side to an angle of 45° *(see fig. a)*. If you use a thin aluminium tube, then form a slight depression below the flat side of the hole, by tapping the tube gently with a ball pein hammer.

3. You can use a piece of wood, or a cork, to form a mouthpiece. Cork is preferable, as it is easy to shape with a craft knife and can also be sandpapered. Pare the cork and sandpaper it smooth, until it fits snugly into the pipe without being compressed. Now cut a flat wind channel. Sand it smooth and insert it into the tube until the end of the cork is level with the top of the wind hole *(see fig. b)*. If necessary, you can push the cork out of the pipe with a length of dowelling.

4. Adjust the cork until you can

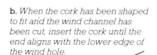

a.

a. First, cut or file the lower edge of the air hole until it is square, then file it to a 45° angle.

b. When the cork has been shaped to fit and the wind channel has been cut, insert the cork until the end aligns with the lower edge of the wind hole.

b.

c.

c. Cut a section off the end to make the mouthpiece.

blow a clear note. Cut off a slice at a sloping angle to form a comfortable mouthpiece *(see fig. c)* and sandpaper until smooth.

5. Stick a length of masking tape along the top of the pipe. You can use it for marking the position of the holes. It will also help to prevent the drill from slipping *(see fig. d)*. If you are using metal tubing, you should make pilot indentations with a bradawl or centre punch before drilling the holes.

6. Drill the second hole 6cm (2⅜in) from the first and the remaining five holes at 25mm (1in) intervals. It is important to drill the holes in an absolutely straight line. Drill a thumb hole on the underside of the tube, 18.5cm (7in) from the open end of the tube.

7. Tune the pipe by carefully enlarging the finger holes one by one with glasspaper. The hole second from the open end should be the largest. If the pipe is out of tune, try adjusting the size of your air inlet. This may mean shaping another cork. Remember that you can flatten the pitch, but you cannot sharpen it. If the pipe is still out of tune, you should probably start afresh, since the materials do not cost much and the pipe is easy to make.

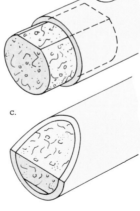

d.

d. Apply a strip of masking tape, mark off the holes, make pilot indentations with a sharp point and then drill the holes.

RATTLE

1. The rattle is an ideal project for using up any left-over scraps of wood. Cut the wood and plywood to the measurements given on the templates. The grain of the wood should run with the length of the clicker. This will give it additional strength.

2. There are two ways of making the rattle wheel. The easiest is to cut a 25mm (1in) length off a piece of dowelling with a diameter of approximately 5cm (2in). The second is to mark a circle onto each end of a block of hardwood, such as beech, and then round it off with chisels and sandpaper.

3. In either case, the next step is to divide the circle into six segments. Use a protractor to mark off angles of 60°. Draw lines from one point to the next until you have formed a star shape *(see fig.b)*.

4. Use a tenon saw to cut notches around the perimeter at the points marked, then carve out the ratchets with a sharp chisel. Sandpaper them until smooth.

5. Round off the bottom and top strips with a coping saw, or a fretsaw, and sandpaper the edges smooth.

6. Drill a 3mm (⅛in) hole in the top strip, a 10mm (⅜in) hole in the bottom strip, and four screw holes in the positions shown at the end of each strip *(see fig. a)*.

7. Now drill a 10mm (⅜in) hole right through the centre of the rattle wheel and a second 10mm (⅜) hole, approximately 19mm (¾in) deep, into the top of the dowelling handle.

8. Drill a hole in one clicker block *(see fig. a)*.

9. Sandpaper all the edges and surfaces until smooth. Now paint all the components,

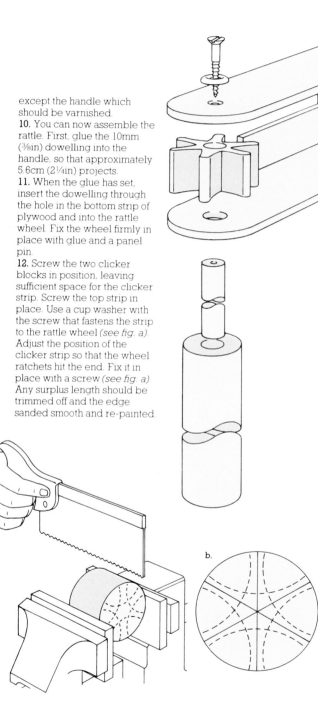

TEMPLATES

TOP/BOTTOM

CLICKER   HANDLE

21cm (8¼in)

25mm (1in)   25.4cm (10in)   15.2cm (6in)

25mm (1in)

CLICKER   5cm (2in)   RATTLE
BLOCK   25mm (1in)   WHEEL

19mm   25mm
(¾in)   (1in)

5.7cm (2¼in)   5cm
(2in)

except the handle which should be varnished.

10. You can now assemble the rattle. First, glue the 10mm (⅜in) dowelling into the handle, so that approximately 5.6cm (2¼in) projects.

11. When the glue has set, insert the dowelling through the hole in the bottom strip of plywood and into the rattle wheel. Fix the wheel firmly in place with glue and a panel pin.

12. Screw the two clicker blocks in position, leaving sufficient space for the clicker strip. Screw the top strip in place. Use a cup washer with the screw that fastens the strip to the rattle wheel *(see fig. a)*. Adjust the position of the clicker strip so that the wheel ratchets hit the end. Fix it in place with a screw *(see fig. a)*. Any surplus length should be trimmed off and the edge sanded smooth and re-painted.

b. Use a protractor to mark off six 60° angles. Draw lines from one point to the next until you have formed a star. Cut notches around the circumference and carve out the ratchets with a chisel.

MATERIALS

Pipe
1 30cm (12in) length uPVC pipe, with internal diameter of 19mm (¾in), or aluminium pipe, with internal diameter of 12mm (½in)
1 cork

Rattle
Softwood:
2 pieces 19 x 25 x 57mm (¾ x 1 x 2¼in) for clicker blocks
Plywood:
2 pieces 6 x 50 x 254mm (¼ x 2 x 10in)
1 piece 3 x 25 x 210mm (⅛ x 1 x 8¼in) for clicker
Dowelling:
1 piece 50 x 25mm (2 x 1in) for rattle wheel
1 piece 10 x 75mm (⅜ x 3in)
1 piece 25 x 152mm (1 x 6in) for handle
Hardware:
woodscrews, panel pin, cup washer
non-toxic paint, PVA glue

TOOLS

Pipe
Hacksaw, wheel brace and bit or power drill and bits, craft knife, bradawl or centre punch, masking tape, glasspaper, sandpaper, file.

Rattle
Tenon saw, coping saw, chisels, mallet, wheelbrace and bit or power drill and bits, screwdriver, paint brushes, sandpaper, protractor.

MAKING A
BABY WALKER

This is basically a sturdily constructed box on wheels with a raised handle at one end. It is a simple toy, which is often a great favourite with toddlers who enjoy using it to ferry their other toys from place to place. It is a toy that also plays a large part in encouraging toddlers to walk. When the handle is grasped for support, the baby walker will start to move forward, inviting the toddler to walk in order to maintain a balance.

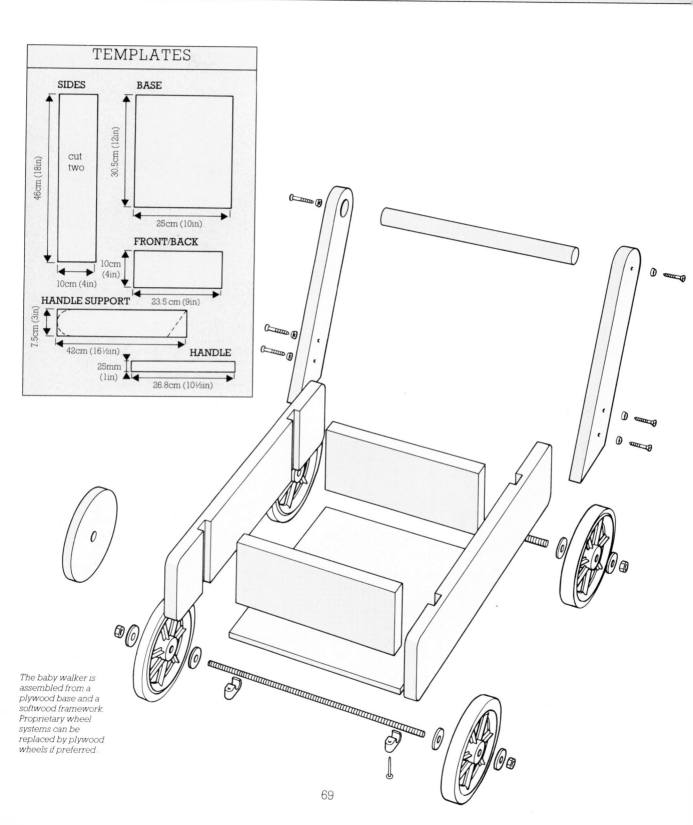

TEMPLATES

SIDES
cut two

46cm (18in)

10cm (4in)

BASE

30.5cm (12in)

25cm (10in)

FRONT/BACK

10cm (4in)

23.5 cm (9in)

HANDLE SUPPORT

7.5cm (3in)

42cm (16½in)

HANDLE

25mm (1in)

26.8cm (10½in)

The baby walker is assembled from a plywood base and a softwood framework. Proprietary wheel systems can be replaced by plywood wheels if preferred.

PROJECT

18

WOODEN TOYS

Buying the wood

Buy prepared wood and have it cut to size. Plywood is used for the base, and good quality knotfree softwood for the framework. If, in place of softwood, you use a hardwood, such as beech, you can allow for a reduction in the thickness used (about 20%) because of its strength. The proprietary wheels can be replaced by plywood wheels if you prefer (see p.58).

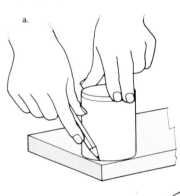

a. *Draw around the base of a circular object for the curved ends of the sides and handle.*

Making the walker

1. If the wood has not been cut to size, saw it to the dimensions given, using a tenon saw or a circular saw. Prepared softwood should be further smoothed with a plane if necessary.

2. Draw around the base of a small jar or glass to mark the curves on the handle ends *(see fig. a).* Use a larger round object to mark the curves on the end of the side pieces. Cut the curves with a coping saw or a power jigsaw and sand smooth.

3. Centre the side pieces with the base and mark the position for the four through-housing joints *(see p.57).* Use a try square and a craft knife to score the edges of the 19mm (¾in) channels and cut with a tenon saw to a depth of two-thirds of the width of the wood *(see fig. b).* Make a central cut

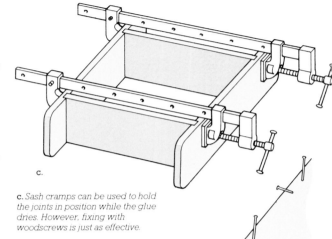

c.

c. *Sash cramps can be used to hold the joints in position while the glue dries. However, fixing with woodscrews is just as effective.*

and chisel out the wood, working from both sides.

4. Now assemble the sides. Glue the grooves and slot the front and back pieces in. Insert woodscrews to hold the joint while it dries (allow at least eight hours). The woodscrews can either be left in place or removed and the holes filled.

Alternatively, use sash cramps to hold the joints fast until the glue has dried *(see fig. c).*

d.

d. *Attach the base with nails dovetailed at alternating angles.*

5. The base can now be fitted. Smooth the edges of the plywood with sandpaper. Glue the edges of the base and place it in position. Nail the base to the frame, dovetailing the nails at alternating angles

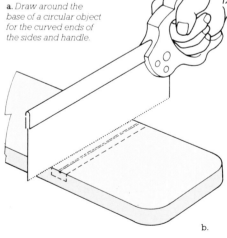

b.

b. *Cut the channels for the through-housing joints with a tenon saw. Chisel out the wood from both sides.*

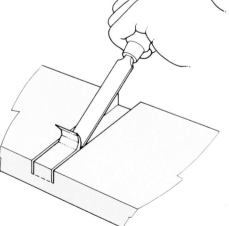

e.

e. *The handle sides are set at an angle. Make sure that you leave enough room for the wheels.*

to give additional strength *(see fig. d)*.

6. The handle can now be assembled. Make pilot holes for the four screws at the base of the handle sides. Use a flat bit to drill a hole 25mm (1in) in diameter through half the depth of the handle sides at the curved end. Assemble the three handle pieces and check for length. Sand the ends of the dowelling handle, glue and slot it into the holes. Countersink a screw into both sides to hold

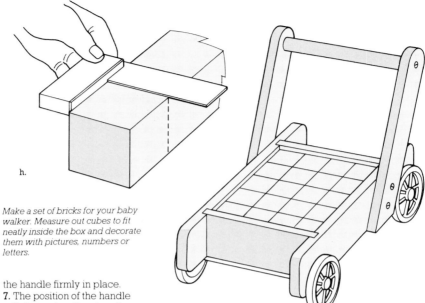

h.

Make a set of bricks for your baby walker. Measure out cubes to fit neatly inside the box and decorate them with pictures, numbers or letters.

the handle firmly in place.

7. The position of the handle will depend on the size of your wheels. Allow a gap of at least 25mm (1in) between the rim and the handle. Screw the base of the handle to the box with two countersunk screws on each side *(see fig. e)*.

8. Before the wheels are fitted the walker should be painted or varnished *(see p.59)*.

9. Place the axles in position just beyond the edge of the base and make pilot holes for the brackets. Place the axles in position and screw down the brackets *(see fig. f)*. Fit the wheels, with a washer on either side, and secure with a locknut (a nut with a nylon collar). Use an epoxy adhesive to keep them in place as shown *(see fig. g.)*.

Proprietary wheels with pushfit caps will make the job of fitting the wheels easier.

Making a set of bricks for the baby walker

Make a special set of cubes for your toddler to carry around in the baby walker. From the measurements given, the box will carry 20 cubes, made from 50 x 50mm (2 x 2in) softwood. A simple method for making these building bricks is given on pp.60-1.

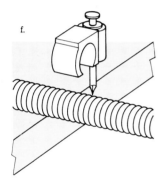

f. *Use brackets to attach the axles to the base of the side pieces.*

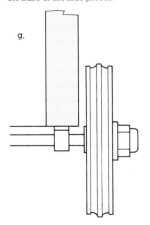

g. *Fit the wheels in position and secure them with washers, locknuts and epoxy adhesive, or with proprietary pushfit caps.*

MATERIALS

Softwood:
2 pieces 19 x 100 x 460mm (¾ x 4 x 18in)
2 pieces 19 x 100 x 235mm (¾ x 4 x 9in)
2 pieces 19 x 75 x 420mm (¾ x 3 x 16½in)
Dowelling:
1 piece 25mm x 268mm (1 x 10½in)
Plywood:
1 piece 6 x 255 x 305mm (¼ x 10 x 12in)
Hardware:
wood glue
2 woodscrews 38mm (1½in) with cup washers
4 woodscrews 25mm (1in) with cup washers
nails
4 wheels at least 10cm (4in) in diameter
2 axles approx. 29cm (11½in) in length
4 brackets and fixing screws
8 locknuts
washers
(proprietary wheels with pushfit caps can be used as an alternative)
epoxy adhesive
PVA wood glue
non-toxic paint

TOOLS

Ruler, pencil, try square and craft knife, tenon saw, set of chisels, smoothing plane, screwdriver, wheelbrace or power drill, brace and bit, hammer, fretsaw, coping saw or jigsaw.

MAKING A
PULL-ALONG DOG

This toy is most suited to very young children up to the age of three. It is big enough to allow two small children to ride on it while an adult, or an older brother or sister, pulls it along. Children older than three will be able to propel the dog along the floor, or the ground, with their feet, just as they would with a scooter. The toy is easy to make, while its sturdy nature makes it suitable for both indoor and outdoor play.

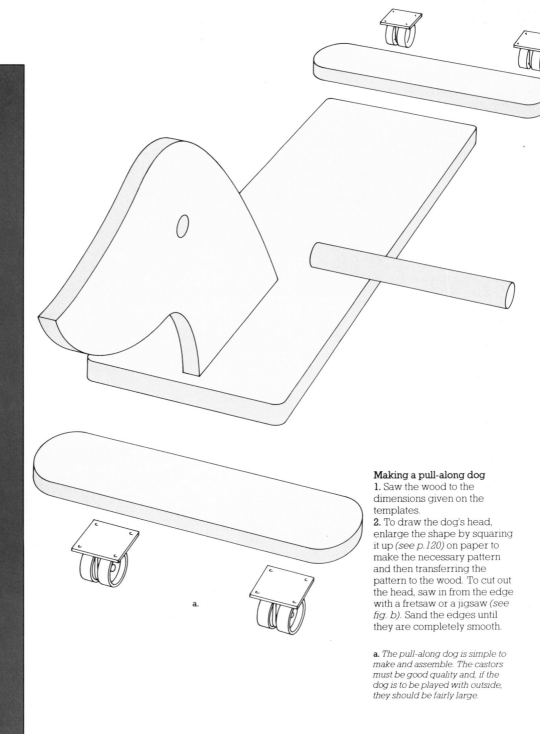

Making a pull-along dog
1. Saw the wood to the dimensions given on the templates.
2. To draw the dog's head, enlarge the shape by squaring it up *(see p.120)* on paper to make the necessary pattern and then transferring the pattern to the wood. To cut out the head, saw in from the edge with a fretsaw or a jigsaw *(see fig. b)*. Sand the edges until they are completely smooth.

a. *The pull-along dog is simple to make and assemble. The castors must be good quality and, if the dog is to be played with outside, they should be fairly large.*

a.

3. Drill a 3.2cm (1¼in) hole for the dowelling that serves as a hand grip (see fig. c).
4. There are two ways of attaching the head to the body. You can drill deeply countersunk holes underneath the body, glue the head in place and secure with screws. You can also cut the 10mm (⅜in) dowelling into six lengths. Measure and mark the centre points of the dowel holes in the head. Drill holes to half the depth of the dowel. The holes must be absolutely vertical. Insert dowels, place in position and mark the corresponding dowel points on the body. Remove dowels and drill another set of holes. Cut a groove along the length of each dowel to allow the glue to escape. Apply glue, insert

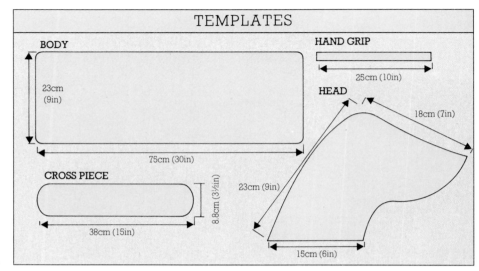

TEMPLATES

BODY 23cm (9in) / 75cm (30in)
HAND GRIP 25cm (10in)
HEAD 18cm (7in) / 23cm (9in) / 15cm (6in)
CROSS PIECE 38cm (15in) / 8.8cm (3½in)

dowels (see pp.57-8) and clamp the pieces together until completely dry.
5. Glue the dowelling hand grip in position.
6. Round the edges of the cross pieces with a fretsaw and sandpaper them smooth.
7. Drill holes in the cross pieces, position them across the body, ensuring that they are square, as it is important for the castors to be straight. Fasten in position with glue

and countersunk woodscrews (see fig. g).
8. Use sandpaper to smooth all sharp or rough edges which might cause injury.
9. Paint and varnish. It is worth giving the dog several coats of varnish for a more durable finish.

10. When the paint has dried, you can attach the castors. If you buy a pre-packed set of four castors, check to see that they are marked with 'l' or 'r'. You must use a left and a right castor on each cross piece, or the castors will not operate properly. Screw them to the ends of the cross pieces as shown (see fig. h).
11. Cut out the fabric ears (see fig. e) and tail. Use tacks to attach the ears to the head and the tail to the back of the body. A staple gun is a useful alternative method of attaching the material.
12. Attach a screw eye to the front of the body and then tie a piece of rope or cord to it, if desired.

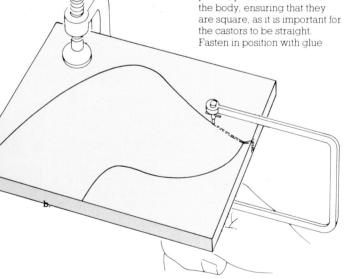

b. Cut out the head by sawing in from the edge with a fretsaw or with a jigsaw.

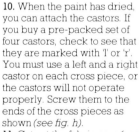

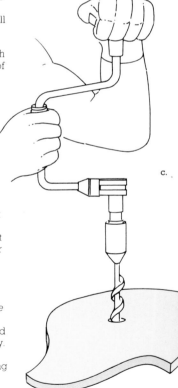

c. Drill a 3.2cm (1¼in) hole for the dowelling handgrip with a brace and bit.

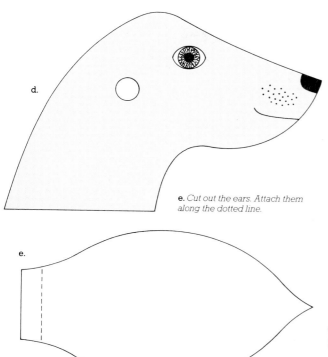

d.

d. Rub the edges of the head with sandpaper until they are completely smooth. Use a fine brush to paint the eyes, nose, mouth and whiskers.

e. Cut out the ears. Attach them along the dotted line.

e.

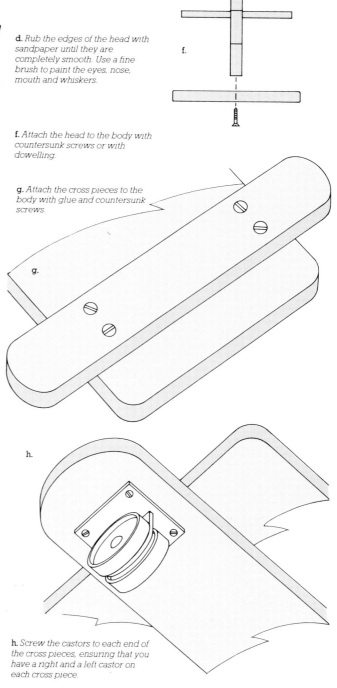

f.

f. Attach the head to the body with countersunk screws or with dowelling.

g. Attach the cross pieces to the body with glue and countersunk screws.

g.

h.

h. Screw the castors to each end of the cross pieces, ensuring that you have a right and a left castor on each cross piece.

MATERIALS

Softwood:
1 piece 32 x 225 x 760mm (1¼ x 9 x 30in)
2 pieces 19 x 88 x 375mm (¾ x 3½ x 15in)
1 piece 32 x 225 x 300mm (1¼ x 9 x 12in)
Dowelling:
1 piece 32 x 250mm (1¼ x 10in)
1 piece 10 x 300mm (⅜ x 12in)
Hardware:
5cm (2in) woodscrews
19mm (¾in) woodscrews
4 good quality castors
1 screw eye
tacks
fabric, such as felt
wood glue
varnish
non-toxic paint

TOOLS

Panel saw, fretsaw or jigsaw, tenon saw, wheelbrace and bit or power drill and drill bits, brace and bit, dowelling jig (optional), screwdriver, G-cramp, bradawl, sandpaper, paint brush.

MAKING A
TRAIN

This pull-along engine and carriage are ideal as toddler toys. They have been designed with a low centre of gravity, a wide track and large wheels, so that they will not overturn easily, even if travelling over carpets. Painting the train is fun and allows a great deal of scope for individual expression. You can, of course, add more carriages, or you can adapt the basic carriage design to form a covered cargo waggon, a flat truck or a passenger coach.

Making the engine
Saw the wood to the dimensions given on the templates. You can make the boiler from one piece of wood or from two pieces which you glue together.

Making the boiler
1. If you want a square boiler, all you do is smooth the edges.

2. To make a round boiler, first draw diagonal lines across both ends of the piece of softwood. Place the compass point at the spot where the lines intersect and draw circles (see fig. b). Round off the corners with a fretsaw and smooth with coarse sandpaper.
3. The boiler should have a flat base so that it will sit squarely

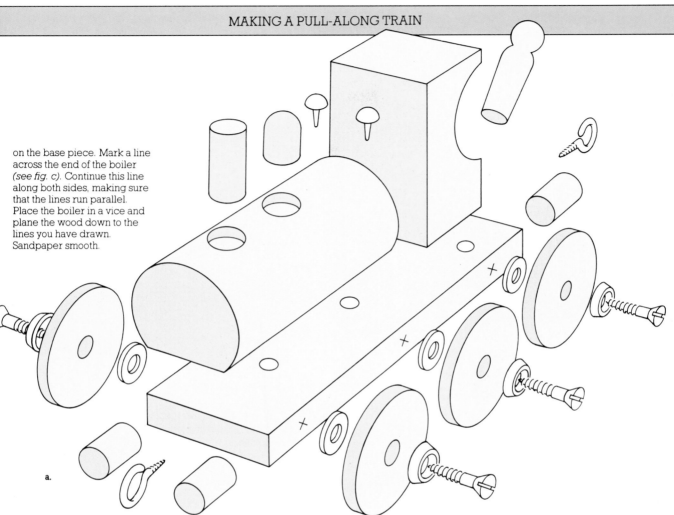

on the base piece. Mark a line across the end of the boiler *(see fig. c)*. Continue this line along both sides, making sure that the lines run parallel. Place the boiler in a vice and plane the wood down to the lines you have drawn. Sandpaper smooth.

a.

TEMPLATES

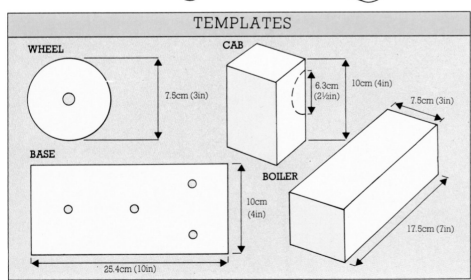

WHEEL

7.5cm (3in)

CAB

6.3cm (2½in) 10cm (4in)

7.5cm (3in)

BASE

BOILER

10cm (4in)

17.5cm (7in)

25.4cm (10in)

4. Drill four holes in the base piece *(see fig. a)*. Drill two holes in the boiler for the steam dome and funnel, using the brace and 19mm (¾in) bit *(see fig. d)*.
5. Fix the boiler to the base with woodglue and countersunk woodscrews *(see fig a.)*.

Making the cab
1. Draw a semi-circle on each side of the piece of softwood.
2. Hold the piece steady in a vice and cut along the curve with a coping saw *(see fig. e.)*. Rub smooth with sandpaper.
3. You can insert the peg figures in either of two ways. If you want them to be removable, drill holes into the curve at an angle and insert the

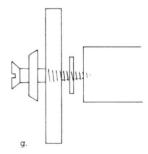

e.

figures from the top. Alternatively, you can drill holes through the bottom of the cab and insert the figures from underneath before attaching the cab. This will ensure that the figures stand upright in the cab, but it will not be possible to remove them.

4. Attach the cab to the base with glue and countersunk screws *(see fig. a)*.

Making the train crew
1. The best way of making the train crew is to use old-fashioned wooden clothes-pegs with a rounded top and split bottom *(see fig. f)*.
2. You can use felt-tipped pens, or paint to draw on the features and clothes.

Making the wheels
1. There are several methods of making the wheels. If you can saw with sufficient accuracy, you can cut sections off a thick length of dowelling with a tenon saw. It is important to make sure that the wheel edges are straight, otherwise not only will the appearance of the train be spoilt, but the wheels will not function properly.
2. You can also draw circles on the sheet of plywood with compasses, and cut them out with a fretsaw or with a power jigsaw.
3. Drill axle holes in each wheel, ensuring that they are exactly centred and straight. The hole should be large enough to allow the wheel to rotate, but not so large that the wheels wobble.
4. You can make wheels up to 7.5cm (3in) in diameter with a hole saw attached to a power drill and a pillar drill stand.

The hole saw automatically drills a hole in the precise centre of the wheel.
5. Paint both the wheels and the train before you attach the wheels to the base.
6. Using a bradawl, make starting holes for the wheel screws in the base. You will require a washer between each wheel and the base and a cup washer on the outside of the wheel *(see fig. g)*. Insert the screws. It is important to make sure that the screws are straight and that they are not screwed in too tightly or the wheels will not turn smoothly.

Finishing touches
1. Cut two lengths of dowelling approximately 25mm (1in) long for the steam dome and the funnel. Shape the end of the steam dome with a craft knife, smooth and glue them in place.
2. Cut four lengths of dowelling

approximately 19mm (¾in) long for the buffers and stick them onto the base *(see fig. a)*.

Hammer upholstery nails into the boiler top *(see fig. a)*.
3. Screw eyes into the front and back of the base. Tie a length of cord to the front eye.

c.

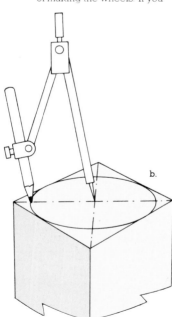

b.

b. To make a round boiler, draw a circle at each end of the block of wood with compasses.

d.

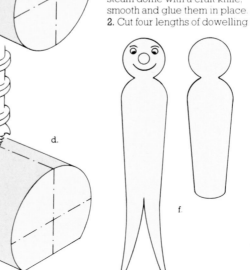

f.

g.

Making the carriage
You make the carriage using the same basic methods as for the engine.
1. Saw the base and sides to the dimensions given.
2. Cut out the wheels, using the same methods as for the engine wheels.
3. Make a paper template for the curved sides of the carriage. Cut out with a coping saw. Smooth the edges.
4. Attach sides to base with glue and pins *(see fig. i)*.
5. Glue the seats in position and fasten securely with pins.
6. Attach the wheels, using the same method as for the engine.
7. Cut four buffers from

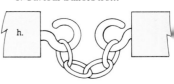

h.

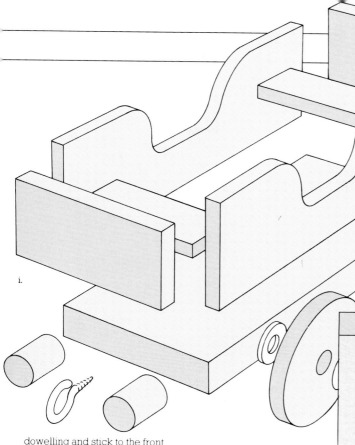

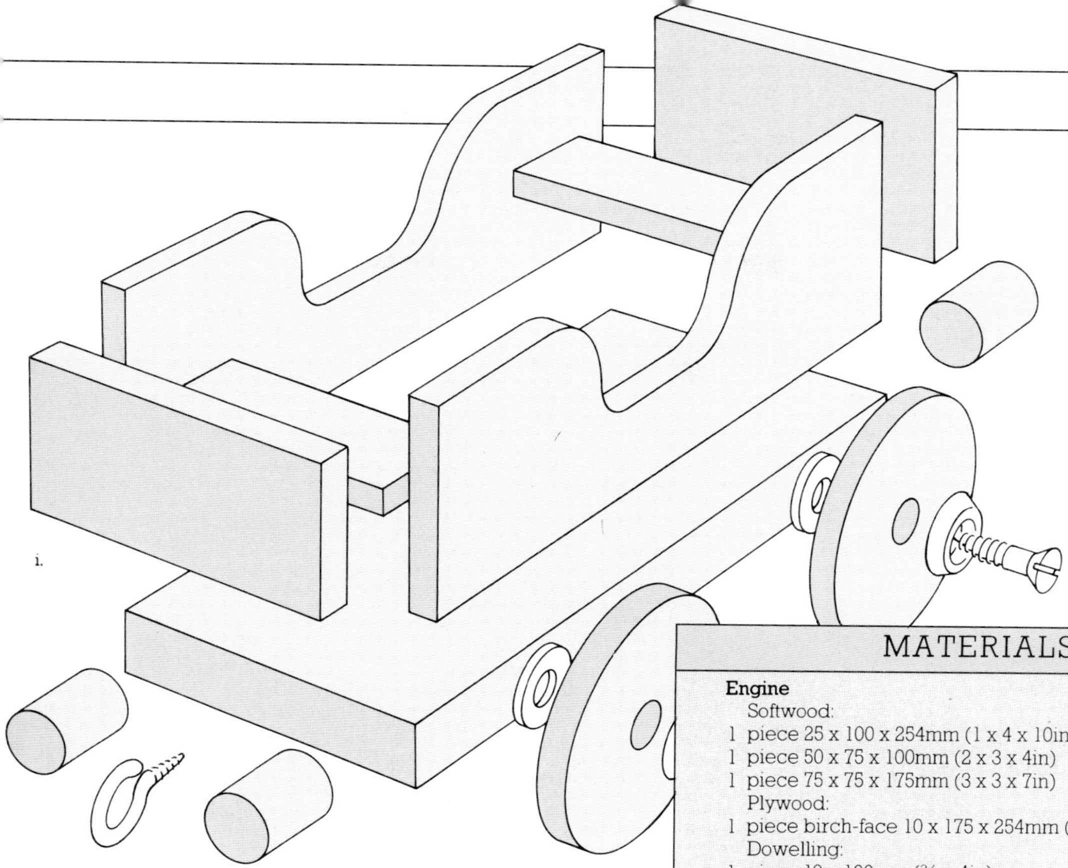

i.

dowelling and stick to the front and back of the base.

8. Make the coupling by screwing a hook into the front of the carriage base and linking it to the engine with chain. The chain should be long enough to prevent the carriage from hitting the engine when turning a corner *(see fig. h).*

Painting
You can copy the colour scheme shown in the picture or you can invent your own. Straight edges can be obtained by using masking tape and coachlines by using a ruling pen *(see p.59)*

MATERIALS

Engine
   Softwood:
1 piece 25 x 100 x 254mm (1 x 4 x 10in)
1 piece 50 x 75 x 100mm (2 x 3 x 4in)
1 piece 75 x 75 x 175mm (3 x 3 x 7in)
   Plywood:
1 piece birch-face 10 x 175 x 254mm (⅜ x 7 x 10in)
   Dowelling:
1 piece 19 x 100mm (¾ x 4in)
1 piece 10 x 100mm (⅜ x 4in)

Carriage:
   Softwood:
1 piece 25 x 100 x 254mm (1 x 4 x 10in)
   Plywood:
2 pieces 10 x 75 x 217mm (⅜ x 3 x 8½in)
2 pieces 10 x 75 x 70mm (⅜ x 3 x 2¾in)
2 pieces 10 x 30 x 70mm (⅜ x 1¼ x 2¾in)
1 piece 10 x 150 x 254mm (⅜ x 6 x 10in)
   Dowelling:
   piece 19 x 100mm (¾ x 4in)
   Hardware for engine and carriage:
   38mm (1½in) woodscrews
   cup washers
   washers
   screw eyes
1 metre (3ft) cord, or shoelace
   screw hook
   chain
2 pegs
   upholstery pins – brass finish
   wood glue
   non-toxic paint

TOOLS

Fretsaw, tenon saw, coping saw, brace and bit, power drill and bits, try square, tape measure, plane, screwdriver, bradawl, compasses or hole saw, hammer, sandpaper, paint brushes, masking tape.

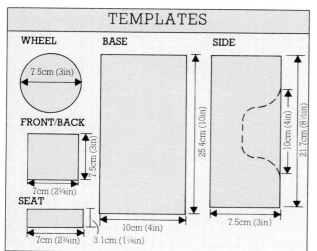

TEMPLATES

WHEEL **BASE** **SIDE**

7.5cm (3in)

FRONT/BACK

7.5cm (3in)

7cm (2¾in)

SEAT

7cm (2¾in)

25.4cm (10in)

10cm (4in)

3.1cm (1¼in)

7.5cm (3in)

10cm (4in)

21.7cm (8½in)

MAKING A
HOBBY HORSE

The hobby horse is one of the most traditional of children's toys, its origins dating back over two thousand years. Although since those far-off times the basic concept of a stick horse has remained unchanged, individual designs naturally vary considerably. This particular design is based upon an 18th century English hobby horse.

Buying the wood
Buy prepared wood. It is important to make sure that the softwood is knotfree.

Making the hobby horse
1. If necessary, cut the wood to size, using a tenon saw or a circular saw. Smooth the edges with a plane if they require it.
2. To make the horse's head you will need a piece of softwood measuring 19 x 230 x 305mm (¾ x 9 x 12in). Draw the outline of a horse's head *(see p.120)* onto the wood and cut out with a fretsaw.
3. Using a brace with a 19mm (¾in) bit, drill a hole in the horse's neck to take the hand grip.
4. Sandpaper the head until it is completely smooth. It is worth spending time on the finish, as the head is the most prominent part of the hobby horse.
5. Use the 19 x 50 x 890mm (¾ x 2 x 35in) piece of softwood to form the crossbar. To join the

a. *Draw diagonal lines across the plywood. Hammer a nail into the centre and draw the circumference of the wheel using a pencil and a length of string.*

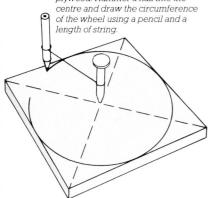

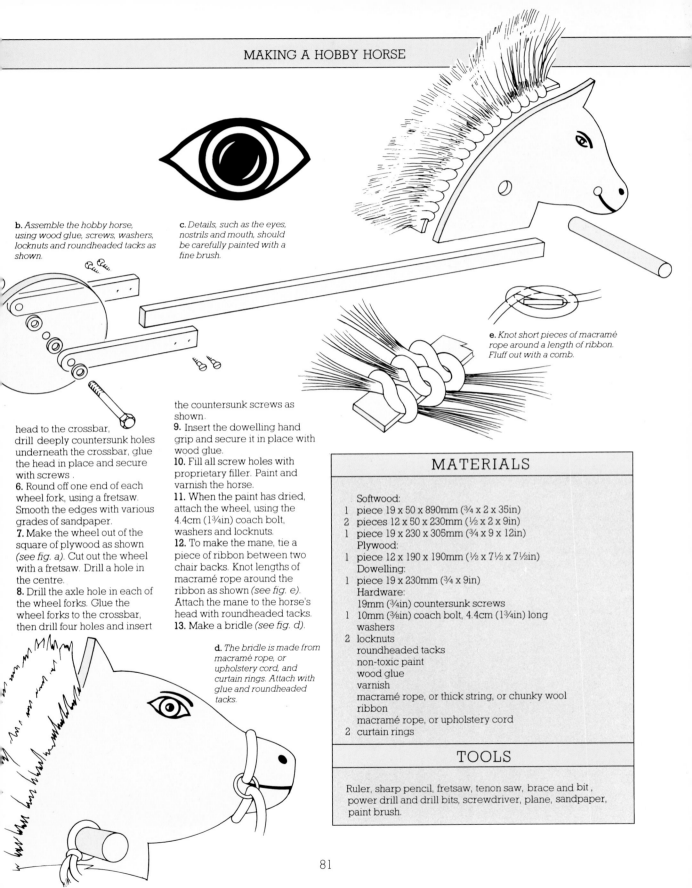

b. *Assemble the hobby horse, using wood glue, screws, washers, locknuts and roundheaded tacks as shown.*

c. *Details, such as the eyes, nostrils and mouth, should be carefully painted with a fine brush.*

e. *Knot short pieces of macramé rope around a length of ribbon. Fluff out with a comb.*

head to the crossbar, drill deeply countersunk holes underneath the crossbar, glue the head in place and secure with screws .

6. Round off one end of each wheel fork, using a fretsaw. Smooth the edges with various grades of sandpaper.

7. Make the wheel out of the square of plywood as shown *(see fig. a)*. Cut out the wheel with a fretsaw. Drill a hole in the centre.

8. Drill the axle hole in each of the wheel forks. Glue the wheel forks to the crossbar, then drill four holes and insert

the countersunk screws as shown.

9. Insert the dowelling hand grip and secure it in place with wood glue.

10. Fill all screw holes with proprietary filler. Paint and varnish the horse.

11. When the paint has dried, attach the wheel, using the 4.4cm (1¾in) coach bolt, washers and locknuts.

12. To make the mane, tie a piece of ribbon between two chair backs. Knot lengths of macramé rope around the ribbon as shown *(see fig. e)*. Attach the mane to the horse's head with roundheaded tacks.

13. Make a bridle *(see fig. d)*.

d. *The bridle is made from macramé rope, or upholstery cord, and curtain rings. Attach with glue and roundheaded tacks.*

MATERIALS

Softwood:
1 piece 19 x 50 x 890mm (¾ x 2 x 35in)
2 pieces 12 x 50 x 230mm (½ x 2 x 9in)
1 piece 19 x 230 x 305mm (¾ x 9 x 12in)
   Plywood:
1 piece 12 x 190 x 190mm (½ x 7½ x 7½in)
   Dowelling:
1 piece 19 x 230mm (¾ x 9in)
   Hardware:
   19mm (¾in) countersunk screws
1 10mm (⅜in) coach bolt, 4.4cm (1¾in) long
   washers
2 locknuts
   roundheaded tacks
   non-toxic paint
   wood glue
   varnish
   macramé rope, or thick string, or chunky wool
   ribbon
   macramé rope, or upholstery cord
2 curtain rings

TOOLS

Ruler, sharp pencil, fretsaw, tenon saw, brace and bit, power drill and drill bits, screwdriver, plane, sandpaper, paint brush.

MAKING A
SWING

Swings are easy to make and give enormous pleasure to children of all ages. If you are making a swing for a toddler it should have safety bars, but a older child will be quite safe on a traditional swing. You can suspend a swing from any tree with a sturdy branch or from a beam in your garage. It is important to test the strength of the branch or beam. The easiest method is to see whether it will bear the weight of an adult.

Positioning the swing
1. Before you buy your materials, you should first decide where the swing is to be positioned, as this will determine the length of rope required.
2. Work out the precise distance between the support branch or beam and the swing seat. The swing should be approximately 56cm (22in) above ground level. Multiply by four, allowing a little extra for knots. This is the length of rope you will need to buy.

Making a swing
1. Swing hooks are especially made for the purpose, with a pronounced curlicue which prevents the swing from unhooking when in use. They also have a very coarse woodscrew thread, which enables them to be screwed securely into the underside of any suitable branch or beam.
2. Drill a generous pilot hole into the horizontal support. To ensure that the screws bite firmly into the wood, the hole should be the same size as the internal diameter of the thread. Screw the swing hooks into the wood.
3. Cut your length of rope in half. To prevent the rope ends from unravelling, play a lighted match, or a cigarette lighter, over each end until the strands

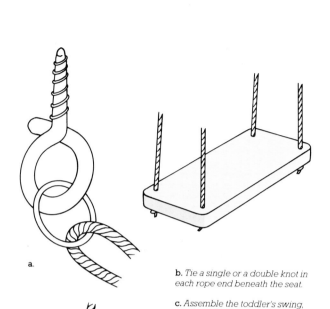

a.

b.

a. *Loop the rope through the steel rings.*

b. *Tie a single or a double knot in each rope end beneath the seat.*

c. *Assemble the toddler's swing, starting with the wooden balls. The rails not only act as a safety measure, but also provide support for very young children.*

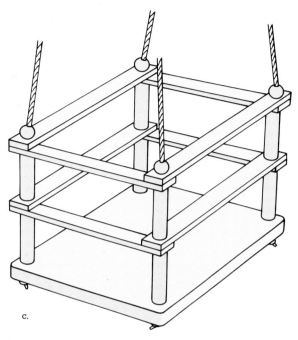

c.

melt together.

4. Drill 10mm (³⁄₈in) holes in each corner of the piece of softwood which will form the seat.

5. Round all corners and edges with coarse sandpaper. Smooth all surfaces with medium and fine sandpaper and then varnish.

6. When the varnish is dry, loop each length of rope through a steel ring (*see fig. a*) and insert the loose ends through each pair of holes in the seat. Tie secure knots underneath (*see fig. b*).

7. Hook the two steel rings over the swing hooks.

Making a toddler's swing
This swing is made using the same basic methods as described above.

1. Round and smooth the corners and edges of all the softwood and plywood.

2. Glue the two squares of plywood together. Drill 10mm (³⁄₈in) holes in each corner of the plywood and at each end of the eight safety bars. Varnish all the pieces.

3. Cut the pvc plastic pipe into eight 90mm (3½in) lengths with a tenon saw and smooth the ends with sandpaper.

4. Loop each length of rope through a steel ring and pass the ends of the rope through the wooden balls, the pvc tube and the safety bars (*see fig. c*). Finally, insert the rope ends through the seat holes and knot as before.

Caution Remember to check the condition of the swing rope from time to time as it may wear through.

MATERIALS

Swing
  Softwood:
1 piece 32 x 230 x 457mm (1¼ x 9 x 18in)
  Hardware:
10 metres (32ft) polypropylene rope, 8mm (⁵⁄₁₆in) in diameter
2 large swing hooks
2 large steel rings
  varnish

Toddler's swing
  Softwood:
8 pieces 25 x 50 x 355mm (1 x 2 x 14in)
  Plywood:
2 pieces 12 x 355 x 355mm (½ x 14 x 14in)
  Hardware:
10 metres (32ft) polypropylene rope 8mm (⁵⁄₁₆in) in diameter
2 large swing hooks
2 large steel rings
1 72cm (28in) length of PVC small bore plastic pipe
4 wooden balls 50mm (2in) in diameter

EQUIPMENT

Tenon saw, wheelbrace and bit or a power drill with a 10mm (³⁄₈in) bit, various grades of sandpaper.

MAKING A
TRUCK AND TRAILER

This toy is intended for very young children. It is robust and stable with large wheels, so that it can be played with outdoors, as well as inside the house. The construction of the truck and trailer is very similar to that of the pull-along train and carriage on pages 76-9. Decorating the truck and trailer allows great scope for individual design. Instant lettering and small coloured sticky labels are useful for providing the finishing touches.

Making the trailer
1. It is important to use good quality knotfree softwood. Saw the softwood and plywood to the dimensions given on the templates. Smooth all the edges with sandpaper.
2. Cut out the wheels, using one of the following methods. If your sawing is very accurate, you can cut sections off a thick

length of dowelling with a tenon saw. It is important to make sure that the wheel edges are straight, both for the sake of appearance and to enable the wheels to function properly.
3. You can also draw circles on the sheet of plywood with compasses and cut them out with a fretsaw or with a power

jigsaw. Sand the edges smooth.
4. Drill axle holes through the centre of each wheel. The holes should be large enough to allow the wheels to rotate, but not so large that the wheels wobble. The holes should also be straight. It is advisable to paint the wheels and the trailer before you attach them together.
5. You can make wheels up to 75mm (3in) in diameter with a hole saw attached to a power drill and a pillar. The advantage of making wheels by this method is that the wheels are perfectly round and the axle hole is automatically drilled in the exact centre.
6. Attach the sides of the trailer firmly to the base with wood glue and pins *(see fig. b)*.
7. Using a bradawl, make starting holes for the woodscrews in the base. You

will require a washer between each wheel and the base and a cup washer on the outside of the wheel *(see fig. e)*. Cup washers with a brass finish will give the wheels an additional sparkle. Insert the screws, ensuring that they go in straight and that you do not screw them in too tightly, otherwise the wheels will not turn smoothly.
8. Screw a hook into the front of the trailer base.
9. Paint with non-toxic paint. You will need a ruling pen *(see p.59)* if you wish to draw coach lines. You can use instant lettering *(see fig. a)* to make up a logo for the sides of the truck.

a. *To apply instant lettering, first make a guiding line with masking tape, then line up the lettering and rub down with a ballpoint pen or a hard point.*

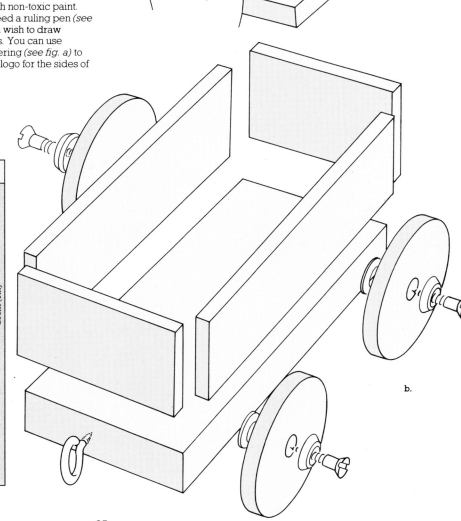

b.

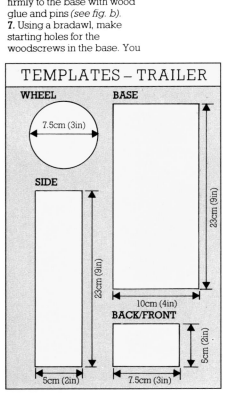

TEMPLATES – TRAILER

WHEEL

7.5cm (3in)

BASE

23cm (9in)

10cm (4in)

SIDE

23cm (9in)

5cm (2in)

BACK/FRONT

5cm (2in)

7.5cm (3in)

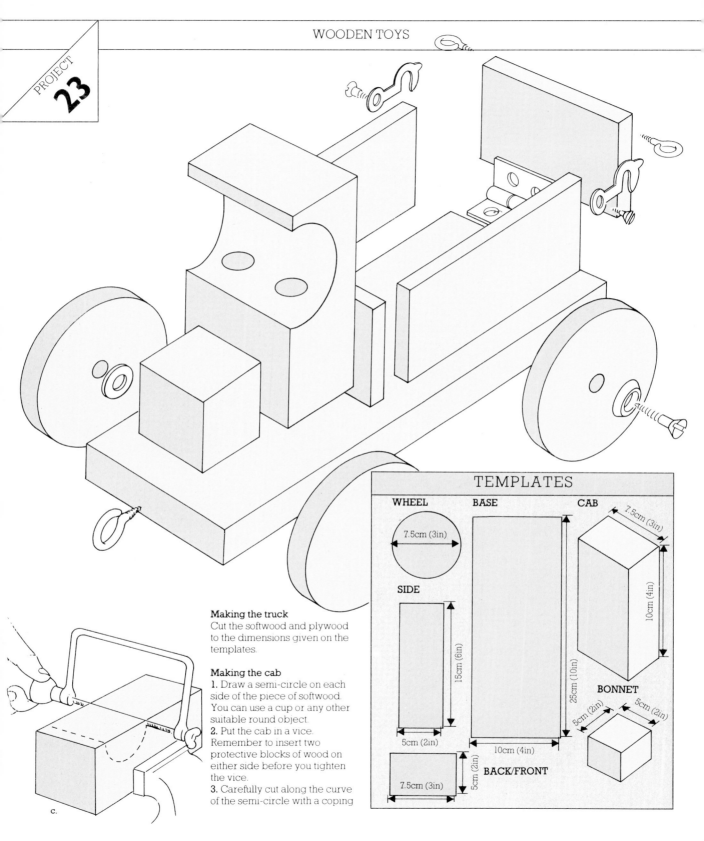

TEMPLATES

WHEEL

7.5cm (3in)

BASE

CAB

7.5cm (3in)

10cm (4in)

SIDE

15cm (6in)

25cm (10in)

5cm (2in)

10cm (4in)

BACK/FRONT

7.5cm (3in)

5cm (2in)

BONNET

5cm (2in)

5cm (2in)

5cm (2in)

Making the truck
Cut the softwood and plywood
to the dimensions given on the
templates.

Making the cab
1. Draw a semi-circle on each
side of the piece of softwood.
You can use a cup or any other
suitable round object.
2. Put the cab in a vice.
Remember to insert two
protective blocks of wood on
either side before you tighten
the vice.
3. Carefully cut along the curve
of the semi-circle with a coping

c.

saw. Rub the sawn curve smooth with sandpaper *(see fig. c)*.

4. You can insert the peg figures in two ways. If you want to make the train crew removable, drill holes into the curve at an angle and insert the figures from the top. Alternatively, you can drill holes through the cab from the bottom and insert the figures from underneath before you attach the cab to the base. This ensures that the figures stand upright, but you will not be able to remove them *(see fig. d)*.

5. Drill two holes in the base *(see fig. f)*. Attach the cab to the base with wood glue and countersunk woodscrews.

Making the driver and mate

1. Old-fashioned clothes-pegs with a rounded top and split bottom are ideal for making the figures. If you are inserting the figures from above, cut the pegs to length so that they can be removed.

2. You can use felt-tipped pens to draw on the features and clothes. Alternatively, you can use paint.

3. Although the figures are too large for young children to swallow, you may prefer to glue them into the cab so that they cannot be chewed or lost.

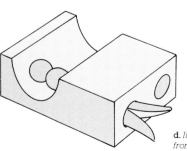

Making the bonnet

Drill holes in the base and attach the bonnet block in position with wood glue and countersunk screws *(see fig. f)*.

Making the open back

1. Attach the sides and back to the base with wood glue and pins *(see fig. f)*.

2. If you would like the back to open up, the sides should each be 10mm (⅜in) shorter and the back piece 19mm (¾in) longer than the measurements given on the templates. Attach a hinge to the back and base

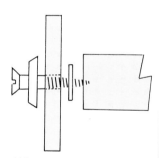

e. Make sure that the wheels are screwed in straight. Have a washer between the wheel and the trailer, and a cup washer on the outside.

d. Insert the peg figures through from the base of the cab. If you want to be able to remove the crew, cut off the base and insert them from above.

with woodscrews *(see fig. f)*. To close the back flap you will require two small hooks and eyes. Screw these in position as shown.

Making the wheels

Make the wheels, using the same methods as for the trailer. Paint them and then attach them to the truck as before.

Finishing touches

1. Screw a hook into the back of the base for coupling the trailer and a hook in the front so that the truck and trailer can be pulled along.

2. Paint and decorate. One method of making a radiator is to buy a sheet of sticky spot transfers, remove the spots and use part of the backing sheet. You can make headlights out of sticky spot transfers or brass-finish upholstery nails.

3. Knot a length of cord or a shoelace to the front eye.

MATERIALS

Trailer:
Softwood:
1 piece 19 x 100 x 230mm (¾ x 4 x 9in)
Plywood:
2 pieces 10 x 50 x 230mm (⅜ x 2 x 9in)
2 pieces 10 x 50 x 75mm (⅜ x 2 x 3in)
1 piece 10 x 175 x 175mm (⅜ x 7 x 7in)

Truck:
Softwood:
1 piece 18 x 100 x 254mm (¾ x 4 x 10in)
1 piece 50 x 75 x 100mm (2 x 3 x 4in)
1 piece 50 x 50 x 50mm (2 x 2 x 2in)
Plywood:
2 pieces 10 x 50 x 150mm (⅜ x 2 x 6in)
2 pieces 10 x 50 x 75mm (⅜ x 2 x 3in)
1 piece 10 x 178 x 178mm (⅜ x 7 x 7in)
Hardware for truck and trailer:
woodscrews 3.2cm (1½in)
washers
cup washers
3.2cm (1½in) pins
2 wooden pegs
wood glue
2 screw eyes
1 screw hook
1 hinge and screws (optional)
non-toxic paint
2 metres (2yds) cord, or shoelace

TOOLS

Fretsaw, tenon saw, wheelbrace and bit or power drill and bits, try square, tape measure, pin hammer, plane, screwdriver, bradawl, compasses or hole saw, sandpaper, paint brushes, masking tape.

MAKING A
PADDLE BOAT

Bring the romance of Huckleberry Finn to life and make something special out of bath night with this miniature version of the traditional paddle boats that still ply the Mississippi river today. The boat is sturdy and durable and will provide your children with hours of innocent fun.

The main requirement is for the boat to be completely waterproof. You can apply several coats of varnish or use waterproof non-toxic paints.

Making the hull

1. Cut the block of softwood to the dimensions given on the template and mark out the shape of the bow and the cut-out for the paddle on it. The classic river boat has a round bow, though you can make it pointed or square, with a chamfered edge, if desired. A suitably-sized paint tin will make an adequate template for the bow, though, for a really accurate curve, you should use the following method.

2. Mark a point which is half the width of the hull and an equal distance from the front and push in a drawing pin. Attach one end of a piece of string to the pin and a pencil to the other end. Keeping the string

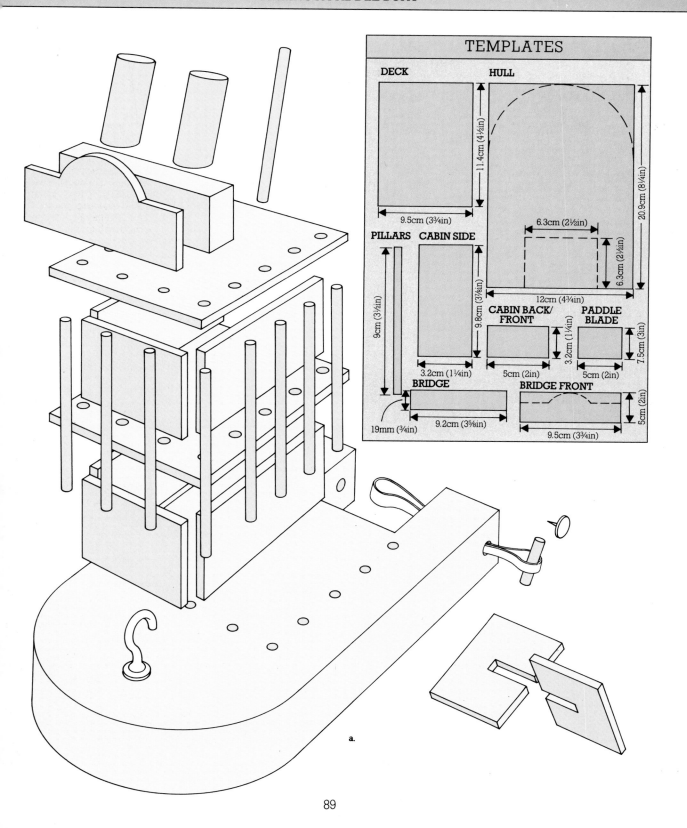

TEMPLATES

DECK

11.4cm (4½in)

9.5cm (3¾in)

HULL

20.9cm (8¼in)

6.3cm (2½in)

6.3cm (2½in)

12cm (4¾in)

PILLARS **CABIN SIDE**

9cm (3½in)

9.8cm (3⅞in)

3.2cm (1¼in)

**CABIN BACK/
FRONT**

3.2cm (1¼in)

5cm (2in)

**PADDLE
BLADE**

7.5cm (3in)

5cm (2in)

BRIDGE

19mm (¾in)

9.2cm (3⅝in)

BRIDGE FRONT

5cm (2in)

9.5cm (3¾in)

a.

taut, draw a semi-circle *(see fig. b)*. Cut out the bow with a fretsaw or a power jigsaw and sandpaper the edge to produce a curve that merges smoothly with the sides of the hull.

3. Place the hull in a vice, remembering to protect the sides with pieces of scrap wood, and cut the two side slots for the paddle cut-out. In order to cut out the back of the cut-out, drill a hole on the inside of one of the slots *(see fig. c)*. Thread the fretsaw blade through the hole and cut across the back of the paddle cut-out. Sandpaper the three edges smooth.

Making the superstructure
1. Cut the decks from plywood to the dimensions given on the templates. On one piece, draw a line 6mm (¼in) in from the edges, around two sides and the front. Starting 6mm (¼in) in from the unmarked side, mark off 25mm (1in) spaces along the lines you have just drawn. These marks indicate the positions of the pillars.
2. To ensure that the holes you drill for the dowelling pillars in the decks and the hull line up exactly, position the two decks carefully on the hull and hold them temporarily in place with a couple of panel pins. The back of the decks should align with the back of the paddle cut-out. Drill 6mm (¼in) holes through both decks and about 6mm (¼in) into the hull *(see fig. e)*. To ensure the holes in the deck are all the same depth, wrap a piece of tape around the drill bit to mark the position down to which you should drill. Insetting the pillars in the hull ensures that the superstructure is firmly anchored *(see fig. d)*.
3. The cabins are simple plywood boxes. Cut the sides

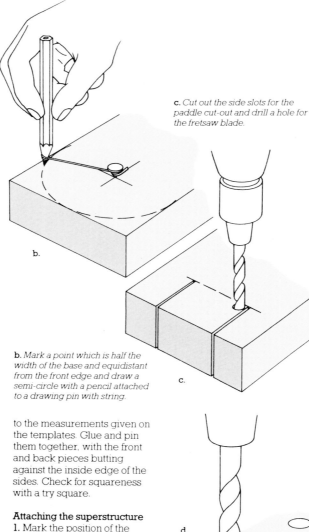

c. Cut out the side slots for the paddle cut-out and drill a hole for the fretsaw blade.

b. Mark a point which is half the width of the base and equidistant from the front edge and draw a semi-circle with a pencil attached to a drawing pin with string.

to the measurements given on the templates. Glue and pin them together, with the front and back pieces butting against the inside edge of the sides. Check for squareness with a try square.

Attaching the superstructure
1. Mark the position of the cabin on the hull, making sure that it aligns with the edges of the paddle cut-out, and glue it in place.
2. Glue the corner pillars into the holes drilled in the hull *(see fig. f)*. The pillars should be cut slightly over length, so that when the top deck is in place, the ends of the pillars can be sanded down to fit flush.
3. Using the corner pillars as a guide, glue the lower deck on top of the cabin. Next, glue the upper cabin and the top deck in place, ensuring that they all line up and that the holes are directly above each other. You

can now insert the remaining pillars through the decks and glue them into the hull.
4. Glue the bridge block in position at the front of the upper deck. Mark out the front of the bridge and name board *(see templates)* and cut out with a fretsaw. Sandpaper the edges smooth and glue it to the softwood block.
5. To make the funnels, cut the 16mm (⅝in) dowelling into 3.8cm (1½in) lengths. Cut one end of each funnel at a slanted angle, so that they rake back slightly when glued in place. Use a scrap of dowelling for the flagpole, drill a hole in the deck and glue it in place.

The propulsion system
1. You will need two pieces of plywood for the paddle blades. Cut the pieces to the dimensions shown. Draw a line through the centre of each blade and cut a slot, to the thickness of the plywood, half way across each one as shown *(see fig. a)*.
2. Apply glue to the blades and slide them into place, checking

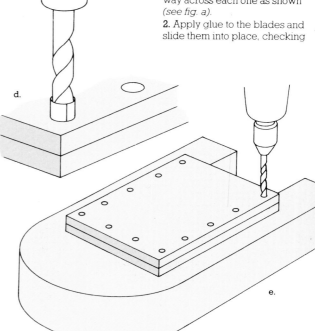

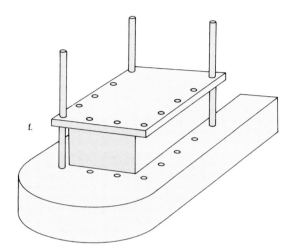

f.

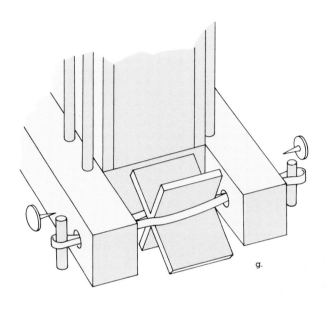

g.

to see that they are at right angles to one another as this ensures an even rotation. Drill a hole through the hull on each side of the paddle cut-out in the position shown (see fig. g). This is important as the position of the elastic band holding the paddle-wheel ensures that the blades bite into the water at the correct depth.

3. The paddle is powered by an elastic band. Use a fairly thick band that stretches across the width of the hull. It is held in place on either side by a piece of dowelling (see fig. g) and is looped across the centre of the blades, so holding them in position. You may find it necessary to insert a nail next to each piece of dowelling, to stop it spinning back as the elastic band is wound up.

Decoration

If you want to keep the natural wood finish, apply at least one coat of clear varnish – you may have to apply further coats on the end grain of the wood to ensure that the boat is completely waterproof. Before doing this you can easily enhance the boat with coloured stickers if you like.

Remember these must be applied before you varnish the boat as they will soak off in water. Alternatively, you can devise whatever colour scheme you like and paint it with waterproof non-toxic enamel paints.

A simpler version

If you feel that this paddle boat design is too complex to build, or that it may not stand up to the rigours of a very young child's bath night, you can simplify the boat's superstructure by using softwood blocks for cabins. Make sure that the blocks are not too heavy or the boat may become unstable.

The maiden voyage

With your riverboat painted or varnished, sea trials can now take place. You may find that the boat needs trimming to make it sit squarely in the water. To deal with this problem, you can either add weight to one side or the other. Alternatively you can drill out small pieces from the underside of the hull. You can also add a cup hook so that your child can tow the boat.

MATERIALS

Softwood:
1 piece 44 x 120 x 209mm (1¾ x 4¾ x 8¼in)
1 piece 19 x 19 x 92mm (¾ x ¾ x 3⅝in)
Plywood:
2 pieces 6 x 95 x 114mm (¼ x 3¾ x 4½in)
4 pieces 6 x 32 x 98mm (¼ x 1¼ x 3⅞in)
4 pieces 6 x 32 x 50mm (¼ x 1¼ x 2in)
2 pieces 6 x 50 x 75mm (¼ x 2 x 3in)
1 piece 6 x 50 x 95mm (¼ x 2 x 3¾in)
Dowelling:
2 pieces 16 x 38mm (⅝ x 1½in)
12 pieces 6 x 89mm (¼ x 3½in)
Hardware:
1 elastic band
1 cup hook
wood glue
panel pins
clear varnish, or waterproof non-toxic paint

TOOLS

Tenon saw, coping saw, fretsaw or power jigsaw, wheelbrace and bits or power drill and bits, sandpaper, paint brush, try square.

MAKING A
LUNAR SPACE STATION

Children can travel to the stars with this inter-stellar galactic space station and save Earth from alien invasion before bedtime. The space station is equipped with the latest triple cluster search and destroy missiles, capable of blasting the alien armada into the terrifying black hole under the coffee table.

Although this toy can be made exactly as shown, it can also be adapted to use up pieces of scrap wood in your workshop. Similarly, you can copy the decoration shown, or invent your own.

Making a space station
1. Make paper patterns of the various shapes, using the dimensions given on the templates and then mark them on the softwood and plywood. Saw out the pieces. You can substitute offcuts – left over from other toys – for any of the pieces listed, or adapt the design to suit the offcuts in your workshop. Sandpaper the edges smooth.
2. Draw a line across the base, 58cm (23in) from one end. Mark the centre point of the near edge and draw two lines from that point to the line you have just drawn *(see templates)*. Saw along the lines

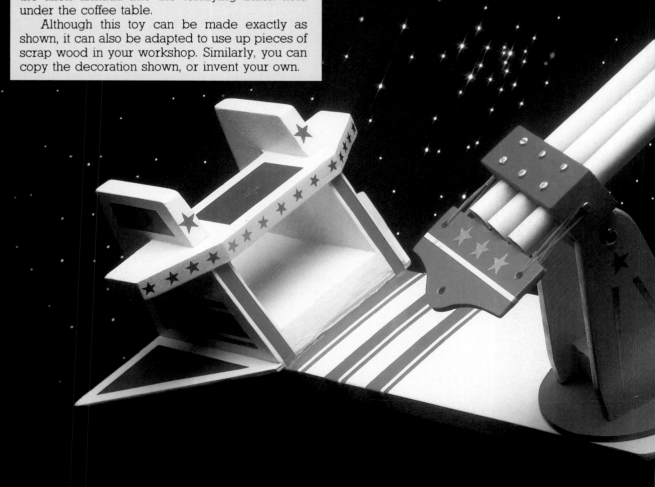

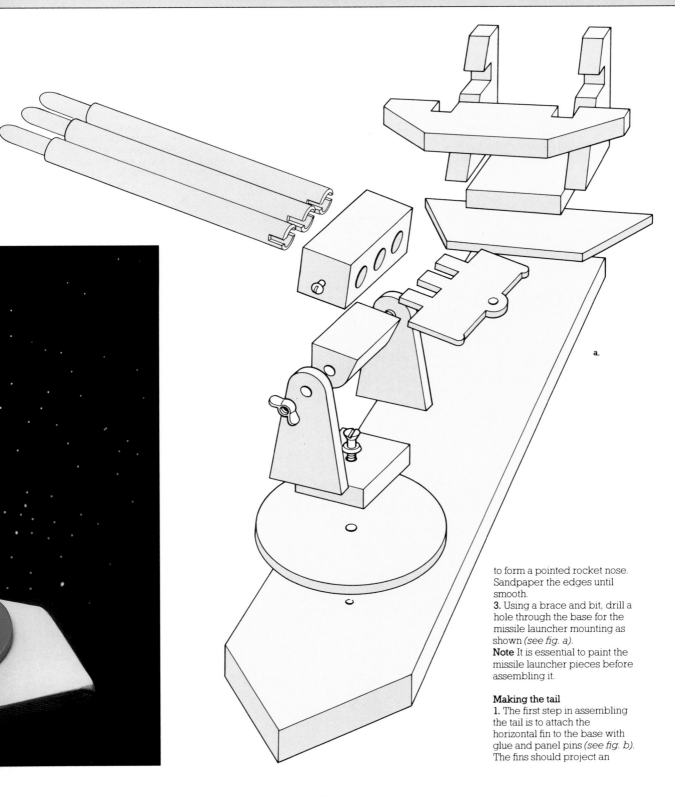

a.

c.

to form a pointed rocket nose.
Sandpaper the edges until
smooth.
3. Using a brace and bit, drill a
hole through the base for the
missile launcher mounting as
shown *(see fig. a)*.
Note It is essential to paint the
missile launcher pieces before
assembling it.

Making the tail
1. The first step in assembling
the tail is to attach the
horizontal fin to the base with
glue and panel pins *(see fig. b)*.
The fins should project an

equal distance on either side of the base.

2. Using a sharp craft knife, mark out the edges of the halving joints on the vertical tail fins and the flying bridge. Cut along the waste edges of the scribed lines with a tenon saw. Remove the unwanted wood with a chisel until the three pieces fit together neatly.

3. Now attach the vertical fins to the tail support with a butt joint, glued and screwed together *(see fig. c).*

4. Glue and screw this assembly in position.

5. Slot the flying bridge into place and fix it with glue *(see fig. d).*

Making the missile launcher

1. Cut the uPVC pipe into three equal lengths of 15.2cm (6in). The plastic is not difficult to cut, but you should use a fine-toothed saw. A hacksaw is ideal, but a tenon saw can be substituted. Smooth the edges with fine grades of sandpaper. Cut slots in one end of each section with a craft knife *(see fig. a).* Sandpaper until smooth.

2. Mark the circumference of the circle on the square piece of plywood with a pair of compasses. Failing this, you can draw diagonal lines from corner to corner and then hammer a nail into the centre point. Attach a pencil to the nail with a piece of string and draw the circumference *(see pp. 80-1).*

3. Drill holes in the barrel mounting large enough to take the uPVC tubes. You can either use a brace and bit, or a power drill mounted on a pillar stand.

4. Drill two screw holes above each barrel hole, plus one on each side of the block. Insert the uPVC tube and screw in round head screws until the points just catch the tubing, but do not actually penetrate it. Screw a round head screw into each side of the barrel mounting, so that elastic bands can be looped around them *(see fig. f).*

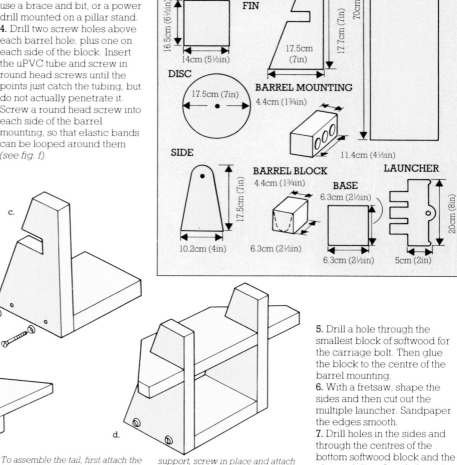

c.

b.

d.

To assemble the tail, first attach the horizontal fin to the base, then butt joint the vertical sides to the support, screw in place and attach the flying bridge with a halving joint.

5. Drill a hole through the smallest block of softwood for the carriage bolt. Then glue the block to the centre of the barrel mounting.

6. With a fretsaw, shape the sides and then cut out the multiple launcher. Sandpaper the edges smooth.

7. Drill holes in the sides and through the centres of the bottom softwood block and the plywood disc. Attach the sides to the bottom block, using glue and countersunk screws. Position this assembly on the plywood disc and fix to the base with a woodscrew and cup washer. The screw should be loose enough to allow the missile launcher to be swivelled to find its target. Now attach the barrel mounting between the side pieces with a coach bolt, washer and wingnut as shown *(see fig. e)*.

8. Drill three holes in the multiple launcher – in the handle to give a better grip and the other two to take the elastic bands, which propel the missiles. Attach the launcher to the mounting barrel with elastic bands *(see fig. f)*.

9. The range of the missile launcher can be altered by adjusting the length of the elastic bands. The range of the missiles should not exceed 1m (1yd), so experiment with different elastic bands until you have the right range.

Making the missiles

1. Cut the 16mm (⅝in) dowelling into three lengths of approximately 7.5cm (3in).

2. Round off one end of each missile with coarse sandpaper *(see fig. g)*.

Decorating the space station

As mentioned earlier, it is essential to paint all the missile launcher pieces before assembling it, but you can now give the space station its final coat of paint and add all the fine detail. Create your own spectacular galactic space station design with the help of self-adhesive paper, or self-adhesive plastic film in different colours, stick-on stars and strips of thin, white, sticky tape.

e. Assemble the missile launcher, using a coach bolt with washers and wingnut, countersunk screws and glue.

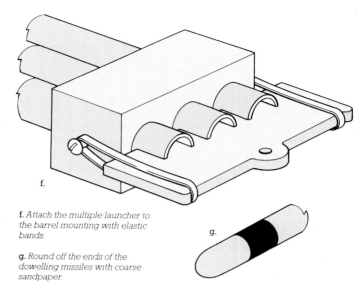

f. *Attach the multiple launcher to the barrel mounting with elastic bands.*

g. *Round off the ends of the dowelling missiles with coarse sandpaper.*

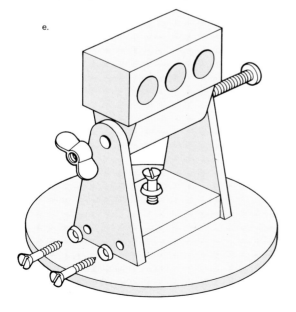

MATERIALS

Softwood:
1 piece 19 x 175 x 700mm (¾ x 7 x 27in)
2 pieces 19 x 175 x 175mm (¾ x 7 x 7in)
1 piece 19 x 140 x 165mm (¾ x 5½ x 6½in)
1 piece 19 x 89 x 300mm (¾ x 3½ x 12in)
2 pieces 12 x 100 x 175mm (½ x 4 x 7in)
1 piece 44 x 44 x 114mm (1¾ x 1¾ x 4½in)
1 piece 32 x 44 x 63mm (1¼ x 1¾ x 2½in)
1 piece 32 x 63 x 63mm (1¼ x 2½ x 2½in)
Plywood:
1 piece 10 x 175 x 406mm (⅜ x 7 x 16in)
1 piece 10 x 175 x 175mm (⅜ x 7 x 7in)
1 piece 6 x 150 x 200mm (¼ x 6 x 8in)
Dowelling:
1 piece 16mm x 225mm (⅝ x 9in)
Hardware:
1 46cm (18in) length uPVC pipe with 19mm (¾in) internal diameter
roundhead screws
countersunk woodscrews
woodscrews
1 coach bolt, with washers and wingnut
cup washer
panel pins
elastic bands
wood glue
non-toxic paint

TOOLS

Panel saw or electric circular saw, coping saw, fretsaw or power jigsaw, tenon saw, brace and bit or power drill with drill bits, screwdriver, try square, hammer, chisels, mallet, craft knife, sandpaper, paint brushes, compasses.

MAKING A
SNAIL CLOCK

This bright, cheerful snail clock is intended to make it fun for young children to learn to tell the time. It will stand on the floor, or on any other suitable flat surface. Alternatively, you can hang it on a wall. It is extremely easy to make and can be adapted if you wish to use up odd scraps of plywood in your workshop. Additionally, using the same basic methods, you can change the snail base to any design you prefer.

Making a snail clock
1. Draw the outlines of the clock pieces on the sheet of plywood. You can use the dimensions given, or alter them to suit the size of your plywood sheet.
2. Start by drawing the circular clock face, leaving enough space for the snail's body. Decide where the centre of the circle will be and, if you do not have compasses, knock in a nail at that point. Attach a 15cm (6in) piece of string to a pencil and then to the nail. Draw a circle (see fig. a).
3. Draw the outlines of the

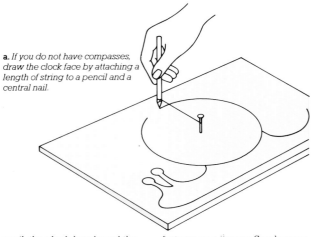

a. *If you do not have compasses, draw the clock face by attaching a length of string to a pencil and a central nail.*

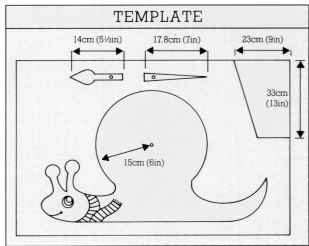

TEMPLATE

14cm (5½in)   17.8cm (7in)   23cm (9in)

33cm (13in)

15cm (6in)

snail, the clock hands and the support bracket by squaring up the shape on a paper pattern *(see p120)* and transferring it to the sheet of plywood.
4. Cut out the shapes with a fretsaw, or a jigsaw. Sandpaper the edges until smooth.
5. Drill holes through the centre of the clock face and in the clock hands.
6. Hinge the support bracket to the back of the clock *(see fig. c)*.

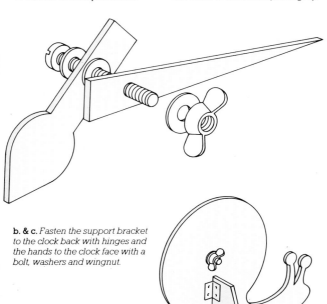

b. & c. *Fasten the support bracket to the clock back with hinges and the hands to the clock face with a bolt, washers and wingnut.*

Use a bradawl to make starting holes for the hinge screws. If the ends of the screws project, it is advisable to file off the sharp points until the ends are flush with the plywood.
7. The clock is now ready for painting. You can use a stencil to paint on the numbers, or instant lettering. You can also mark the minutes, if desired.
8. When the paint is dry, attach the clock hands to the face, using the 6mm (¼in) bolt, two washers, and a wingnut *(see fig. c)*.
9. If you wish to hang the clock on the wall, attach screw eyes, or picture hooks to the back.

MATERIALS

Plywood:
1 piece approx. 6-10 x 480 x 710mm (¼-⅜ x 19 x 28in)
Hardware:
2 small brass hinges, with screws
2 small screw eyes, or picture hook
1 6mm (¼in) bolt 3.2cm (1¼in) long
2 washers
1 wingnut
non-toxic paint

TOOLS

Pencil, tape measure, try square, fretsaw or jigsaw, wheelbrace and bit or power drill and drill bits, screwdriver, bradawl, compasses, sandpaper, paint brush, hammer, file.

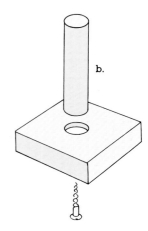

— MAKING —
MIXED MEDIA TOYS

Because so many different materials and skills are required to make the puppets in this section, they have been used to demonstrate the principles of mixed media toymaking. Once you have mastered the techniques involved, you can apply them to other toymaking areas.

Using mixed media for making puppets

Start with some glove puppets, as these are less complicated to make than the other varieties. Children also find them relatively easy to operate, so even the simplest design can provide them with many hours of amusement and fun. String puppets or marionettes, on the other hand, are more sophisticated. Because of their size, their intricate articulation and their stringing, they are complex to make and correspondingly difficult to operate. They thus present a challenge.

In both cases, however, the very wide range of modern materials that can be used makes the task less demanding. Though puppets are traditionally made of papier mâché, wood and cloth, for instance, why not use self-hardening clays, polystyrene, foam plastic and cold cure rubber as speedier alternatives; modern adhesives and paints also help to make life easier. Let your imagination run free as well – you can use all sorts of junk materials to create instant, low cost characters that will appeal to children of every age group.

Making puppet heads

Traditionally, papier mâché is an excellent medium for making lightweight yet durable puppet heads. What you do is to model the basic shape you need in plasticine or self-hardening clay and then

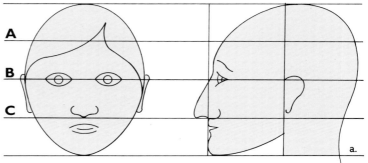

cover this with pieces of paper. When the paper dries, the resulting hard shell is cut in half, removed from the plasticine and pasted together again. Allow sufficient time between the various stages for drying out.

You do not have to be an expert modeller to model the face – the important thing is to get the proportions of the various features more or less correct. Here, the following guidelines will help you. Remember that all puppets should have relatively large heads to make the face more visible to an audience. Consequently the features should be bold and simple, so that they can convey the various kinds of emotion. Think of the head as an oval divided into four equal parts *(see fig. a)*. The eyes lie halfway down the head and are separated by a distance equal to their width. Line A represents the hairline; the nose lies between B and C together with the ears, which can be seen in the side view. Thus the

bottom of the ears are level with the tip of the nose. The mouth lies in the lower quarter section of the head – model this partly open so the puppet looks as if it is speaking.

These guidelines apply to both glove and string puppets, but, when it comes to the neck, things are different. A glove puppet's neck should have a flange to help secure the glove, while you should allow sufficient room to accommodate the fingers that will be manipulating the puppet. The design of a string puppet's neck depends on the type of movement required and the media used to make the head.

Making the modelling stand

A modelling stand is an essential prerequisite before you get down to business. Such a stand makes the task easier, as it provides a steady base of exactly the right height on which to work. You will need a 25mm (1in) thick wooden block about 15cm (6in) square; a length of dowel rod or

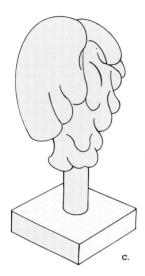

c.

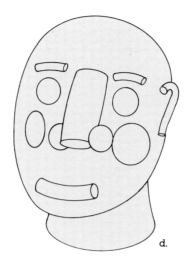

d.

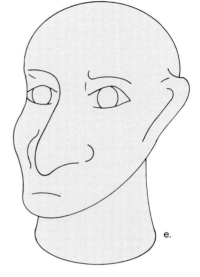

e.

broomstick approximately 20cm (8in) long and 19mm (¾in) in diameter; woodworking glue; a brace with 19mm (¾in) flat bit; a hammer or a screwdriver and 5cm (2in) screw.

1. Drill a hole through the middle of the block and smear a little glue inside the hole and around the rod's base *(see fig. b)*. Then hammer the rod home into the hole. Alternatively, glue the rod to the centre of the block and then secure by screwing it in place from underneath. Countersink the screw, as otherwise the base will wobble.

Modelling with plasticine
You will need your stand, newspaper, household cling film, about 681g (1½lbs) of plasticine and a few modelling tools.
1. Scrunch up a few sheets of newspaper to make a ball about 10cm (4in) tall.
2. Cover the ball with a layer of cling film, then place it on top of the stand. Hold it in place by covering with more cling film, wrapping the ends around the rod *(see fig. c)*.

Modelling with plasticine *The newspaper core is held in place on the stand with cling film. Features are built up with sausages of plasticine and then modelled in an exaggerated style.*

3. Work the plasticine in your hands until it is warm and pliable. Roll out a strip just long enough to wrap around the rod. This is the neck.
4. Cover the paper core with plasticine, smoothing into the neck.
5. Add plasticine to the head piece by piece to build up the basic shape.
6. Press the eye sockets out with your thumbs. Then roll out two eyeballs and gently push them home.
7. Use plasticine sausages to build up the eyebrows, lips and ears *(see fig. d)*.
8. The nose is made from a large sausage, with two balls attached on each side of the base for nostrils.
9. Assess what you have done critically before proceeding further – this means looking at the head upside down as well. The detail should be bold and deep *(see fig. e)*, as otherwise it will be lost under the layers of paper added at the next stage.

Modelling with self-hardening clay
There are many self-hardening clays suitable for modelling on the market, all of which set hard after a few days at room temperature. The clay is easy to work with and gives a very smooth surface, especially if it is brushed with water at the end of modelling. Use it as a modelling medium like plasticine, although you should bear in mind that the heads may be too heavy for the puppets. *(See also p.122.)*

Laminating with papier mâché
To create the laminated effect described earlier, you will need to cover the head you have modelled in layers of newspaper, torn into postage stamp sized squares. You will also need a release agent, such as petroleum jelly or liquid soap; cellulose paste as used for wallpapering; surgical bandage or muslin; PVA glue; mixing bowl; water; a paste brush; and a craft knife.

1. Mix cellulose paste with water according to manufacturer's instructions. Use a heavy duty paste

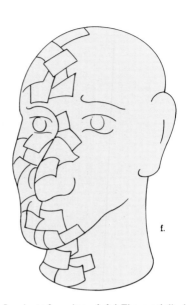

Laminated papier mâché *The modelled plasticine head is pasted with several layers of paper squares. When dry, cut the shell in half and glue strips of bandage in place, ready to join the two halves together.*

containing anti-fungicide as this will prevent mould growing on the paper. Rub the surface of the head with petroleum jelly.

2. Cover head with a layer of paper squares, pressing these firmly down into place *(see fig. f)*. Paste over the paper and cover with a further layer of squares. Use plenty of paste, rubbing it over the surface with your fingers, so that it really soaks into the paper. Build up at least six layers, ideally stopping half way through to let the paper dry, although this is not essential.

3. Leave the head to dry in a warm place, though you should avoid direct heat. Some shrinkage will inevitably occur and characteristic ridges will result.

4. Use a craft knife to cut through the paper shell *(see fig. g)*. This is generally done from side to side, passing behind the ears, although in some cases the design may involve

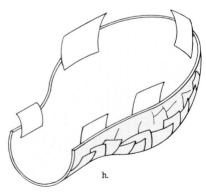

working from front to back. If you have any difficulty prising the papier mâché apart a further cut from side to side, quartering the head, will help.

5. Leave the head pieces to dry on the inside for a few hours and then hold them up to the light to check for any weaknesses. If necessary, glue on strips of bandage on the inside, or use more paste and paper.

6. Glue strips of bandage around a

cut edge with half the bandage width projecting beyond the edge *(see fig. h)*. Leave to dry. Glue the matching cut edge, then bring the two halves together, and press bandage into the glue, using the handle of a long paint brush to reach right inside the head if necessary. Cover the join on the outside with more paste and paper and leave to dry. Neatly trim the neck edge.

Painting papier mâché

Before you start painting the head, prepare the surface by rubbing it down with very fine sandpaper. Then seal it – the sealant stops the paint soaking into the paper. Ideally a white acrylic gesso primer should be used, but, if this is unavailable, use white acrylic primer or emulsion paint instead.

Paint the features with acrylic paints; these are waterproof, fast drying and very easy to use. Thin them with water if you need to and clean your brushes with water when you have finished painting. To obtain a good flesh tone, mix red and white to get a basic pink, to which you add a little yellow and brown. Coat the entire head with the mixture, using two coats if necessary to get a good covering. Paint the eyeballs white with a very small amount of yellow added to take away the starkness. The features can now be painted according to the chosen character. Avoid excessive detail, as this simply will not be visible. Go for bold make up, eliminating the iris if necessary. You are aiming to create a sense of theatre.

The final finish may need some attention as acrylics dry flat. Because of this, you may decide to varnish the eyes and mouth to make them sparkle. The finished head can also be polished with clear furniture polish.

MAKING
GLOVE
PUPPETS

Glove puppets have a universal appeal, especially when it comes to the fast-moving action of a Punch and Judy show. Here, Punch and Judy are the puppets – the baby cannot be operated, even though its head is made of papier mâché. All it consists of is a stump bundled up in a wrap, a head and a bonnet, so start with this.

Judy is just a little more complicated, with a modelled head and a glove which acts as a dress. By the time that you have made her you will be able to tackle the challenge of Punch and his strongly modelled features confidently.

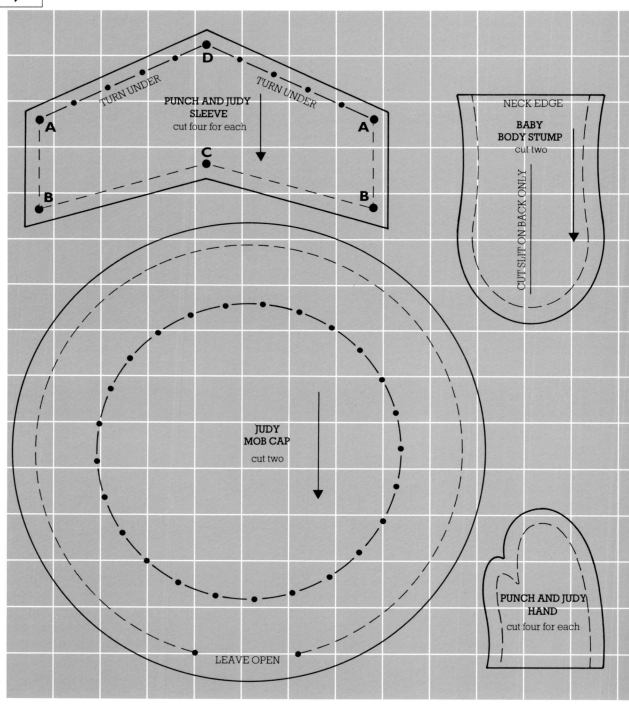

TURN UNDER

TURN UNDER

**PUNCH AND JUDY
SLEEVE**
cut four for each

D

A

A

C

B

B

NECK EDGE

**BABY
BODY STUMP**
cut two

CUT SLIT ON BACK ONLY

**JUDY
MOB CAP**

cut two

LEAVE OPEN

**PUNCH AND JUDY
HAND**

cut four for each

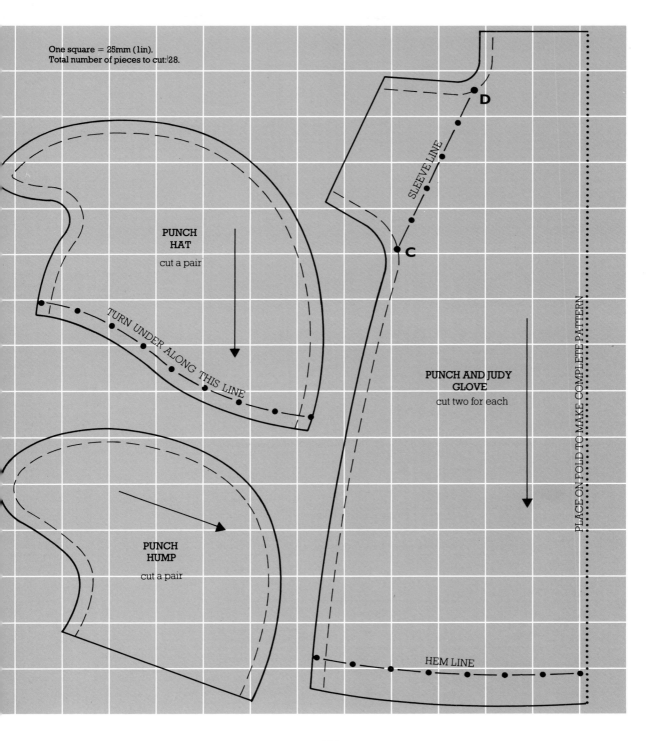

One square = 25mm (1in).
Total number of pieces to cut: 28.

PUNCH
HAT

cut a pair

TURN UNDER ALONG THIS LINE

D

SLEEVE LINE

C

PUNCH AND JUDY
GLOVE

cut two for each

PLACE ON FOLD TO MAKE COMPLETE PATTERN

PUNCH
HUMP

cut a pair

HEM LINE

PROJECT 27

Making the baby
Form a plasticine ball for the head and then embed a vinyl face mask (available from toymakers' suppliers) onto its front.
1. Follow the instructions given on the previous pages to make the papier mâché head. The neck needs a circumference of 15cm (6in) to take the body stump (see fig. a).
2. Paint on the features, starting with brown pupils and continuing with lighter brown eyebrows and a soft, pink, rosebud-shaped mouth. Put a dot of red in the inside corner of each eye and a spot of white on each pupil as a highlight. Fill the head with stuffing.
3. Make a full-size pattern (see p.12) of the body stump from the pattern grid and cut the two pieces you will need from the white cotton. Sew them together around the curved edge, then turn right side out. Make a narrow hem on the neck edge by folding towards the inside and tacking.
4. Fit the stump onto the neck and check for size, resewing if necessary. Glue in place. Stuff the stump through the slit in the back, then close the opening with ladder stitch.
5. Wind wool over two fingers to make a cluster of loops for the hair (see fig. b). Backstitch

Vinyl face mask
Plasticine head and neck

15cm (6in) circumference

a.

the loops together at one end, then glue on forehead.
6. Cut a piece of cotton 20cm (8in) wide by 15cm (6in) long for the bonnet and a circle 7.5cm (3in) in diameter for the crown. Fold bonnet in half across the width and sew both short sides together in turn. Turn right side out.
7. Cut lace into three equal lengths. Gather two to fit the width of the bonnet. Sew one in place along the folded edge

and the other just behind it (see fig. c).
8. Run a gathering thread along the open edge and pull up until the bonnet fits the head. Overlap the ends slightly and fasten off (see fig. d). Run a gathering thread around the edge of the crown circle and pull up tightly. Fasten off. Flatten to form a small disc.
9. Gather edge of the third length of lace and sew it around three-quarters of the crown (see fig. e). Place crown over gathers of bonnet, thus concealing them, and sew in place. Sew ties onto each side of bonnet, then place bonnet on head and fasten.
10. Fold Icelandic wool square diagonally in half and wrap around the baby as a shawl. Stitch in place.

Making Judy
Make a full-size pattern (see p.12) of the glove, sleeve, hand and mob cap from the pattern grid. Cut glove and sleeves from striped cotton, hands from felt and mob cap from white cotton.
1. When you model the head, give it a strong nose and prominent chin. There is no need to model ears as they will not be seen. You can even leave the mouth area flat if this is your first attempt at modelling.
2. Paint the eyes blue with black pupils and outline the upper edge of each eye with a line of red, putting a dot of red in the inside corners and finishing with white highlights

c. Gather up two lengths of lace and sew onto the bonnet. **d.** *Gather up the open edge of the bonnet to fit the head and fasten off.* **e.** *Sew the gathered edge of the third length of lace onto the crown circle.*

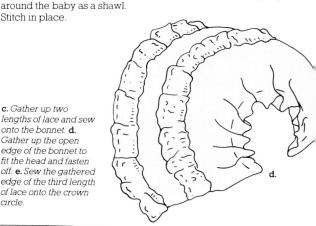
d.

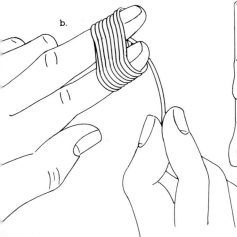
b.

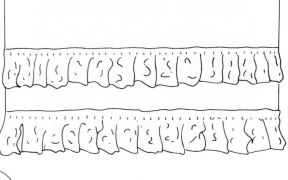
c.

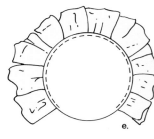
e.

on the pupils. Paint the mouth. Finally give the cheeks some colour by rubbing a little lipstick on them.

3. Cut a strip of card 20cm (8in) by 5cm (2in) and roll to fit the neck opening, which is approximately two fingers wide *(see fig. f)*. Glue edges of roll with rubber latex to hold it in place. Cover one end of the roll with scrap fabric and glue. Now glue the roll inside the neck opening, with the covered end right inside the head. Hold with clothes pegs until the glue sets.

4. Glue a strip of felt around the outside of the neck and a second strip inside the roll. Sew the lower edges of both strips together for further security.

5. Sew glove pieces right sides together across shoulders and down each underarm and side seam. Make a double hem along the lower edge. Turn right side out, then fold under neck edge, making a single hem. Gather to fit over the neck. Backstitch in place, carefully working into the felt collar. Work a second row of stitching to secure. Cover stitching with gathered lace, which you glue in place with clear-drying glue.

6. Sew around the two felt hand pieces with a 3mm (⅛in) seam. Snip corner between thumb and fingers, turn right side out and stuff finger area lightly. Stab stitch finger divisions *(see p.14)*.

7. Cut two pieces of card 15cm (6in) by 3cm (1¼in). Roll these up, coat one end of each piece with glue and cover with scrap fabric. Glue the outside of the roll and gently ease the covered end inside wrist edge of hand *(see fig. g)*. Complete the second hand in same way.

8. Feed hands into arm openings of glove with thumbs

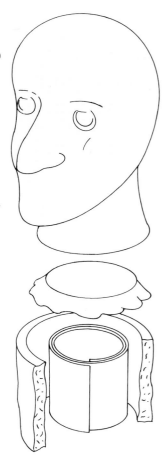

f. For strong support at the neck, glue together a roll of card and cover with a glued circle of fabric at one end. Glue the roll and insert into the head. Reinforce with strips of felt inside and around the neck.

uppermost. Backstitch in position. Cover joins with gathered lace, again glueing into place.

9. Take two sleeve pieces and sew each underarm seam by folding A to A and B to B, then sewing from A to B. Turn one sleeve right side out and feed it inside the other sleeve, so that

PAINTING FACES

Prepare the surface by rubbing with fine sandpaper and seal with a water-based primer. Use acrylic paint to mix a basic flesh tone, then add the features, keeping them simple and bold. Varnish the eyes and mouth and polish the flesh with clear furniture polish (see p.100).

PROJECT 27

right sides are together, seams pressed flat and all edges level *(see fig. h)*. Sew wrist edges together from B through C to B. Open sleeve out so that all right sides are facing, then turn one sleeve inside the other, so that wrong sides are together.
10. Fold under a narrow hem on the shoulder edge of the

sleeve and tack. Feed sleeve over hand and onto the glove, with D on neck seam and A on side seam of glove *(see fig. i)*. Hem in place. Make and attach second sleeve in the same way.
11. Wind wool into a 30cm (12in) long hank, using a book of the same height as the

g. *Position of card roll glued to the inside of the hand.*

OPERATING A GLOVE PUPPET

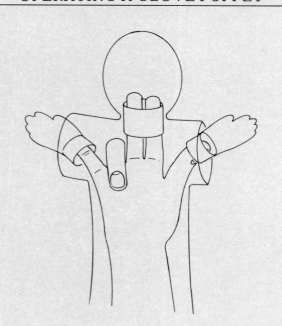

Punch and Judy are planned to fit a large hand. The index and second finger support the head, while the thumb and little finger each operate an arm. The third finger remains bent down towards the palm. The cardboard rolls – called finger stalls by puppeteers – should ideally reach no further than the second joint of each finger and the first joint of thumb. This arrangement ensures maximum freedom of movement.

Practise clapping without hitting the chin, picking up and passing baby, hitting with the stick or even waving hands convincingly and bowing. Try operating two gloves together. Punch traditionally stays on the right hand, while all other members of the cast take turns on the left.

h. *Place one sleeve piece inside another with right sides together, seams pressed and aligned between B and A. Sew the wrist edges together from B through C to B.*

template. Wrap wool over book 57 times, then slip hank off book and tie each end securely with strong thread. Backstitch a parting through the centre of the hank *(see fig. j)*. Now glue parting to the top of the head and then glue down each side of the face and around to back where the tie ends should come together. If there is a gap, conceal it with a bun.
12. Make the mob cap by sewing two circles together around the edge with right sides facing. Leave a small opening. Turn right side out, close opening and press cap.

i. *The sleeve is positioned over the glove, ready for hemming between D and A.*

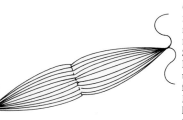

j. The hair is wound into a hank, tied off at each end and sewn through the centre to make a middle parting. The ties can be used to fasten the hank at the back of the head.

Sew gathered lace around edge. Now run a strong gathering thread all round cap, 3cm (1¼in) in from the edge. Pull up to fit head. If necessary, put more stuffing in mob cap to give it shape, then sew cap in place through the gathering to the hair beneath. As a finishing touch you can sew ribbon to each side of the mob cap and bring it down to tie under the chin.

Making Punch

Make a full-size pattern *(see p12)* of the glove, sleeve, hand, hump and hat from the pattern grid. Cut hands from felt and all parts of the costume from needle cord.

1. Because the head is so complex you may have to cut it off in four sections from the plasticine. Stress the characteristic curves of the nose and chin in your modelling and do not forget to model ears.

2. Paint the eyes brown with black pupils and outline the upper edge of each eye with a flamboyant red eyebrow. Finish eyes with white highlights. Paint the mouth with the same red as the eyes and paint the mouth opening white. You may like to add a black grid indicating teeth. Blush the cheeks and chin with more red paint or rub a little lipstick into them to heighten the colour.

3. Make the neck roll, glove, hands and sleeves as you did for Judy, but this time using ric-rac for decoration, not lace.

4. Sew the two hump pieces together, turn right side out and stuff firmly. Run a strong gathering thread around the edge and pull up to roll raw edges inwards. Cover seams with ric-rac. Ladder stitch the hump in place on the back of the glove.

5. To make the hair, you will need to cut a 23cm (9in) by 1cm (½in) central slot in the strong piece of card as shown. Wrap wool over card approximately 130 times, then backstitch or machine the curls together through the slot. Break one end of the card and pull string of curls free. Glue hair around head, leaving a gap over the forehead.

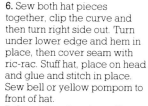

k. Card template used for making a row of curls from wool.

6. Sew both hat pieces together, clip the curve and then turn right side out. Turn under lower edge and hem in place, then cover seam with ric-rac. Stuff hat, place on head and glue and stitch in place. Sew bell or yellow pompom to front of hat.

7. Attach head to glove. Cover the join by glueing a simple collar over it, decorating the collar with ric-rac or a gathered ruff. If you like, you could even make a collar with tiny bells attached to it.

8. Finally take a length of dowelling and sandpaper each end until really smooth. Then tuck it under Punch's arm.

MATERIALS

For the baby:
plasticine
acrylic paints
a 6cm (2½in) long by 6cm (2½in) wide vinyl face mask
1m (1yd) wool for curls
56g (2oz) stuffing
31cm (12in) square white cotton
61cm (24in) cotton lace
46cm (18in) square of Icelandic wool
31cm (12in) white baby ribbon

For Judy:
a papier mâché head measuring 10cm (4in) from chin to top of head
ball of mohair wool
23cm (9in) square of flesh-coloured felt
0.5m (½yd) of 92cm (36in) wide striped cotton
1.5m (1½yd) gathered lace
30cm (12in) of 92cm (36in) wide white cotton
56g (2oz) stuffing
20cm (8in) square of thin card

For Punch:
a papier mâché head measuring 11cm (4½in) from chin to top of head
mohair yarn for hair
23cm (9in) square of flesh-coloured felt
69cm (27in) of 92cm (36in) wide red needle cord
168g (6oz) stuffing
20cm (8in) square thin card
approximately 2m (2yd) yellow ric-rac
strong piece of card 30.5cm (12in) by 6.5cm (2½in)
small bell or yellow pompom for hat
length of dowelling for stick

EQUIPMENT

Dressmaking shears, pins, needles, thread, tape measure or ruler, pattern-making equipment, paint brushes, knife, fabric and paper glue.

MAKING A
PUPPET THEATRE

This toy theatre is based on the traditional 'Punch and Judy' glove puppet theatre. However, it can also be used for small string puppets if it is turned upside down. It is designed to be easily adaptable – the removable playboard will provide both the external playboard needed for glove puppets, and the internal playboard used for string puppets.

The size of your theatre

There are two things to consider before building your puppet theatre: firstly the size of the puppeteer (the measurements for this theatre are suitable for a small child), and secondly the size of the puppets, which will determine the size of the stage opening. If you want to make a theatre to be used by adults for children's entertainment, simply enlarge the measurements. The string puppet described on p.112 is a large puppet that will require a much larger theatre, so adapt the measurements of either the puppet or the theatre. There is a wide range of commercially available string puppets that can be used with this theatre.

Cutting the wood

Mark out the largest sheet of plywood and cut out the front, the two sides and the backboard. Use a panel saw, an electric circular saw or a power jig saw.

Make templates for the shelf supports. From the second piece of plywood cut out the parts for the string puppet shelf; cut the parts for the playboard from the third piece. Cut battens to size if this has not already been done.

Mark the fixing slots in the

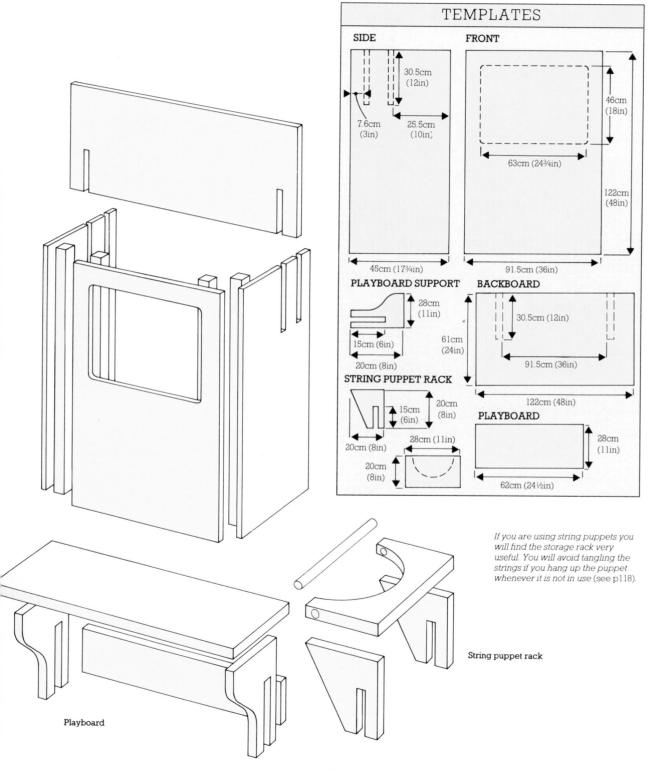

TEMPLATES

SIDE

30.5cm (12in)

7.6cm (3in)

25.5cm (10in)

45cm (17¾in)

FRONT

46cm (18in)

63cm (24¾in)

122cm (48in)

91.5cm (36in)

PLAYBOARD SUPPORT

28cm (11in)

15cm (6in)

20cm (8in)

BACKBOARD

30.5cm (12in)

61cm (24in)

91.5cm (36in)

122cm (48in)

STRING PUPPET RACK

15cm (6in)

20cm (8in)

20cm (8in)

28cm (11in)

20cm (8in)

PLAYBOARD

28cm (11in)

62cm (24½in)

If you are using string puppets you will find the storage rack very useful. You will avoid tangling the strings if you hang up the puppet whenever it is not in use (see p118).

Playboard

String puppet rack

109

PROJECT
28

Recess the hinges on the battens to give a smoother finish.

shelf supports, the sides and the backboard and make 10mm (⅜in) wide cuts.

Now mark out the outline of the proscenium opening. Drill small holes in each corner and cut out the shape with a pad saw or a power jig saw. Smooth all of the edges with sandpaper before assembling the pieces.

Assembling the theatre

The front and sides are put together first.

1. Pin the battens in position. Before screwing the pieces together mark the position of the hinges. Use a pencil to outline each hinge and score around each outline with a chisel to half the depth of the hinge. Chisel out the wood and tidy up the edges.

2. Attach the front to the side pieces by countersinking the screws from the front, making sure that the recesses for the hinges are accurately aligned. Screw on the hinges.

3. To assemble the playboard screw the crossbar to the two side supports, just in front of the slot. Glue the supports on the playboard and secure with

small nails or screws.

4. When the glue has dried screw the cuphooks onto the playboard. The glove puppets should be hung from these hooks when awaiting use.

5. The string puppet rack can now be assembled if it is required. Glue and screw the components together in the same way as for the playboard shelf (step 3). Drill a recess for the dowelling and glue it in position.

Fix cuphooks on the underside of the playboard shelf.

Finishing and painting

6. All the sawn edges should be well rubbed with sandpaper for a smooth finish. Check that none of the nails are protruding. Fill any holes with a proprietary filler.

7. Seal the surface of the wood with a water-based primer. When dry apply a coat of white emulsion to all the pieces except the backboard. Give the playboard and the string puppet shelf a second coat of white paint, and paint the backboard a colour of your choice or paint a decorative background to add to the scenic effect. To paint neat and well-spaced stripes on the sides of the theatre you will need to mask with tape. Tear off strips of masking tape to strips of 1220mm (48in) and stick them at regular intervals down the length of the three sides of the theatre. Give one coat of emulsion paint and when quite dry carefully peel off the tape. This will give a crisp edge to the lines.

8. Seal the paint with a coat of full strength polyurethane varnish.

Making the curtain

9. Hem the edges of the material and sew curtain rings along one long edge. Thread

the rings onto a piece of dowelling. (If felt is used for the curtains there is no need to make a hem.)

10. Screw cuphooks into the back of the front board of the theatre at all four corners. You will need to be able to hang the curtain from either end of the opening, depending on how the theatre is being used.

Using the theatre for glove puppets

The theatre should be assembled with the opening at the top. The backboard should be slotted into the back slot to allow room for the puppeteer to sit inside the theatre. Fit the playboard onto the lower edge of the proscenium opening with the shelf projecting out of the theatre. The puppets are hung on the cuphooks, where they are easily accessible.

Using the theatre for string puppets

The theatre should be set up so that the proscenium is in the lower half, the backboard is fitted into the slots positioned in the middle of the side pieces, the playboard faces the interior of the theatre to form a stage. Put the puppet rack in position on one of the sides.

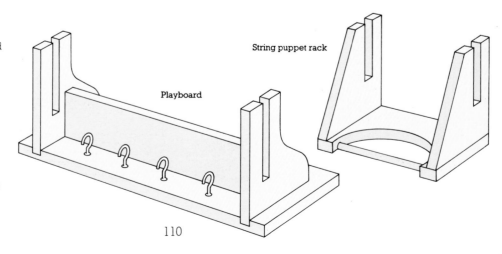

String puppet rack

Playboard

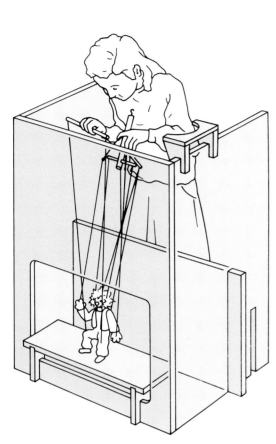

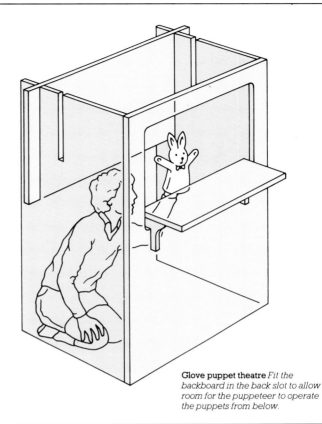

Glove puppet theatre *Fit the backboard in the back slot to allow room for the puppeteer to operate the puppets from below.*

String puppet theatre *Stand the theatre on a raised surface to add height, making viewing more comfortable for the audience.*

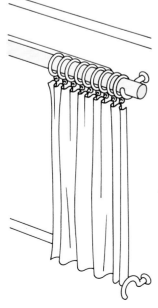

Cuphooks fitted at all four corners of the stage opening will allow the curtain to be hung from either direction, depending on how the theatre is being used.

MATERIALS

	Plywood:
1	sheet 10 x 1220 x 2400mm (⅜ x 48 x 96in)
1	piece 10 x 200 x 610mm (⅜ x 8 x 24in)
1	piece 10 x 280 x 1020mm (⅜ x 11 x 40in)
	Softwood:
1	pieces 25 x 25 x 1220mm (1 x 1 x 48in)
1	piece 25 x 50 x 600mm (1 x 2 x 23¾in)
1	piece 25 x 50 x 200mm (1 x 2 x 8in)
	Hardware:
	cuphooks
4	hinges and small fixing screws
	32mm (1¼in) woodscrews
	emulsion paint (white and colours of your choice)
	For the curtain:
4	large cuphooks
	curtain rings
	piece dowelling 70cm (27½in)
1	99 x 53cm (39 x 21in) piece of fabric (cotton or felt)

TOOLS

Panel saw, power jigsaw or pad saw, wheelbrace and bit, or power drill and drill bits, chisels, bradawl, tenon saw, screwdriver, ruler, masking tape.

MAKING A
STRING PUPPET

Here is a character that is sure to delight any audience, for clowns not only seem to have a natural charm all of their own but also are well able to hold the stage on their own. The stretch knit fabric used for the body has been deliberately chosen to enable you to employ the typical puppet movement more often associated with carved wooden puppets.

Preparing the pattern for the body

Prepare a full-size pattern (see p.12) from the pattern grid. Cut head, face panel, body, arms and legs from jersey. Draw round hand piece on a rectangle of doubled fabric, twice, for hands. Leave uncut until they have been sewn together. Cut shoes from squares of felt, keeping toes and soles in one colour and remainder from second colour. The finished clown stands 56cm (22in) tall from feet to top of head.

Making the body

1. Start by sewing the front to the back body piece, from A to B on each side. Turn right side out and top stitch the double row that forms the waist hinge, either by machine or hand-sewn stab stitch. This hinge allows the clown to bow and bend naturally.

2. Stuff upper portion of body through the neck opening and the lower portion through the bottom one. Close each opening with ladder stitch. Stitch three weights, such as heavy buttons, across the lower portion of the back.

3. Sew two leg pieces together on each side in turn from top edge to lower ankle edge.

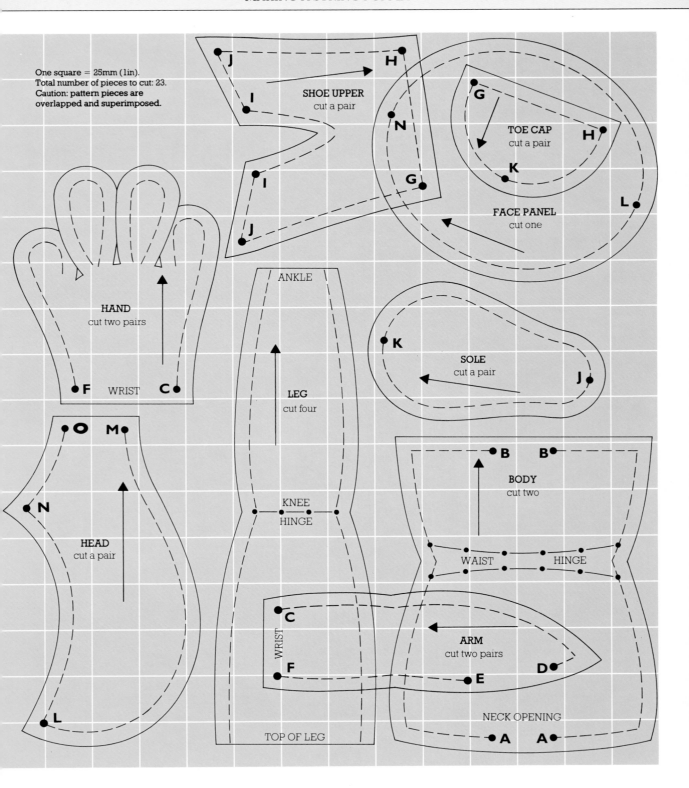

One square = 25mm (1in).
Total number of pieces to cut: 23.
Caution: pattern pieces are
overlapped and superimposed.

SHOE UPPER
cut a pair

TOE CAP
cut a pair

FACE PANEL
cut one

HAND
cut two pairs

WRIST

ANKLE

LEG
cut four

KNEE
HINGE

SOLE
cut a pair

BODY
cut two

WAIST   HINGE

HEAD
cut a pair

WRIST

ARM
cut two pairs

NECK OPENING

TOP OF LEG

PROJECT
29

Turn right side out and top stitch knee hinge. Stuff upper and lower sections of leg, then turn in top raw edges and ladder stitch closed. Hold stuffing in lower leg temporarily with a pin. Cut an oval-shaped knee cap from foam and sew in place across the front of the knee hinge by catching on each side only. This knee cap will ensure that the knee only bends in the correct direction. Extra strength can be provided by glueing a small square of card to the back of the foam, after first scoring it in half.

4. Make the second leg in the same way, then attach each leg to the lower edge of the body with buttonhole bars. These are simply strong thread straight stitches worked between body and leg, which are strengthened by having buttonhole stitch worked along the length.

5. Complete legs by sewing shoes. Sew toe cap to shoe upper from G to H, then make back seam by bringing I to I and J to J and sewing. Run a gathering thread around front edge of the toe cap, pull up until the shoe fits the sole between J and K and then sew in place. Turn completed shoe right side out and stuff toe area firmly. Wrap weights in stuffing and place in foot, directly below leg. Finish stuffing the foot.

6. Turn under ankle edge of leg, and then hand sew in place to the top of the shoe, covering the slit. Test to see that both leg and foot move freely by pinching the knee between your fingers and 'walking' the leg along a table. If the toe drags when the leg 'walks forward', the toe is overweight. When satisfied with the weighting, complete second shoe and attach in the

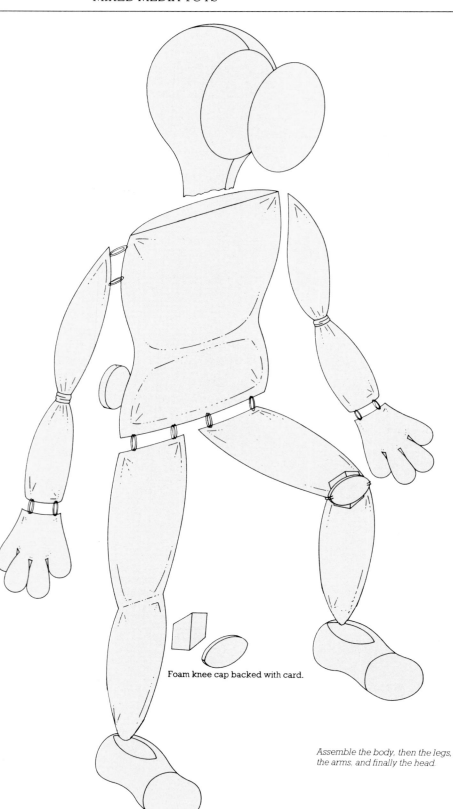

Foam knee cap backed with card.

Assemble the body, then the legs, the arms, and finally the head.

Use two pieces of fur fabric for the hair. Attach with glue, or by sewing.

same way.

7. Sew a pair of arm pieces from C to D and E to F. Turn right side out and lightly stuff, taking care not to distort the shape. Close opening between D and E with ladder stitch and draw up waist opening with raw edges turned in. Now wind strong thread tightly around elbow and fasten off. This makes a flexible joint. Make the second arm in the same way.

8. Sew around hand pieces on rectangle of fabric, then cut out carefully, snipping corners between the fingers at the bottom of the slash. Turn hands right side out and stuff, again taking care not to distort the shape. Insert a weight into the palm of each hand. Turn in wrist edge, close and then attach to end of arm with buttonhole bars.

9. Place the arms at the side of the body and attach with buttonhole bars at the shoulders. If you feel that the arm is too long, you can compensate by shortening the shoulder. If it looks too short, make longer buttonhole bars.

10. Sew head pieces together from L to M and N to O. Run a gathering thread around the edge of the face panel and pull up to fit opening on head. Keep most of the gathers on the lower part around the chin area. Fit face to head matching

M to M and N to N then sew.

11. Turn head right side out and stuff face first, carefully rounding out its shape, before tackling the rest of the head. Leave neck area empty – this is essential as otherwise it will be impossible for you to nod the head and turn it from side to side. Turn under raw edges at bottom of neck and ladder stitch to top of body.

12. Cut out felt shapes for mouth and eyes, glue together and then glue in place on face, using clear-drying glue or latex. Glue a sequin to the centre of each eye. These will catch the light when the puppet moves. Cut a circle of red felt of around 3cm (1¼in) diameter for the nose, gather up and stuff to make a ball. Sew in place with ladder stitch. Blush cheeks with face rouge.

13. Cut fur into a strip and wrap this around the head. Then cut a circle of fur to cover the top of the head. Glue or stitch fur hair pieces in place and brush into shape.

Preparing the pattern for the costume

Draw up a full-size pattern *(see p12)* from the grid provided for

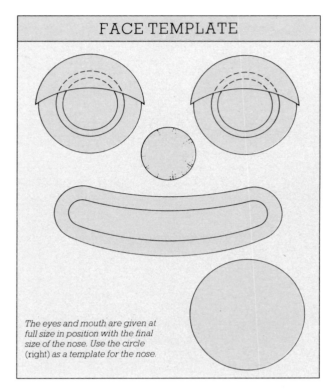

FACE TEMPLATE

The eyes and mouth are given at full size in position with the final size of the nose. Use the circle (right) as a template for the nose.

the jacket and the rest of the costume. Before cutting out the latter, check the size by laying the body of the clown against the pattern, as stretch fabrics alter so much in size when stuffed. Pay particular attention to length of sleeve and legs. Cut jacket pieces from felt.

Making the costume

1. Make a slit for the neck and then cut the centre front open from neck to heel. The centre back is only slit from heel to crotch. Hem the wrist edges of each sleeve. Sew underarm and side seams down to ankle, then seam each inside leg seam. Hem ankle edges.

2. Slip clown into costume and check again for fit. Gather each ankle edge and sew securely to leg beneath. Now sew a 2m (2yd) length of strong thread to each leg, just above the knee.

Do this beneath the costume by working through the front opening. These threads are for stringing the puppet and so must be attached securely. Pass threads through costume to outside and leave hanging for the time being.

3. Close front opening of costume and sew neck edge to body beneath. Cover neck join by making a mandarin collar – this is simply a strip of material long enough to pass around the neck. It should be cut to twice the required height. Sew collar into a tube, then fold in half, turn under raw edges and sew in place.

4. Make the jacket by sewing front pieces to back on shoulders and sides. Edge jacket and sleeves with braid, then sew on sequins. Like the eyes, these sequins will catch the light.

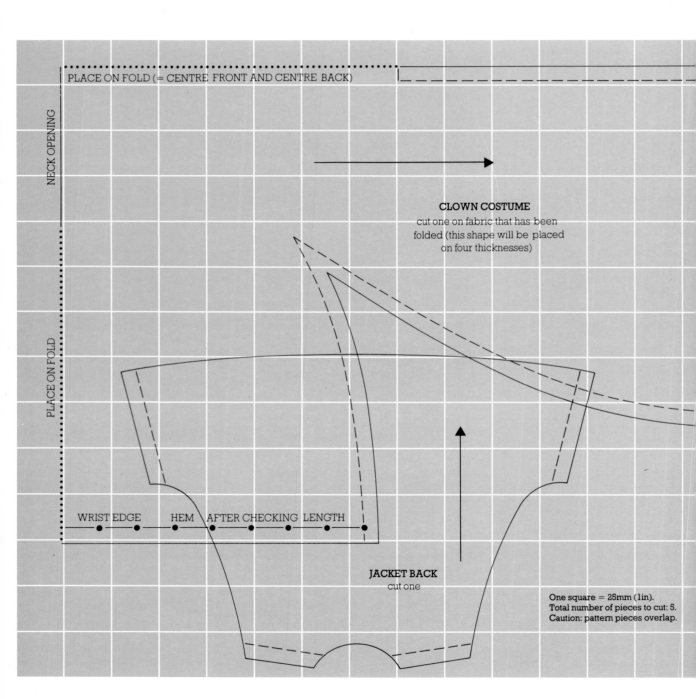

PLACE ON FOLD (= CENTRE FRONT AND CENTRE BACK)

NECK OPENING

PLACE ON FOLD

CLOWN COSTUME
cut one on fabric that has been
folded (this shape will be placed
on four thicknesses)

WRIST EDGE ● ● HEM ● AFTER CHECKING LENGTH ● ● ● ● ●

JACKET BACK
cut one

One square = 25mm (1in).
Total number of pieces to cut: 5.
Caution: pattern pieces overlap.

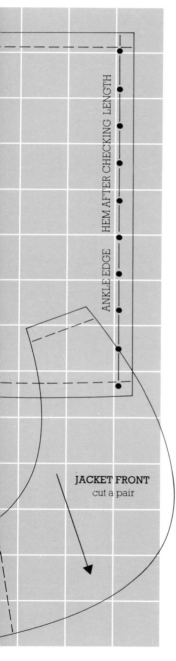

ANKLE EDGE — **HEM AFTER CHECKING LENGTH**

JACKET FRONT
cut a pair

Making the control

1. Sand all the pieces of dowelling so that the ends are smooth. The 20cm (8in) section of dowelling is the upright control to which all other parts are attached.
2. Drill a hole across the bottom of the upright and glue the head dowelling in place. This is the 16.5cm (6½in) length.
3. Now drill a hole at an angle in the back of the upright, just above the head bar. Glue shortest length of dowelling in place. This is the shoulder bar.

4. The remaining 27cm (10½in) piece of dowelling is the detachable leg bar, which is attached to the upright by a hook and ring. Tie a ring to the centre of the bar with a fine piece of wire, then screw the smallest hook into the front of the upright.
5. The largest hook is screwed into the top of the upright. Use this to hang the puppet up when it is not performing.
6. The wires control the arms. Attach these to the upright by drilling two holes through the

control, one above the other and both, just below the leg hook. Bend the top of each wire at right angles, push the short end through the hole and bend over at the other side to stop it being pulled out. Make a loop with thin-nosed pliers at the lower end of each wire for attaching the hand strings. Make sure that the wires are long enough to rest on the head bar and insert from opposite sides, as in the

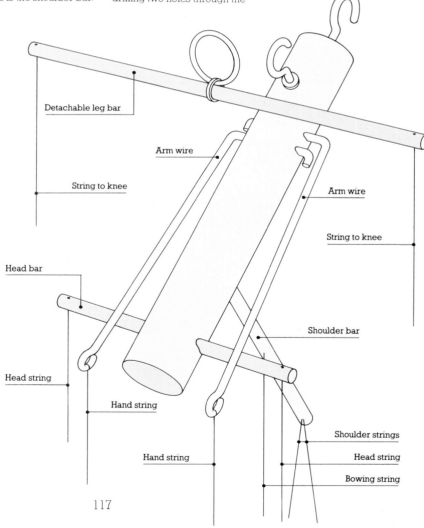

Detachable leg bar

Arm wire

String to knee

Arm wire

String to knee

Head bar

Shoulder bar

Head string

Hand string

Shoulder strings

Head string

Hand string

Bowing string

117

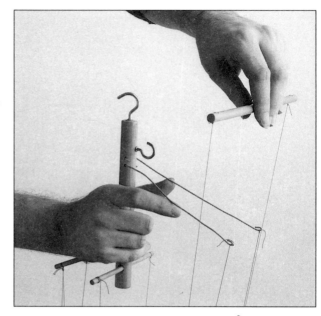

diagram.

7. Small holes must be drilled in the dowelling to take the strings. Position the holes at each end of the leg and head bars, the end of the shoulder bar and 5cm (2in) from the end of the shoulder bar.

Stringing the puppet

Use dark coloured thread – button thread or crochet cotton are both suitable – to string your puppet. The thread should be rubbed with beeswax to protect it from fraying and becoming brittle. The strings should be long enough to support the puppet either on the floor or on stage when you have your arm bent at the elbow.

1. Attach head strings to puppet by sewing long threads on each side where the ears would be. Thread these head strings through the holes in each end of head bar and tie off at required length. Leave thread ends for any alterations that might be needed, including final tightening.

2. Together with the head strings, shoulder strings take the weight of the puppet and also control height. Sew a long thread to each shoulder, making sure that the thread bites into the body beneath the costume. Now put jacket on clown and pass threads through shoulder seams on each side of the jacket. Tie off both shoulder strings through the hole in the end of the shoulder bar.

3. Sew string to top of hand and then tie off through loop in end of wire. Repeat for other hand.

4. Sew string to the bottom and tie off on the shoulder bar through the centrally placed hole. This is the bowing string.

5. Now thread the leg strings, which you have already stitched in place, through the

holes in each end of the leg bar and tie off. Make sure that the leg strings are long enough to allow the leg bar to be unhooked without moving the puppet when it is performing.

6. Your puppet is now fully strung. Test the support, height and movement, making any final adjustments, if required. Knots can be sealed with glue and ends cut off if desired.

Operating your puppet

Hold the control in your right hand with second, third and fourth fingers wrapped around the upright, beneath the wires.

Nodding

Bowing

Turning head

The wires sit over the thumb and index finger. The left hand can be used to operate the leg bar, bowing string and individual hand strings

Sometimes it is more convenient to hold the puppet in the left hand and operate with the right. Decide for yourself which position you find more comfortable.

You are now ready to practise all the movements needed to produce a convincing performance. Tilt the control forward to nod and bow the head. Pull on the bowing string and lower the control to bow the clown. Turn the control from side to side and tilt slightly to get the head turning. Raise your thumb or index finger to lift an arm. Pull up on a hand string to make the clown wave.

Next, try walking. Unhook the leg bar and paddle it from side to side with your free hand. This will lift each leg in turn and, provided that your puppet is correctly weighted, return it to the floor in a natural walking rhythm. Having mastered walking forwards, try walking the clown in a circle without moving yourself. Now try to get the clown to sit on a chair, kneel down and lie down.

Looking after your puppet
By following this simple procedure, you will keep your puppet from tangling when not in use. Spin clown so that strings wind up in a twist. Now wind twist over a key, which can be made from a piece of strong card or plywood. Store the puppet in a large bag and fasten the bag around the key with a pipe cleaner. Hang the puppet in a cupboard from the hook in the top of the control.

Waving

Walking

MATERIALS

For the body:
    46cm (½yd) of 138cm (54in) wide cotton jersey or cotton stockinette
    556g (1lb 4oz) stuffing
    small pieces of white, red, blue, black and flesh-coloured felt
 2 large blue sequins
 2 23cm (9in) squares of PVC or felt for shoes
    selection of weights such as dressmaker's lead discs or heavy buttons
    30cm (12in) square of blonde, long pile fur for hair
    small piece of card
    face rouge
    15cm (6in) square of 1cm (approx ½in) thick foam

For the costume:
    46cm (½yd) of 92cm (36in) wide fur fabric that drapes well and is not stiff
    30.5cm (12in) square of felt for jacket
    152cm (5ft) braid
    sequins

For the control:
    20cm (8in) of 20mm (¾in) dowelling
    16.5cm (6½in) of 5mm (³⁄₁₆in) dowelling
    11cm (4½in) of 5mm (³⁄₁₆in) dowelling
    27cm (10½in) of 8mm (⁵⁄₁₆in) dowelling
 2 23cm (9in) long 14 gauge galvanised wires
    length of fine wire to hold ring in place
 1 2.5cm (1in) brass hook
 1 1.8cm (¾in) brass hook
    curtain ring
    woodworking glue or epoxy resin adhesive

EQUIPMENT

For the body and costume: dressmaking shears, embroidery scissors, pins, needles, thread, measure or ruler, pencil, pattern-making equipment. For the control: saw, drill, wirecutter, pliers, fabric and wood glue, sandpaper.

MAKING

ADVANCED TOYS

The toys in this section present a new challenge for you, since there are extra factors to take into account. When children grow older they become more active, so their toys should reflect this fact. The Wendy house and go-cart are two examples of what you can create to meet this need. Remember, however, that toys like these are subject to wear and tear, so make sure that the materials you use are strong enough for their tasks – and do not be surprised if you are asked to build new, larger versions when the originals have been outgrown.

Your growing child will also be fascinated by the intricate miniature world of make-believe. The doll's house is a perennial favourite, since it gives your children the opportunity to create a world of their own.

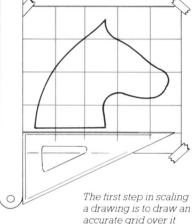

The first step in scaling a drawing is to draw an accurate grid over it using a ruler and set square, or a T-square and set square.

When enlarging, tape the picture onto a larger sheet of paper of a similar shape. Extend the base line to the required length and draw a vertical line from it. The intersection of the diagonal line with the vertical will give you the height of the enlargement.

Enlarging and reducing

The measurements for all the toys can be adapted to suit your growing child quite simply by enlarging all the measurements given by a fixed proportion, taking into consideration the fact that stronger materials should also be used. However, for more complicated parts it is useful to know how to 'square up' patterns. This works on the same principle as the grids for the soft toy patterns *(see p.12)*, but the method here allows for more flexibility (the soft toys are all enlarged by the same proportion).

This is also a useful method for enlarging or reducing a picture and preparing it for a jigsaw *(see pp.62-3)*, or as a template for a doll's house ornament.

Squaring up

1. Draw an accurate grid over the drawing with a T-square, set square and a ruler.
2. Fix the drawing to the bottom left-hand corner of a larger piece of paper of a similar shape and align the grid with the T-square. Extend the bottom line to the width you require and draw a line at right

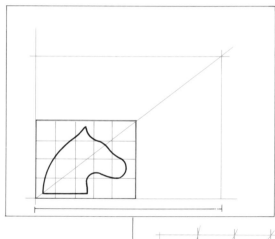

Draw a line from the bottom left corner of the picture, through the furthest points of the original grid to mark the new positions on the enlarged grid.

angles to it. Then extend the diagonal of the original grid to intersect this vertical line. This will mark the height of the enlargement from which you can then draw the rectangle. Draw the grid on the enlargement rectangle by placing one end of a ruler at the bottom left-hand corner of the rectangle and aligning it with the furthest point of each vertical and horizontal line of the grid, then marking with a pencil where the ruler meets the edge of the larger rectangle. You can draw the enlarged grid using these markers.

3. The lines and shapes within each original square can now be plotted by eye in the corresponding square on the larger grid.

Working in miniature
Before you begin to construct the doll's house it is essential that you understand the basic principles

relating to working to scale and working in miniature. Basically, this is simply a development of the squaring up method, but because of the size of the original measurements involved it means transferring those measurements from actual size, to another medium. These principles can also be adapted to making furniture and furnishings for the doll's house.

Scaling in proportion
The traditional doll's house is often based on a real home and it is relatively simple to recreate your own, or a friend's home, in miniature. All traditional doll's houses are built to a scale of 1:12, so that 25mm =

30cm (1in = 12in), and all fixtures, fittings and furniture that can be bought are made to this scale. This makes producing a realistic replica relatively easy.

Ideally, you should measure the house and draw up the plans accordingly. However, since this is generally not practical the best way to overcome the problem is to take a series of photographs of the side and front elevations of the house, as square-on as possible and scale up your plans from these using the method described earlier. To maintain the 1:12 scale, the squares of the grid that you draw over the photograph should correspond to a known dimension – the front door

Transfer the drawing onto the enlarged grid, plotting it out square by square. Your enlarged drawing is now a full-sized template, ready to be transferred onto the wood and cut out.

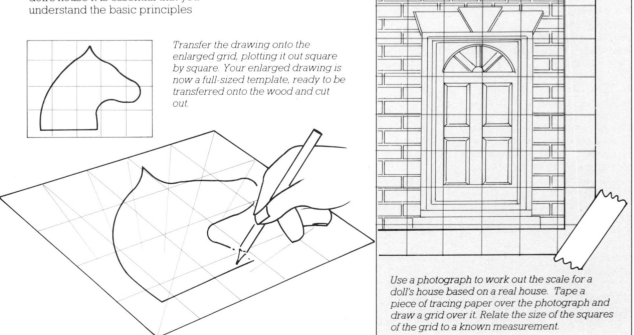

SCALING A HOUSE

Use a photograph to work out the scale for a doll's house based on a real house. Tape a piece of tracing paper over the photograph and draw a grid over it. Relate the size of the squares of the grid to a known measurement.

provides a convenient unit of measurement as it is probably the easiest to measure.

If for example, the front door is 180cm (6ft) high, then it should measure 15cm (6in) high on your plans. So, ideally you should draw up your grid with the total height of the door corresponding to six squares. Whatever the size of the squares on the photo, you can easily work out how much they need to be enlarged by to make 25mm (1in) squares on the plans. This may mean drawing a grid, depending on the size of the photograph, that has so many squares on it that it becomes impractical. If this is the case, halve the number of squares so that the 180cm (6ft) door corresponds to three squares on the grid, making each one worth 5cm (2in) on the plan.

Another method, which is not so accurate, is to take individual measurements from the photograph and increase each one by the percentage that you have worked out with the door – if the door in the photograph is 25mm (1in) high, multiply all measurements by six.

Whatever method you use, you will achieve a perfect scale replica of your chosen house. However, allowances have to be made when transferring real life to miniature. The average height of a modern room is about 240cm (8ft) but this will make the rooms in a doll's house too shallow to easily place and manoeuvre objects as well as making the room appear to be out of scale. There is no hard and fast rule, but it is safe to increase the height of the rooms by about 20% to give you plenty of space and a natural looking room. Remember to take into account the fact that this will increase the overall height of the house.

Miniature finishes

Wood is used for the basic construction of most doll's houses, but they get their individual character from the exterior and interior decoration that you give them. On pp.136-9 you will find details of external finishes and architectural details that will enable you to create anything from a stone cottage, or a half-timbered Tudor manor house to a modern brick building. Several materials are used, but the most versatile of all is self-hardening clay.

Self-hardening clay

This material is frequently used in the construction of both the exterior and interior of the doll's house. There are a number of clay-like modelling materials that are very convenient to use because they include binding and hardening additives which do away with the need to bake the clays at high temperatures in special kilns. Drying occurs over a period of days, the exact time dependant on a number of factors such as the thickness of the clay, the size of the object made, atmospheric humidity, room temperature and the exact composition of the clay being used.

Surface cracking

The clays dry without losing their shape although there is sometimes a slight reduction of volume and some surface cracking. This is not quite the problem it might seem, for gaps and cracks are easily filled with glue and fresh clay.

The hardened surface is rather like plaster of Paris to work with and consequently you may find yourself sawing, grinding, drilling and filling.

Preparing the clay

Self-hardening clays are sold in sealed packets which usually contain instructions for use. Read these carefully before starting, noting any special requirements. Prepare the work surface by laying down a plastic sheet and have ready a bowl of water so that fingers and modelling tools can be kept moist.

Start by gently kneading the clay to make it pliable and if necessary, add a little water. Work on small pieces at a time, combining them with each other until you have a sufficient quantity for your project. Any left over clay can be wrapped in a plastic bag and stored in an airtight tin for future use.

Forming

Clay can be shaped in many traditional ways. Perhaps the most popular method is pinching it to shape. More detailed shaping can be achieved by using the same modelling tools as are used with plasticine (see p.99). A craft knife is particularly useful. Clay can also be flattened by hand, or with a rolling pin to make sheets for forming or for cutting out flat shapes.

Yet another method of forming is to make long worms of clay which are then built into shapes by coiling. This is the method used to make the flower borders in the doll's house garden (see p.142).

Self-hardening clay can be modelled on a base or around a framework of a different material. Support can be provided by a wire framework (see tree making on p.144), cocktail sticks and even pencils. This saves on the amount of clay used and also strengthens the object being made. Experiment, and if you do not like the form you arrive at first time, simply roll it up and start again.

Surface textures

A smooth surface can be achieved by gently rubbing the clay with a moist sponge or damp finger before it dries. For a project that has dried you can use very fine-grade sandpaper and rub gently, wipe with a damp sponge then polish with a finger and dry with a soft cloth. Repeat this process several times if necessary to get a really smooth surface.

Interesting textures can be obtained by brushing the surface with different kinds of brushes, by stippling and even by drawing a comb or fork over the clay.

Patterns can be imprinted by pressing on lace or buttons, or simply by drawing with a fine knitting needle.

Drying

Allow air to circulate on all surfaces by placing the object on a foam rubber base or similar permeable substance.

If you want to change the shape or add a small piece, simply moisten the surface with a brush, smear with a little washed clay, then press the pieces together firmly and support them while they dry. Multipurpose glue can be added to the washed clay if necessary.

Sealing and painting

Self-hardening clays should be sealed with a coat of lacquer or paint to protect them from water. For painting, use acrylics (as used for the papier mâché projects, *see p.100*), tempera colours and emulsions or undercoat followed by gloss.

Miniature style

The external finish of the doll's house you build will have to be matched by its windows and doors. Close attention must be paid to these details if you want your doll's house to be an exact replica. On pp.136-9 alternative doors of different periods are shown which may fit in with your plans, otherwise it is a matter of reproducing in balsa wood the door of your chosen house. There is not as much detail to consider in the

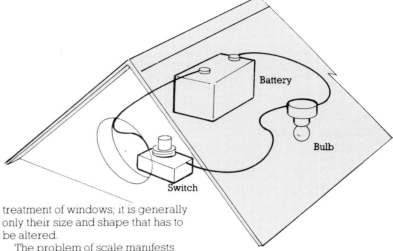

treatment of windows; it is generally only their size and shape that has to be altered.

The problem of scale manifests itself most in the interior of the house with the wallpaper and carpets. Real carpet is too thick and the designs on most wallpaper only really work when they are on full size walls. Felt is a good substitute for carpet. It can be obtained in many different colours, off-cuts may be all you need, and it has the right texture for carpet. For wallpaper, wrapping paper often works well as long as the pattern is small and not too bold.

Lighting in miniature

A miniature lighting system will give the perfect finishing touch to your doll's house.

For the doll's house described in this section you will need just one central bulb fixed in the ceiling above the stairwell to illuminate the landing, stairs, hall and bedrooms.

You will need 91cm (36in) of thin flex, one small torch bulb and holder, one small toggle-type switch, and one large square torch or wireless battery, preferably with screw-down terminals.

Drill a 3mm (⅛in) hole through the landing ceiling section before the roof is put in place. This will take the two wires from the bulb in the landing ceiling to the battery and switch which are placed in the attic area.

A simple miniature lighting system is arranged by fixing a screw-mounted bulb on the landing ceiling of the doll's house. The light is controlled by a toggle switch located in the attic.

SAFETY TIPS

For all their fun and suitability for the older child, these toys will almost certainly be used by younger brothers and sisters and by groups of children playing together. They are, after all, toys that encourage social contact. In this respect there is cause for concern. Check frequently that the Wendy house is safe and sound and free from splinters, with all hooks firmly in place. Remember too, that small objects in the doll's house, especially pretend food, might well prove dangerous to very young toddlers who may be tempted to swallow them.

MAKING A
WENDY HOUSE

All children love having a home of their very own. This Wendy house will give hours of enjoyment, not only keeping your children amused, but also providing them with something very important – an environment that is truly their own. The house can be used both indoors and outdoors. Made from oil-tempered hardboard, it is weatherproof, yet lightweight, and, since it is hinged, it can be dismantled and easily stored.

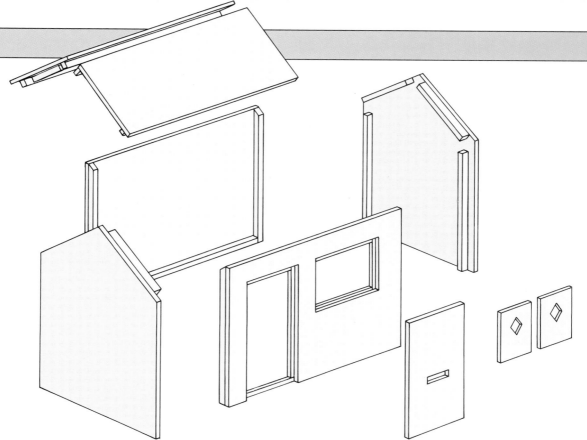

The battens strengthen the structure of the Wendy house and provide the support for hinges and hooks.

Cutting the wood

Mark out the pieces for the sides, the front and back and the roof of the Wendy house and cut out from oil-tempered hardboard. Cut one roof, one side and a front or back from one sheet of hardboard (plywood can be used as an alternative for the sides and roof).

Mark out the door and window on one of the long sides. Drill holes at the corners and cut out with a jigsaw. Take care when cutting out these pieces. Cut the softwood battens to size if you have not bought them pre-cut to size.

Assembling the Wendy house

1. Saw the tops of the four 99cm (39in) battens that will be the vertical supports for the back and front of the house at an angle of 45°, and sand them smooth (see fig. a). Make a

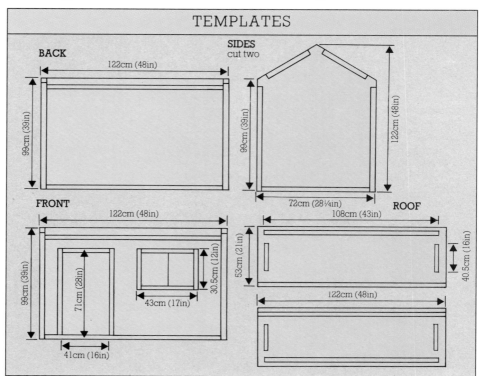

TEMPLATES

BACK

122cm (48in)

99cm (39in)

SIDES
cut two

99cm (39in)

122cm (48in)

72cm (28¼in)

FRONT

122cm (48in)

99cm (39in)

71cm (28in)

30.5cm (12in)

43cm (17in)

41cm (16in)

ROOF

108cm (43in)

53cm (21in)

40.5cm (16in)

122cm (48in)

frame with two side pieces and a batten for the base using halving joints, nails and glue *(see fig. f)*, or a simple butt joint *(see p.58)* – you will need to cut the wood to size first if you use this alternative method. Screw the frame in position on the hardboard.

2. Make the frame for the front of the Wendy house in the same way. Then make a frame for the door. Use the 81cm (32in) and 51cm (20in) pieces of 25 x 50mm (1 x 2in) wood. Fix the frame to give an overlap of 12mm (½in) so that it will stop the door from opening inwards.

3. Construct a frame for the window with the 53.3cm (21in) and 41cm (16in) battens, using halving joints. This frame should also be fixed to give an overlap of 12mm (½in). Screw the frame in position on the inside of the window *(see fig. g)*.

4. Now make the frames for the sides. The vertical pieces should be 38mm (1½in) shorter than the sides at the top edge and they should be positioned 38mm (1½in) in

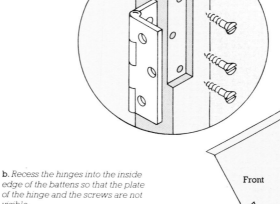

b. *Recess the hinges into the inside edge of the battens so that the plate of the hinge and the screws are not visible.*

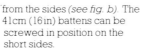

c. *The vertical battens on the sides are cut 38mm (1½in) shorter than those on the front and back.*

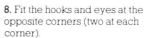

d. *Hooks are fitted onto battens at two of the corners and at the sloping sides of the roof.*

from the sides *(see fig. b)*. The 41cm (16in) battens can be screwed in position on the short sides.

5. Smooth all the edges with sandpaper.

6. The front, back and sides can now be assembled. Two diagonally opposite corners should be hinged and the other two corners fitted with hooks to make a Wendy house that can be dismantled. Match up the pieces and mark the position for the fixings.

7. Fit the hinges. There should be three at each corner. Chisel a recess for each hinge on the inside edge of the batten and screw the hinges in position.

8. Fit the hooks and eyes at the opposite corners (two at each corner).

9. The roof can now be assembled. The 108cm (43in) battens should be used. Screw one pair to the edges that will form the apex of the roof – one at the very edge of the roof piece, the other 38mm (1½in) from the edge. Screw on the second pair of battens 25mm (1in) from the opposite long edges of the roof pieces. Screw on the 41cm (16in) battens to the short edges of the roof, 38mm (1½in) from the edge.

10. Hinge the apex of the roof,

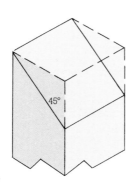

a. *Saw the ends of the vertical battens for the front and back to an angle of 45° and sand them smooth.*

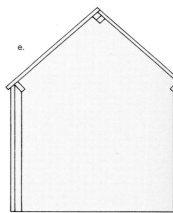

e. *The roof battens rest on the angled ends of the vertical battens at the corners of the Wendy house.*

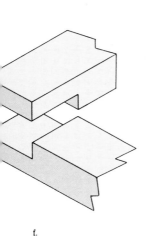

f.

f. *Assemble the frames with halving joints and then glue. They can be assembled independently and then screwed in position, or fixed directly on the main pieces.*

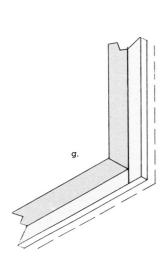

g.

g. *The frame for the interior of the window should be 25mm (1in) smaller than the actual opening so that the shutters will close against it.*

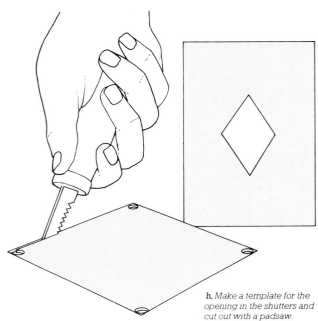

h. *Make a template for the opening in the shutters and cut out with a padsaw.*

using three hinges (follow the method in step 7).

11. Place the roof in position on the walls of the Wendy house. The long battens rest on the angled vertical supports. Mark the position for the four hooks (two on either side, at the midpoint of the short sides) that will hold the roof firmly in position. Screw them in place.

12. The shutters can now be fitted. If you cut out the front piece carefully, you will be able to use the offcut for the window; otherwise cut a new piece from hardboard. Cut the wood in two halves and make a pattern for the diamond shape. Cut the shape from the two pieces, using a padsaw *(see fig. h)* or jigsaw. Mark the position for the hinges and screw them in place (they do not have to be recessed).

13. Hinge the door in place.

Painting the Wendy house

Prepare the Wendy house for painting by filling any holes with proprietary filler and then

sanding all edges smooth. Apply a coat of oil-based primer, paying particular attention to the sawn edges. When dry apply an undercoat, and then a final topcoat of paint.

Decide on a colour scheme for your Wendy house. Paint the walls inside and outside, and add brightly coloured borders around the window and door frames. You might like to add details such as a brick or wood finish for the walls, or to create the illusion of a tiled roof.

Storing the Wendy house

Simply unhook the roof and the two corners and fold up the three sections.

Making a permanent structure

If you intend to keep your Wendy house outside in all weathers, give it extra weather protection by sealing all the joins with PVC tape. Put in extra screws to strengthen the joints.

MATERIALS

2 sheets 1220 x 2400mm (48 x 96in) oil-tempered hardboard
Softwood:
8 pieces 38 x 38 x 1000mm (1½ x 1½ x 39in)
2 pieces 38 x 38 x 1220mm (1½ x 1½ x 48in)
2 pieces 38 x 38 x 720mm (1½ x 1½ x 28¼)
8 pieces 38 x 38 x 410mm (1½ x 1½ x 16in)
4 pieces 38 x 38 x 1080mm (1½ x 1½ x 43in)
2 pieces 38 x 38 x 1200mm (1½ x 1½ x 48in)
1 piece 38 x 38 x 600mm (1½ x 1½ x 24in)
2 pieces 25 x 50 x 533mm (1 x 2 x 21in)
2 pieces 25 x 50 x 410mm (1 x 2 x 16in)
1 piece 25 x 50 x 810mm (1 x 2 x 32in)
2 pieces 25 x 50 x 510mm (1 x 2 x 20in)
Hardware:
8 hooks
9 hinges with fixing screws
6 face-fixing hinges with fixing screws for the windows and door
PVA glue
woodscrews and nails
roll of PVC tape 50mm (2in) wide (optional)
oil-based primer, undercoat and topcoat

TOOLS

Panel saw, padsaw or electric jigsaw, wheelbrace, or power drill and suitable drill bits, hammer, screwdriver.

MAKING A
GO-CART

Though you can make a go-cart from any sturdy pieces of wood you have to hand, it is essential to use good quality, knotfree wood and to test the strength of the seat and the sturdiness of the construction before you allow your children to play with it. You can use any type of wheel, as long as it has a strong axle. In fact, because pram wheels have ball-bearings, they will go faster than bought wheels. If you are making the go-cart for very young children, it is a good idea to fix a pram handle onto the back so that the go-cart can be pushed by an adult.

Making the go-cart
1. Saw the pieces of wood to the dimensions given on the templates.
2. It is important to round off all sharp corners and edges of the go-cart, as children will be jumping on and off it. Using a fretsaw, or a power jigsaw, round off the top front corners of the side pieces and the front corners of the centre board. This is not only for reasons of safety, but because it will give

the go-cart a racier appearance. It is a good idea to shape the ends of the brake levers to give a good hand grip. Sandpaper them smooth.
3. Make the steering disc out of the square of plywood (*for method see pp. 80-1*). Drill a 10mm (⅜in) hole through the centre. The steering disc is not essential, but it will make the steering smoother.
4. To assemble the cockpit floor, position the side seats on

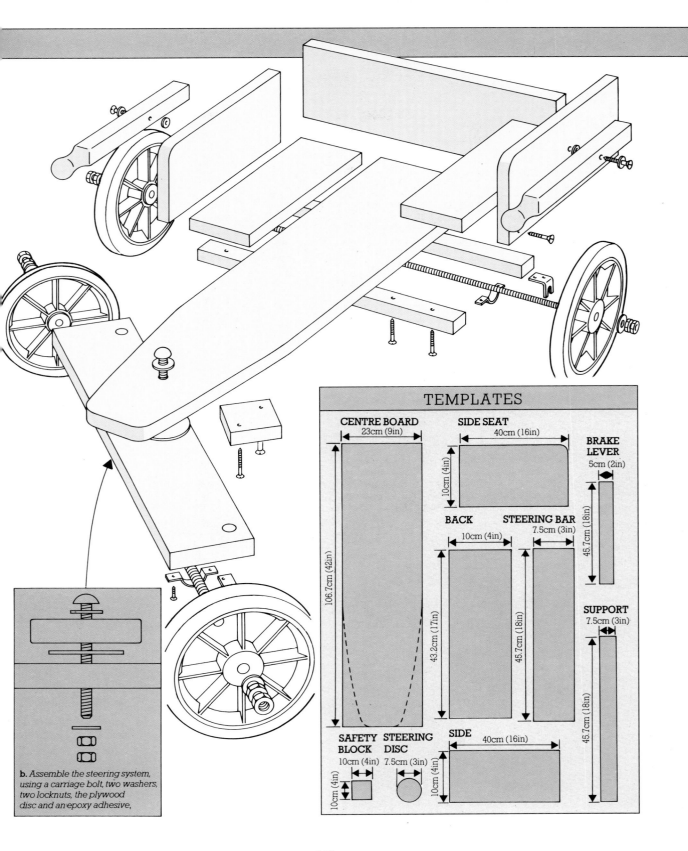

TEMPLATES

CENTRE BOARD
23cm (9in)
106.7cm (42in)

SIDE SEAT
40cm (16in)
10cm (4in)

BRAKE LEVER
5cm (2in)
45.7cm (18in)

BACK
10cm (4in)
43.2cm (17in)

STEERING BAR
7.5cm (3in)
45.7cm (18in)

SUPPORT
7.5cm (3in)
45.7cm (18in)

SAFETY BLOCK
10cm (4in)
10cm (4in)

STEERING DISC
7.5cm (3in)

SIDE
40cm (16in)
10cm (4in)

b. *Assemble the steering system, using a carriage bolt, two washers, two locknuts, the plywood disc and an epoxy adhesive,*

either side of the centre board. Drill holes in the supports. Mark the centre of each support and of the centre board. Lay the supports across the cockpit floor, ensuring that they are square to the centre board, as it is important for the back axle to be straight. They should also project beyond the edges of the side seat pieces, so that the wheels will clear the cockpit sides. Insert countersunk screws and screw the supports to the centre board and side seats (see fig. c). Make sure that none of the screws project through the seat. If they do, file the ends flush with the surface of the wood.

5. To attach the back axle to the rear support, drill pilot holes for the brackets and saddle clips. The brackets prevent the wheels from hitting the sides of the go-cart and they should project slightly over the edge of the support. Place the axle, brackets and

saddle clips in position and firmly screw in place (see fig. d). If you use a proprietary wheels and axles set, it will come complete with the necessary fittings. It is important to make sure that the axle is rigid and cannot move laterally.

6. Drill holes in the sides and back of the cockpit and attach them to the cockpit floor with wood glue and countersunk screws. (see fig. e).

7. Drill 4mm (³⁄₁₆in) holes through the brake levers. It is important to position the brake levers correctly or they will not work effectively. The screw holes should be approximately 25mm (1in) from the outer rim of the wheel (see fig..g). You will require washers on either side of the brake levers to ensure free movement. Insert screws as shown (see fig. f). To prevent the brake levers from dropping forward, you should insert two support screws into the sides just below the levers.

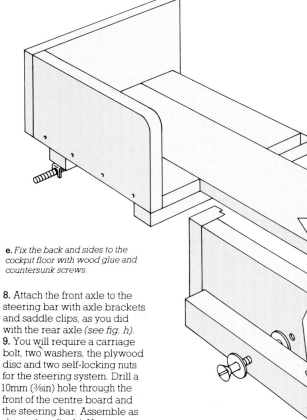

e. Fix the back and sides to the cockpit floor with wood glue and countersunk screws.

8. Attach the front axle to the steering bar with axle brackets and saddle clips, as you did with the rear axle (see fig. h).

9. You will require a carriage bolt, two washers, the plywood disc and two self-locking nuts for the steering system. Drill a 10mm (³⁄₈in) hole through the front of the centre board and the steering bar. Assemble as shown (see fig. b). Use an epoxy adhesive to keep the locknuts securely in place.

10. The safety block will

f. Fasten the brake levers to the sides with washers and screws.

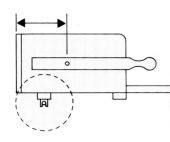

g. The position of the screw should be approximately 25mm (1in) from the edge of the wheel.

d. Fix the rear axle to the back support with brackets and saddle clips.

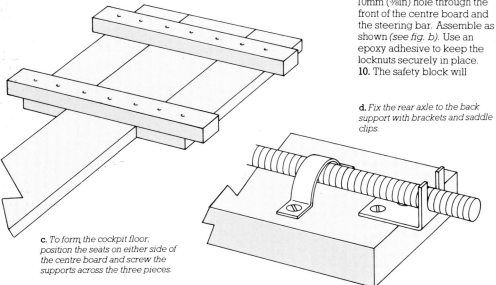

c. To form the cockpit floor, position the seats on either side of the centre board and screw the supports across the three pieces.

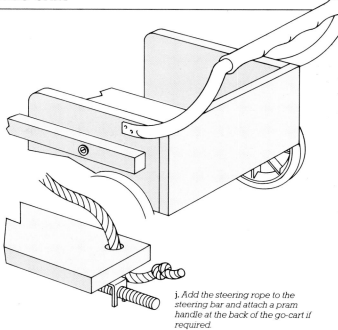

prevent the steering bar from swivelling too far back and the wheels from hitting the centre board. Find the correct position for the block by moving the steering bar. Drill holes in the safety block and fix in place with countersunk screws *(see fig. h)*.

11. There are several methods of attaching the wheels to the axles. If the axle is threaded, you can use a single locknut – a nut with a nylon collar which holds it securely – or two ordinary nuts which are tightened against each other when in position. Use an epoxy adhesive as before. If the axle is unthreaded, drill a small hole through the ends of the axle, insert a split pin and bend up its ends. Whichever method you use, position a washer on either side of the wheel as shown *(see fig. i)*.

12. Drill 7mm (⁵⁄₁₆in) holes in each end of the steering bar. Insert the ends of the length of polypropylene rope through the holes. To prevent the rope ends from unravelling, play a lighted match, or a cigarette lighter, over each end until the strands melt together. Tie secure knots underneath the steering bar *(see fig. j)*.

13. If the go-cart is intended for very young children, drill holes in the sides and attach the pram handle with countersunk screws *(see fig. j)*. This is an ideal method of controlling the go-cart, as well as making it easier to push.

14. Paint or varnish the completed go-cart. It is worth applying several coats of polyurethane varnish to obtain a hardwearing surface.

Caution Check regularly the locknuts holding the axles and the steering system. Also check the rope for signs of fraying.

j. *Add the steering rope to the steering bar and attach a pram handle at the back of the go-cart if required.*

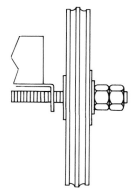

i. *Attach the wheel to the axle with washers, locknuts and epoxy adhesive.*

MATERIALS

Softwood:
1	piece 25 x 230 x 1067mm (1 x 9 x 42in)
1	piece 25 x 100 x 432mm (1 x 4 x 17in)
4	pieces 25 x 100 x 400mm (1 x 4 x 16in)
2	pieces 32 x 75 x 457mm (1¼ x 3 x 18in)
2	pieces 25 x 50 x 457mm (1 x 2 x 18in)
1	piece 25 x 75 x 457mm (1 x 3 x 18in)
1	piece 25 x 100 x 100 (1 x 4 x 4in)

Plywood:
1	piece 6 x 75 x 75mm (¼ x 3 x 3in)

Hardware:
1	10mm (⅜in) coach bolt, 6.3cm (2½in) long
2	10mm (⅜in) locknuts
2	washers
	3.8cm (1½in) woodscrews
1	metre (1 yd) 6mm (¼in) polypropylene rope
1	pram handle
4	wheels at least 15cm (6in) in diameter
2	axles approx. 61cm (24in) in length
4	brackets
4	saddle clips
8	axle locknuts
8	axle washers
	epoxy adhesive
	varnish or paint
	wood glue

TOOLS

Tape measure, pencil, panel saw, try square, wheelbrace and bit or power drill and drill bits, screwdriver, spanner, paint brush, sandpaper.

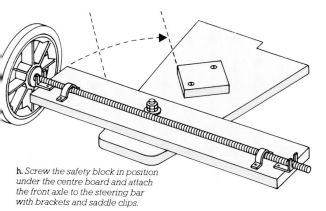

h. *Screw the safety block in position under the centre board and attach the front axle to the steering bar with brackets and saddle clips.*

PROJECT
32

MAKING A
DOLL'S HOUSE

Doll's houses hold a special appeal for children of all ages, since they are the key to a whole miniature world of make believe. Here is a particularly appealing example of an 18th-century house with interior decoration and furnishings based on those of a modern family home, though, of course, its design can be modified to suit other periods and styles of house – including your own. The construction has been kept as simple as possible and the finished house is sturdy and durable.

Preparing the basic structure

1. With pencil and ruler, measure and mark out on tracing paper the 16 units that make up the house. The scale used is 1:12 (25mm to 30cm or 1in to 1ft).

2. Cut out the templates for the units and position them on the sheet of plywood using drawing pins to secure them. Draw around the templates.

3. Before you start sawing the wood, secure it to your work bench with a G-cramp. This is both helpful and a safety precaution. Now cut out the units using a medium cross-cut saw. Rub down all the rough edges with sandpaper and label each unit for further reference.

4. When all the units have been sawn out and sanded, you can cut out the doors and windows. Drill two 6mm (¼in) holes in

diagonal corners of each door and window. Insert the tip of a keyhole saw into one of the holes and cut to a corner. Then, from the same hole, cut to the other corner. Repeat this process from the second hole. Continue, until you have cut out all the doors and windows, with the exception of the gable windows. These are made with a brace and 25mm (1in) bit. Lightly smooth all rough edges as before. Be sure you save the offcuts as some of them will be needed at a later stage of construction.

The chimney stacks and fireplaces should be constructed and fixed to the inner walls before the house is put together, as it will be difficult to work on them later.

Preparing the inner walls
1. You will need two blocks of wood 7.6cm (3in) wide, 25mm (1in) deep and 21.7cm (8½in) long. Using wood glue, stick one of them to the centre of a first floor inner wall. Cut the second block in half, sandwich the bathroom wall unit between the halves and then glue and panel pin together. Now glue them to the other first floor inner wall.
2. Next, cut out two blocks 7.6cm (3in) wide, 25mm (1in) deep and 23cm (9in) long. These will be used for the fireplaces in the drawing room and kitchen. Using a fretsaw, cut out a section for the fireplace measuring 7.6cm (3in) high and 5cm (2in) wide. Stick each chimney stack to the centre of the ground floor inner walls.
3. The kitchen fireplace has a brick finish. Use the same method as for the outside wall of the house (see p.136) and then go over it lightly with white emulsion. Give the inside of the drawing room fireplace a

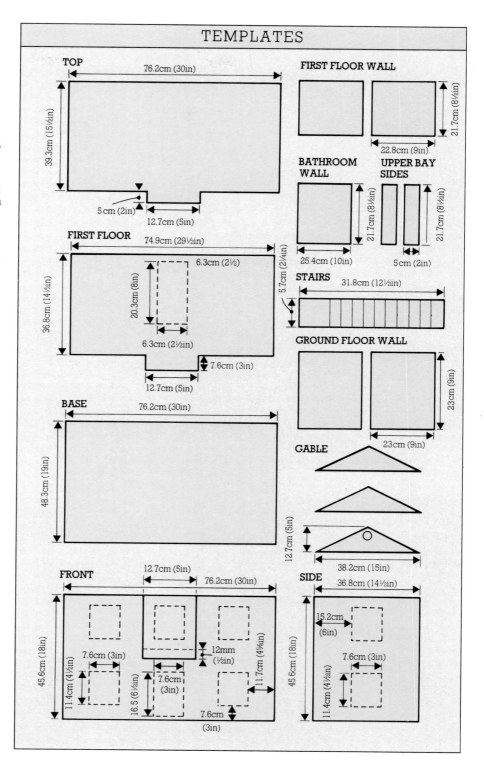

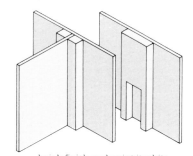

Attach the chimney stacks, fireplaces and the bathroom wall to the inner wall units

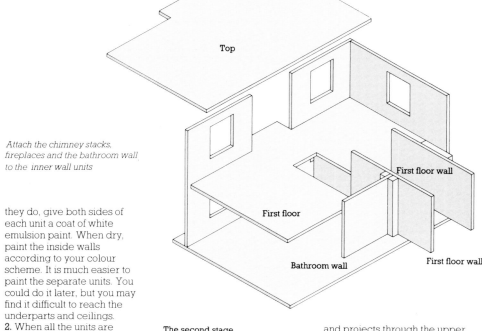

brick finish and paint it white as before. Paint the chimney stack the same colour as the drawing room walls, leaving the front strip on either side of the fireplace unpainted. The mantel is made from an offcut of wooden architrave. Cut off a piece 7.6cm (3in) long. With a fret saw cut a section measuring 5 x 2.5cm (2 x 1in) out of the centre. Glue the mantel above the fireplace, leaving it unpainted to create a stripped-pine look. Use two flat lolly sticks for the pillars. Glue them in place with the rounded ends at the top.

Putting the house together
1. Before you start fixing the parts together permanently it is essential to check whether they all fit. When you are sure

they do, give both sides of each unit a coat of white emulsion paint. When dry, paint the inside walls according to your colour scheme. It is much easier to paint the separate units. You could do it later, but you may find it difficult to reach the underparts and ceilings.
2. When all the units are completely dry, glue and panel pin them together. Use plenty of wood glue. Wipe off any drips with a damp cloth before the glue sets. Start the panel pin holes with a bradawl. You only need a few pins – one near the corner of each unit and one in the middle should be enough.
First, attach the front to the side. Fix them to the base, leaving a 10cm (4in) overlap in

The second stage
The first floor should rest firmly on the ground floor walls. Position the first floor walls and add the top.

front. Next, position the two inner ground-floor walls so that they are aligned on either side of the gap left for the upper bay. Leave a 7.6cm (3in) corridor between the inner walls and the front unit. Fix the first floor so it rests firmly on the inner ground-floor walls

and projects through the upper bay gap. Now position the inner first-floor walls so that they are directly above the ground-floor walls. The first floor wall, with its previously attached bathroom wall, should be above the drawing room. Add the top unit and glue and pin two of the triangular roof supports to it. Leave the open end support loose to allow access to the flashlight battery in the attic. (This powers the lights and is inserted at a later stage, *(see p.123)*. Use small blocks of wood to strengthen the roof supports. Position and fix the blocks to the inside of the end roof support and on both sides of the middle roof support. Leave the house to dry overnight.
If you plan to leave the floors bare, the stairs can be made and inserted at this late stage of construction. But if you are planning a complicated décor you may wish to make them when decorating *(see p139)*.
3. The roof is made from hardboard. Cut two rectangles, each measuring 77.5 x 23cm (30½ x 9in). Tape them together. Glue a strip of canvas

The first stage
Attach the front to the side. Fix them to the base, leaving a 10cm (4in) overlap in front. Next, position the ground floor inner walls. Glue and panel pin after each step.

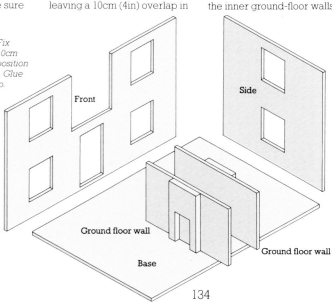

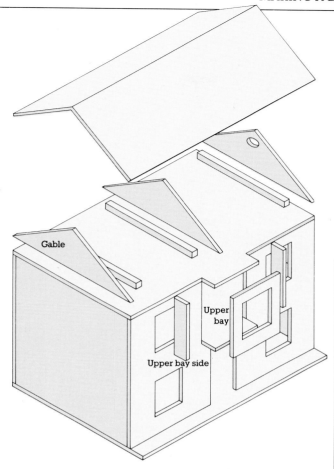

Gable

Upper bay

Upper bay side

where it meets the 6mm (¼in) squares of wood. Place a pillar on either side of the door opening. Glue to the top step. Fill the spaces between the tops of the pillars and the upper bay with two 38mm (1½in) cubes of wood.

3. Create an arch between the pillars to give the portico that final finishing touch. Measure the distance between the cubes of wood and draw an arch on thick card. Cut out, using a craft knife. Paint with white emulsion. Next, cut a thick section of card to form the underside of the portico. Shape the piece of card into a curve and trim to fit the space. Glue into place and then glue the arch in front.

MATERIALS

- 1   2.4 x 1.2m x 12mm (8 x 4ft x ½in) sheet plywood
- 1   1.2 x 1.2m x 12mm (4 x 4ft x ½in) sheet plywood
- 1   61 x 61cm (24 x 24in) sheet 3-ply
- 1   small piece 3mm (⅛in) plywood
- 1   51 x 81cm (20 x 32in) sheet hardboard
- 1   30cm (12in) length dowel
  small pkt mixed balsa wood sheets – 2mm, 3mm, 6mm, 10mm sq (1/16in, ⅛in, ¼in, ⅜in sq)
  strips 12mm (½in) lath
- 1   length wooden architrave
- 1   3mm (⅛in) perspex sheet
  cardboard (thick and thin)
  pva glue (non-toxic, multipurpose)
  balsa wood glue
- 1   small pkt self-hardening clay
- 1   small pkt polyfilla
- 1   tin white emulsion paint
  powder watercolour paints or liquid poster paint
- 1   brass split pin
- 2   short strips leather (or inner tube)
- 33   6mm (¼in) round wooden beads
- 33   tubular wooden beads, 6mm (¼in) long, 3mm (⅛in) diameter
- 2   flat lollypop sticks
- 1   roll masking tape (or bias binding)
  tracing paper
  small strip of canvas
- 1   pkt drawing pins
- 1   box 25mm (1in) panel pins
  sandpaper

TOOLS

Medium cross-cut saw, fretsaw/jigsaw/coping saw, keyhole saw, hammer, G-cramp, brace and 25mm (1in) bit, bradawl, hand or power drill, 6mm (¼in) and 2mm (1/16in) bits, spoke shave, craft knife or scalpel, 25mm (1in) household paint brush, no.1 pure sable paint brush, pencil, 1m (1yd) rule, tape measure.

The final stage
Fix two gables to the top and leave one loose. Construct the roof and attach it firmly to the gables. Add the three upper bay units.

to the underside of the join so that the unit is hinged like a book. When the glue has dried place the roof on the triangular supports. Glue and panel pin. Remember to leave the open side roof support loose.

Insert the upper bay unit between the first floor and top unit projection. Fix it 12mm (½in) in from the edge. Put the two side strips in place. Glue and pin to fix.

Front steps and pillars
1. Cut out and sand two strips of plywood, 12mm (½in) thick. One strip should measure 23 x 10cm (9 x 4in), the other 19 x 7.6cm (7½ x 3in). Centre the larger strip in front of the door opening and glue it to the projecting section of the base. Centre the smaller strip and glue to the first one.

2. The pillars are decorative rather than functional, so they could be made from a variety of materials, such as a roll of stiff cardboard tube, rolled clay or papier-mâché. The best material however is dowel wood with a diameter of 25mm (1in) – a broom handle would do. Cut two 14cm (6in) lengths. Using a spoke shave, taper each pillar slightly and then sand them. Glue a square of 6mm (¼in) plywood to the ends of each pillar. Roll a thin band of self-hardening clay and coil it around each pillar end. Glue it to the dowel

DOLL'S HOUSE

DECORATION

Finishing touches make all the difference to the final appearance of the doll's house and whether or not it has a professional look. You will have great pleasure making the slate roof, brick exterior or window and door surrounds, knowing that ultimately these simple procedures will result in a truly period look. The colour scheme for the interior has been left to your own personal choice, but, if you decide to follow the period style, keep to pink and blue for walls and white for ceilings.

The finishing touches

Allow all the glue used during construction to set before you start painting the exterior of the doll's house.

Roof - slate finish

1. Cut thin card into long strips 19mm (¾in) wide then cut off 3.8cm (1½in) lengths. This will give you tiles with the correct proportions.
2. Now, draw a line 3.8cm (1½in) from the bottom edge of the roof. Brush this strip with glue and stick a row of tiles across the roof. When this row is dry, pencil another line across the roof, 19mm (¾in) above the row of tiles.
3. Apply multipurpose glue and stick on a second row of tiles. These tiles will overlap the row below. They should be staggered so that each new tile is centred on the gap between two tiles in the row below. Continue until you reach the ridge of the roof. Repeat the process on the other side.
4. The roof ridge is made by folding a 19mm (¾in) wide strip of card lengthwise. Glue along the top of the roof so that there is an equal amount of card on each side of the ridge. Mix up some blue-grey paint using white emulsion as a base and adding powder watercolour or liquid poster paint. When coated over the paper tiles it will give the effect of slates. Paint the roof ridge grey so it looks like lead. Or, with a ruler and grey felt-tip pen rule parallel lines the length of the ridge before you glue it to the roof. If the pen is worn, the effect will be more realistic.

Walls - brick finish

1. First, brush a thin coat of multipurpose glue over the front and side of the house. When the glue is dry, cover it with a thin (approximately 3mm or ⅛in) skim of proprietary filler. If you mix the filler yourself, add the powder to the water and mix to a creamy paste.
2. While the filler is still slightly damp, you can score the brick lines using a nail. The bricks are 23 x 8cm (9 x 3in). You are working to a scale of 1:12 so you require 6 x 19mm (¼ x ¾in) lines. Pencil 6mm (¼in) marks on either side of the areas requiring a brick finish. Using a rule, score horizontal lines across the walls. Continue until both walls have been completely scored with lines 6mm (¼in) apart.
3. Now score short vertical lines 19mm (¾in) apart, between the horizontal lines. When you have done one row,

---

ALTERNATIVE ROOF FINISHES

Flat tile
1. Cut long strips of card 10mm (⅜in) wide, then cut off 25mm (1in) lengths. 2. Lay the tiles in the same way as the slate tiles, applying glue along a pencil line drawn every 25mm (1in). 3. Paint a terracotta colour with poster paint.

Ridge tile
*1. Cut long strips of corrugated card 25mm (1in) wide.
2. Draw lines every 25mm (1in) from the edge of the roof and overlap the tiles.
3. Paint with terracotta poster paint.*

Thatched roof
*1. Cover the roof with multipurpose glue.
2. Apply self-hardening clay and while still wet, texture with a comb or stiff brush to give a thatched look.
3. Paint with yellow emulsion.*

Roof ridge

Slate roof

stagger the next row so that each vertical line is centred on the brick below. This will make the bricks look truly realistic. If the plaster surface becomes too dry and difficult to score, dampen it with a brush dipped in water.

5. Paint the wall surfaces with a terracotta emulsion or water paint. Make sure you paint lightly over the surface because you want to cover the bricks, but leave the deep scoring clear to create the effect of mortar pointing.

Plaster edges and window surrounds

1. Using a sharp blade, cut 12mm (½in) strips of thick white card for the corners, edges and central divisions of the house. (Detergent packets are ideal.) Glue in place and cover with multipurpose glue to seal them.

2. Make paper templates for the gable, top and bottom floor windows from the diagram measurements. Position them on card and cut out using a sharp blade. Glue the surrounds in place and seal with multipurpose glue. When all the card is dry it can be painted with white emulsion.

Windows

Perspex makes an ideal substitute for glass. It is safe for children to play with and can be scored easily with a blade and then snapped off.

1. Make paper templates of the window spaces. Place the templates on the perspex, score round them and snap off.

2. The window frame can be made from white card, balsa wood or semi-rigid foam plastic. Cut with a sharp blade and glue to the perspex. Use a clear balsa glue. Position each window centrally in its space and glue into place.

ALTERNATIVE WALL FINISHES

Stone wall
Make stone shapes and strips from clay and attach with glue, then paint grey and white.

Weather-board
Cut lengths of card 12mm (½in) wide, overlap in the usual way then paint.

Half-timbered
Cut balsa wood strips as shown. Paint with black poster paint and glue onto a pre-painted surface.

Flint wall with brick edge
1. Make blobs of clay and attach with glue, then paint white with dabs of black.
2. For the bricks, cut strips of card alternately 10mm (⅜in) and 25mm (1in) wide and 12mm (½in) long. Paint terracotta and glue to the wall alternating long and short.

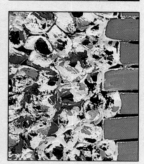

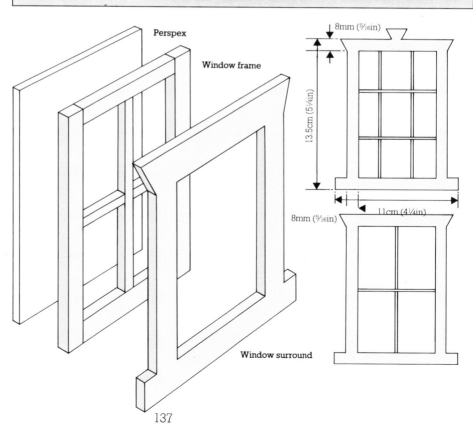

Perspex

Window frame

Window surround

8mm (⁵⁄₁₆in)

13.5cm (5¼in)

11cm (4¼in)

8mm (⁵⁄₁₆in)

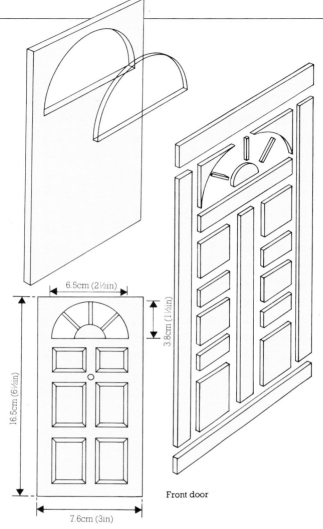

Front door

1. Cut out a rectangle 7.6 x 16.5cm (3 x 6½in) from a piece of 3mm (⅛in) plywood. Test it for size in the door space and trim if necessary.

2. Draw the shape of the fanlight using the measurements in the diagram. Drill a small hole. Insert the tip of your fret saw into the hole and cut out a semicircle.

3. Next, cut a semicircle of perspex, increasing its size by 6mm (¼in) all round.

4. The trim and small detail of the door are made from thin balsa sheet, cut with a sharp blade, then sanded and glued into place as shown. Cut 6mm (¼in) strips for the edges and divisions. Cut six rectangles for the panels and carefully cut the trim for the fanlight.

5. Glue the edges of the perspex, place over the fanlight space and sandwich it between the plywood backing and the balsa trim.

6. Give the door an undercoat and a topcoat of oil paint, just as you would a full-size door.

7. A brass split pin makes a good door knob. Two small

strips of leather or inner tube will serve as hinges. Attach them to the inside of the door frame and to the back of the door. You can use a staplegun or glue. Leave overnight to dry.

Balustrade

There are various ways of constructing the short pillars that make up the balustrade. They can be made in wood turned on a lathe or moulded and cast in plaster. However the easiest and most effective method of producing uniform pillars is to assemble them from wooden beads, balsa wood, pins and clay. For each 19mm (¾in) pillar you will need: one round bead with a 6mm (¼in) diameter, one 6mm (¼in) long tubular bead with a 3mm (⅛in) diameter, two 9mm (⅜in) squares of 6mm (¼in) deep balsa wood, a pin and a tiny piece of clay.

1. Assemble abacus-fashion, following the diagram.

2. Next cut 4 blocks of wood 8.8cm (3½in) long, 19mm (¾in) high and 13mm (½in) thick and two blocks 19mm (¾in) long.

6.5cm (2½in)

3.8cm (1½in)

16.5cm (6½in)

7.6cm (3in)

Front door

ALTERNATIVE DOORS

Cottage door

1. Make plank lines 12mm (½in) apart with a shallow saw cut.
2. Cut ply for the cross members and glue on. Paint.

Art Deco door

1. Cut two pieces of semi-rigid foam plastic and one piece of perspex to size. Glue together then cut a shaped section at the top to show the perspex.
3. Glue three flat ice lolly sticks to the door as shown. Paint the door and paint the perspex to create a stained glass effect.

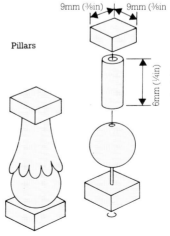

9mm (⅜in) 9mm (⅜in)

Pillars

6mm (¼in)

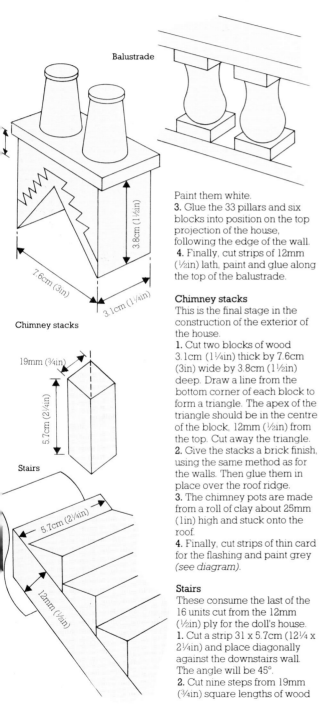

Balustrade

3.8cm (1½in)

7.6cm (3in)

3.1cm (1¼in)

Chimney stacks

19mm (¾in)

5.7cm (2¼in)

Stairs

5.7cm (2¼in)

12mm (½in)

Paint them white.
3. Glue the 33 pillars and six blocks into position on the top projection of the house, following the edge of the wall.
4. Finally, cut strips of 12mm (½in) lath, paint and glue along the top of the balustrade.

Chimney stacks
This is the final stage in the construction of the exterior of the house.
1. Cut two blocks of wood 3.1cm (1¼in) thick by 7.6cm (3in) wide by 3.8cm (1½in) deep. Draw a line from the bottom corner of each block to form a triangle. The apex of the triangle should be in the centre of the block, 12mm (½in) from the top. Cut away the triangle.
2. Give the stacks a brick finish, using the same method as for the walls. Then glue them in place over the roof ridge.
3. The chimney pots are made from a roll of clay about 25mm (1in) high and stuck onto the roof.
4. Finally, cut strips of thin card for the flashing and paint grey (see diagram).

Stairs
These consume the last of the 16 units cut from the 12mm (½in) ply for the doll's house.
1. Cut a strip 31 x 5.7cm (12¼ x 2¼in) and place diagonally against the downstairs wall. The angle will be 45°.
2. Cut nine steps from 19mm (¾in) square lengths of wood

cut every 5.7cm (2¼in) then cut diagonally and glued. In the flat they resemble a row of tents.
3. With wood glue attach the steps to the strip and finish with dark wood stain.
4. Sandwich a piece of cloth between the stairs and landing before glueing in place.

Walls, ceilings and floors
Walls and ceilings require three coats of emulsion paint except when wallpaper is used, then only one as a sealant.

Wallpaper
Patterned wrapping paper is used for this and is ideal because the designs are simple, small and suit the scale of the house.
1. Make a paper template of the wall area first then cut the patterned paper to the correct size.
2. Lightly paste with wallpaper paste and attach.

Carpets
You will probably want to carpet the drawing room, small bedroom, large bedroom and

bathroom.
Coloured felt, sold in squares 61cm (24in) square is best for this but iron before cutting because if you leave until afterwards it can shrink, especially with a steam iron.
1. Make a paper template of the area to be covered then cut felt to the pattern.
2. Test for fit then brush the floor lightly with multipurpose glue and attach.

Tile and wood floors
A floor board and tile look can be achieved with semi-rigid foam plastic and lines drawn on this with ball point pen and ruler. This has the advantage of keeping the level with the carpets. It is suitable for the kitchen and bathroom.
1. Cut a paper template to fit the floor area.
2. Cut foam to shape and fix with multipurpose glue.
3. Paint the desired colour. The foam plastic will take both oil and water paints. For a quarry tile effect, paint with terracotta coloured poster paint. For wooden areas such as the hall and landing, leave the ply as it is, stain or varnish.

DOLL'S HOUSE
GARDEN

No doll's house, least of all this one, is complete without an appropriate setting. To complement the classical lines of its 18th-century facade you can create a walled garden with a central drive and lawns with flowerbeds at each side. The whole garden is contained in a detachable base which fits onto the front of the house.

Preparing the base and walls

1. With tracing paper, pencil and ruler, measure and cut out the templates for the base unit and six wall units, all of which are cut from 12mm (½in) plywood.

2. Now cut the units with a cross-cut hand saw. Then, cut out the curves in the wall units with a jig saw. Smooth with sandpaper.

3. Glue the wall units to the base using wood glue. Set the front walls 5cm (2in) back from the front edge of the base. When dry, the wall units should be given a brick finish with proprietary filler in the same way as the house (see p.136).

4. Now that the wall units are in place make the two gate posts. Cut two 20.1cm (8in) lengths of 6mm (¼in) deep balsa wood and glue to the front wall ends. When dry, smooth clay over them.

Cap and orb

1. With self-hardening clay, mould two caps 3.8cm (1½in) square. Now mould two balls of

clay 3.2cm (1¼in) in diameter. Pin and glue each cap and orb together when soft and leave to dry.

2. To finish, paint with stone grey emulsion mixed with a touch of sharp sand. When dry, pin to the top of the gate posts.

Assemble the basic garden area (right) *following the proportions given before going on to add the decorative caps and orbs* (far right) *to the gateposts* (bottom right) *for a touch of authentic 18th century elegance.*

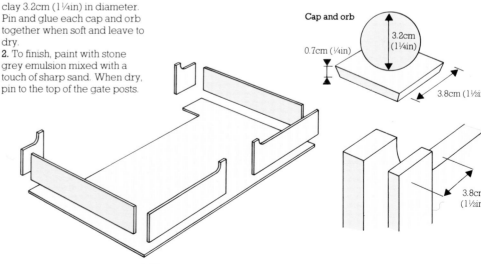

Cap and orb

3.2cm (1¼in)

0.7cm (¼in)

3.8cm (1½in)

3.8cm (1½in)

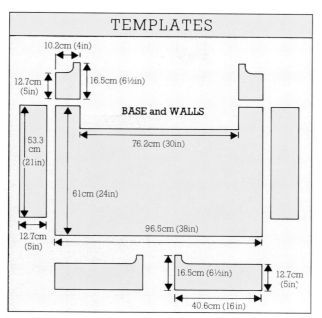

TEMPLATES

BASE and WALLS

10.2cm (4in)
12.7cm (5in)
16.5cm (6½in)
53.3 cm (21in)
76.2cm (30in)
61cm (24in)
12.7cm (5in)
96.5cm (38in)
16.5cm (6½in)
12.7cm (5in)
40.6cm (16in)

The gate

This is made from 1cm (³⁄₈in) thick balsa wood.

1. Carefully measure and cut out three strips 1 x 12.7cm (³⁄₈ x 5in) for the horizontal slats, one strip 1 x 7.6cm (³⁄₈ x 3in) for the right-side support, one piece 1 x 16cm (³⁄₈ x 6¼in) the diagonal support, and one curved piece 1 x 3 x 10cm (³⁄₈ x 1¼ x 4in) for the left-side support. Cut the two small internal slats 5 x 19mm (¼ x ³⁄₄in).

2. Glue the pieces together with wood glue and when dry, paint with undercoat, followed by a white gloss finish.

3. To make the gate hinge, bend two 19mm (³⁄₄in) nails at side of the gate. These will fit into two staples secured on the left-side gatepost at the same level.

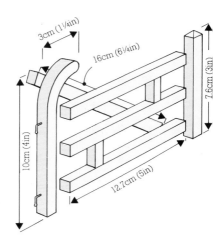

3cm (1¼in)
16cm (6¼in)
7.6cm (3in)
10cm (4in)
12.7cm (5in)

Garden plan

Before you begin to construct the components inside the garden, it is essential to draw a plan on the garden base. With a pencil and ruler, mark the correct dimensions and positions of everything within the garden as shown on the garden plan diagram.

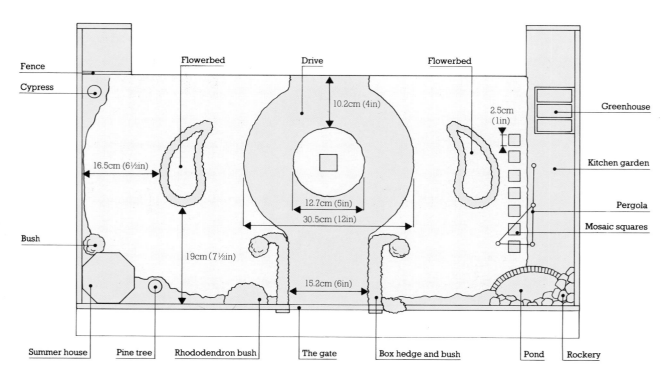

Fence
Cypress
Flowerbed
Drive
Flowerbed
Greenhouse
10.2cm (4in)
2.5cm (1in)
Kitchen garden
16.5cm (6½in)
12.7cm (5in)
30.5cm (12in)
Pergola
Mosaic squares
Bush
19cm (7½in)
15.2cm (6in)
Summer house
Pine tree
Rhododendron bush
The gate
Box hedge and bush
Pond
Rockery

141

The lawns

These are made with self-hardening clay.

1. Brush multipurpose glue onto the area which is to be grass.
2. Cut irregular outlines to form clear borders, then texture by brushing over with an old toothbrush. When the clay dries it will shrink and crack, so fill the gaps with glue, plug in more clay, and then texture in the same way.
3. When dry, paint with green emulsion mixed with a little sharp sand for more texture.

Hedges, borders, bushes and shrubs

1. Model clay to make the shapes shown in the diagram and texture the surface by scraping with a comb or kitchen fork.
2. Glue in place with wood glue and when the clay is still soft, hand paint with green oil or emulsion paint.
3. To make rhododendron

flowers, stick pieces of coloured sponge here and there on the bush.
4. To create the tear drop shape of the flower border, make a roll of clay 35.5cm (14in) long, 15mm (⅝in) wide and 25mm (1in) deep. Fix in place on the garden base with multipurpose glue. Texture with a toothbrush.

Flowerbeds, kitchen garden, rock garden

1. You have already marked their positions on the base. Now dig up a piece of dry earth from your own garden and pick out the stones.
2. Mix the earth with a good amount of wood glue to make a glutinous mixture and press in place. At first it will look grey, but, when the glue dries, the earth will return to its natural

colour and be held and sealed in place.
3. For the border plants and flowerbeds cut sponge shapes and soak in water paint. Then fix. For the vegetable garden, simply glue pieces of green sponge in straight rows. Tomato plants can be modelled in plasticine or clay.
4. A convincing rock garden can be made by cutting small chips of stone then fixing into clay with lots of multipurpose glue.

For plants, finish off with blobs of different coloured sponge and dabs of paint. The best setting is in a corner with the wall for support.

Gravel drive

First brush wood glue over the surface and while still wet, sprinkle with sharp sand.

Pond

1. Cut a small semi-circular shape 12.7cm (5in) across, from a sheet of perspex. Fix in place with multipurpose glue.
2. Paint blue and green then varnish.
3. To make a brick border for the pond, cut a 15.2cm (6in) strip of clay 12mm (½in) wide and 6mm (¼in) deep. Paint brown to match the garden wall and mark off the bricks with a knife.

The summer house

This is an octagonal building built mainly from balsa wood strips and set on a raised plywood base. All parts are secured with multipurpose glue.

1. Draw the eight-sided base onto a piece of 12mm (½in) plywood, 10.2cm (4in) in diameter, with each side measuring 3.8cm (1½in)
2. Cut eight balsa wood strips 10.2cm (4in) long and 6mm (¼in) wide. Glue to the base

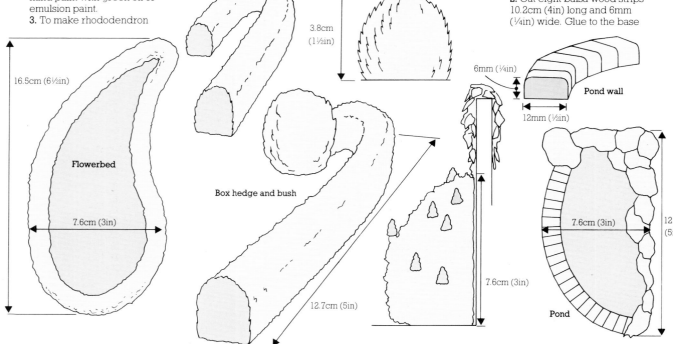

16.5cm (6½in)

3.8cm (1½in)

Flowerbed

7.6cm (3in)

Box hedge and bush

12.7cm (5in)

1cm (⅜in)

6mm (¼in)

Pond wall

12mm (½in)

7.6cm (3in)

7.6cm (3in)

Pond

12 (5i

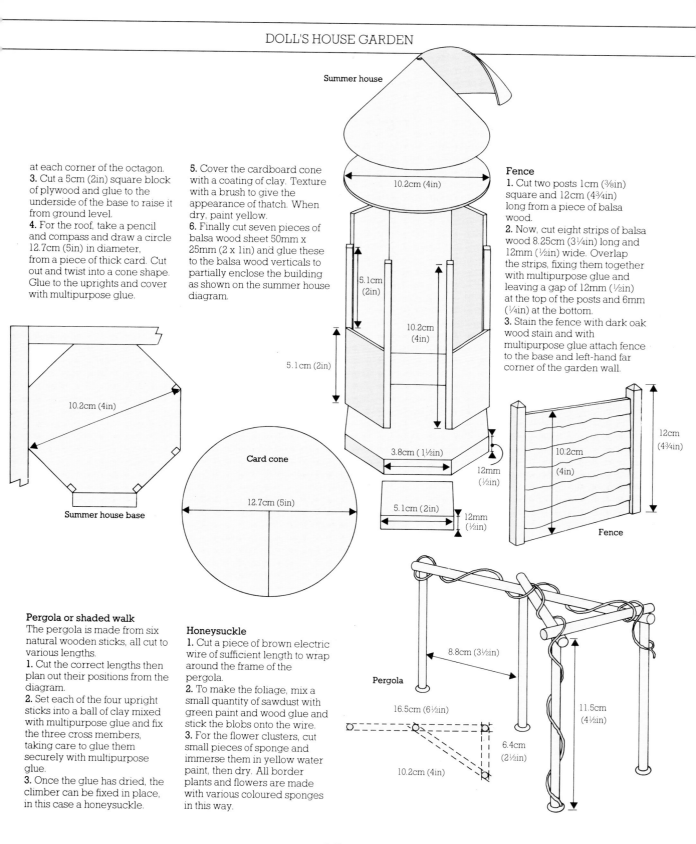

Summer house

10.2cm (4in)

5.1cm (2in)

10.2cm (4in)

5.1cm (2in)

3.8cm (1½in)

12mm (½in)

Card cone

12.7cm (5in)

Summer house base

10.2cm (4in)

5.1cm (2in)

12mm (½in)

at each corner of the octagon.
3. Cut a 5cm (2in) square block of plywood and glue to the underside of the base to raise it from ground level.
4. For the roof, take a pencil and compass and draw a circle 12.7cm (5in) in diameter, from a piece of thick card. Cut out and twist into a cone shape. Glue to the uprights and cover with multipurpose glue.

5. Cover the cardboard cone with a coating of clay. Texture with a brush to give the appearance of thatch. When dry, paint yellow.
6. Finally cut seven pieces of balsa wood sheet 50mm x 25mm (2 x 1in) and glue these to the balsa wood verticals to partially enclose the building as shown on the summer house diagram.

Fence
1. Cut two posts 1cm (⅜in) square and 12cm (4¾in) long from a piece of balsa wood.
2. Now, cut eight strips of balsa wood 8.25cm (3¼in) long and 12mm (½in) wide. Overlap the strips, fixing them together with multipurpose glue and leaving a gap of 12mm (½in) at the top of the posts and 6mm (¼in) at the bottom.
3. Stain the fence with dark oak wood stain and with multipurpose glue attach fence to the base and left-hand far corner of the garden wall.

12cm (4¾in)

10.2cm (4in)

Fence

Pergola or shaded walk
The pergola is made from six natural wooden sticks, all cut to various lengths.
1. Cut the correct lengths then plan out their positions from the diagram.
2. Set each of the four upright sticks into a ball of clay mixed with multipurpose glue and fix the three cross members, taking care to glue them securely with multipurpose glue.
3. Once the glue has dried, the climber can be fixed in place, in this case a honeysuckle.

Honeysuckle
1. Cut a piece of brown electric wire of sufficient length to wrap around the frame of the pergola.
2. To make the foliage, mix a small quantity of sawdust with green paint and wood glue and stick the blobs onto the wire.
3. For the flower clusters, cut small pieces of sponge and immerse them in yellow water paint, then dry. All border plants and flowers are made with various coloured sponges in this way.

Pergola

8.8cm (3½in)

11.5cm (4½in)

16.5cm (6½in)

6.4cm (2½in)

10.2cm (4in)

PROJECT 34

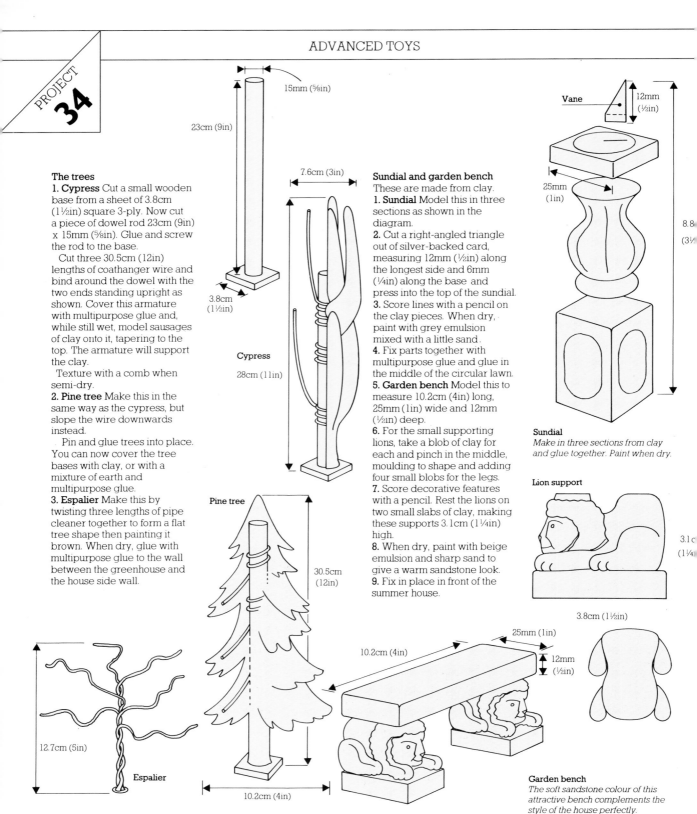

The trees
1. Cypress Cut a small wooden base from a sheet of 3.8cm (1½in) square 3-ply. Now cut a piece of dowel rod 23cm (9in) x 15mm (⅝in). Glue and screw the rod to the base.

Cut three 30.5cm (12in) lengths of coathanger wire and bind around the dowel with the two ends standing upright as shown. Cover this armature with multipurpose glue and, while still wet, model sausages of clay onto it, tapering to the top. The armature will support the clay.

Texture with a comb when semi-dry.
2. Pine tree Make this in the same way as the cypress, but slope the wire downwards instead.

Pin and glue trees into place. You can now cover the tree bases with clay, or with a mixture of earth and multipurpose glue.
3. Espalier Make this by twisting three lengths of pipe cleaner together to form a flat tree shape then painting it brown. When dry, glue with multipurpose glue to the wall between the greenhouse and the house side wall.

Sundial and garden bench
These are made from clay.
1. Sundial Model this in three sections as shown in the diagram.
2. Cut a right-angled triangle out of silver-backed card, measuring 12mm (½in) along the longest side and 6mm (¼in) along the base and press into the top of the sundial.
3. Score lines with a pencil on the clay pieces. When dry, paint with grey emulsion mixed with a little sand.
4. Fix parts together with multipurpose glue and glue in the middle of the circular lawn.
5. Garden bench Model this to measure 10.2cm (4in) long, 25mm (1in) wide and 12mm (½in) deep.
6. For the small supporting lions, take a blob of clay for each and pinch in the middle, moulding to shape and adding four small blobs for the legs.
7. Score decorative features with a pencil. Rest the lions on two small slabs of clay, making these supports 3.1cm (1¼in) high.
8. When dry, paint with beige emulsion and sharp sand to give a warm sandstone look.
9. Fix in place in front of the summer house.

15mm (⅝in)
23cm (9in)
3.8cm (1½in)

7.6cm (3in)

Cypress
28cm (11in)

Pine tree
30.5cm (12in)
10.2cm (4in)

12.7cm (5in)
Espalier

Vane
12mm (½in)
25mm (1in)
8.8 (3½)

Sundial
Make in three sections from clay and glue together. Paint when dry.

Lion support
3.1c (1¼

3.8cm (1½in)

25mm (1in)
10.2cm (4in)
12mm (½in)

Garden bench
The soft sandstone colour of this attractive bench complements the style of the house perfectly.

Greenhouse

This is made from perspex 2mm (³⁄₁₆in) thick as used in the house windows.

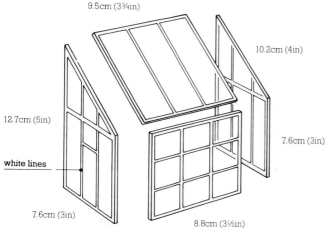

9.5cm (3¾in)

10.2cm (4in)

12.7cm (5in)

white lines

7.6cm (3in)

7.6cm (3in)

8.8cm (3½in)

1. Cut out the four sections with a craft knife – two side sections 12.7 x 7.6cm (5 x 3in); top section 10.2 x 9.5cm (4 x 3¾in): and front section 7.6 x 8.8cm (3 x 3½in).

2. To create the white wooden frame effect, cover the units with masking tape and draw on the white parallel lines.

3. Split the tape with a scalpel and peel off the strips, then spray the perspex underneath them with white cellulose paint. When dry, scratch the criss-cross lines for panes.

4. Glue the two side sections to the garden wall 8.8cm (3½in) apart. When dry, glue on the front section.

5. Hinge the roof in place with masking tape and multipurpose glue.

GARDEN TOOLS

No garden is complete without tools. You can easily make a small spade and garden rake
1. For the spade handle, make a 6mm (¼in) hole in the centre of a piece of 12mm (½in) dowel with an electric drill. Then cut in half.
2. Fix a 5cm (2in) lollipop stick into the handle with multipurpose glue.
3. Cut a spade shape from a piece of silver-backed card to measure 25 x 19mm (1 x ¾in). Glue the flap round the stick to fix.
4. To make the rake head, cut a similar pattern from a piece of 25mm (1in) wide card and glue the flap round a lollipop stick of 8.8cm (3½in).

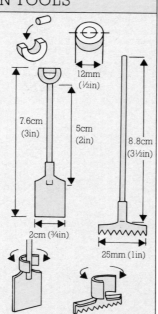

12mm (½in)

7.6cm (3in)

5cm (2in)

8.8cm (3½in)

2cm (¾in)

25mm (1in)

MATERIALS

1 97 x 61 x 10mm (38 x 24 x ⅜in) sheet plywood
2 53.3cm x 12.7cm x 12mm (21 x 5 x ½in) strips of plywood
2 16.5cm x 10.2cm x 12mm (6½ x 4 x ½in) strips of plywood for two small curved side walls
2 40.6cm x 16.5cm x 12mm (16 x 6½ x ½in) strips of plywood for the two front walls
1 pkt proprietary filler
   self-hardening clay
   all-in-one pkt mixed balsa wood sheets 10mm, 6mm, 12mm, (⅜, ¼, ½in) thick for the summer house
1 tin undercoat; white gloss, green, grey and beige emulsions; yellow water paint; copper paint
1 10.2cm x 10.2cm x 12mm (4 x 4 x ½in) block plywood for the summer house base
1 5cm x 12mm (2 x ½in) summer house block support
   sandpaper
   masking tape
   piece of silver-backed card 5cm (2in) square
1 piece of thick card
   multipurpose glue
7 natural wooden sticks of pencil thickness and length approx. for the pergola
1 box 25mm (1in) panel pins
   brown electric wire
1 sheet sponge rubber
   dowel and wire armatures for trees
1 pkt pipe cleaners
   stone chips mosaic squares
1 sheet perspex 3mm (⅛in) thick for the glasshouse
1 can white enamel spray paint
   plasticine
2 lollipop sticks
   varnish
2 screws 25mm (1in) to fix trees to the block

TOOLS

Pencil, jig saw, keyhole saw, craft knife, screwdriver, small household paint brush, glue, brush, scissors, comb, compass, toothbrush.

PROJECT
35

DOLL'S HOUSE
FURNITURE

Realism is all-important when you are creating a world in miniature for your children. If you have chosen to make a replica of your own home, you will enjoy the challenge of recreating its contents and décor. Here are some simple methods using a wide variety of materials and ranging in style and period from a jardinière to a T.V. set, from Chippendale to the 'chip'. They include soft furnishing, simple wooden furniture, clay work and ideas for adapting found objects.

The kitchen units
The oven, hob and sink are made with 4.5cm (1¾in) square soft wood.

1. Cut three pieces – one 19cm (7½in) long for the oven, and two shorter measuring 17cm (6¾in) for the hob and sink sections. Sand these blocks smooth and ensure that the ends are accurately squared.

2. Place the longer of the three blocks on end to make the oven, and arrange the other two longways around it as you think best, according to your overall kitchen design.

3. Draw up an area 4.5cm (1¾in) square for the hob. Paint it silver grey and stick on four flat red buttons without holes, or red spot transfers, for the hotplates. To make the outlines of the cupboards, sawcut vertical lines every 4.5cm (1¾in) on the hob and sink sections, making three along the hob and two along the sink side.

4. To make the sink, chisel out a block 7.6 x 4cm (3 x 1⅜in) from the section to form a square cavity. Glue a lump of self-hardening clay firmly into the space. Pat into shape, scooping out a rounded rectangular shape with a teaspoon to a depth of 3cm

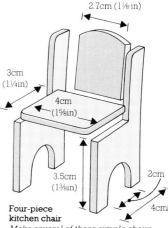

2.7cm (1⅛in)

3cm (1¼in)

4cm (1⅝in)

3.5cm (1⅜in)

2cm

4cm

Four-piece kitchen chair
Make several of these simple chairs to furnish a busy family kitchen.

(1³⁄₁₆in). Press drain and overflow holes into the clay with a nail head and for the plug hole, press in the female part of a silver press stud. Glue a cup hook into the wall side corner for a tap. When the clay has dried, paint with two coats of aluminium primer. Paint some thin card with the same paint and cut two strips for the work tops next to the sink and hob. Glue in place.

5. To make the 'see-through' oven door, saw two 5mm (³⁄₁₆in) cuts one level with the work surface, the other parallel with it 5.5cm (2³⁄₁₆in) above. Cut away the unwanted centre with a 25mm (1in) wood chisel and into the recess stick a picture of food cooking cut from a catalogue or magazine.

To cover this, cut a piece of thick perspex (as used in the doll's house windows), and fix in place with multipurpose glue.

6. When all the sawing has been done and the sink made, paint the units with undercoat, followed by two top coats of household gloss paint.

Wooden furniture
Most of the furniture has been made with 3-ply, a light, pine-

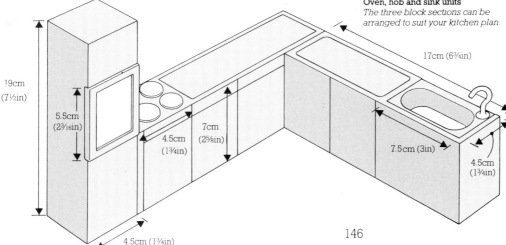

Oven, hob and sink units
The three block sections can be arranged to suit your kitchen plan.

19cm (7½in)

5.5cm (2³⁄₁₆in)

4.5cm (1¾in)

7cm (2⅝in)

17cm (6¾in)

7.5cm (3in)

4.5cm (1¾in)

4.5cm (1¾in)

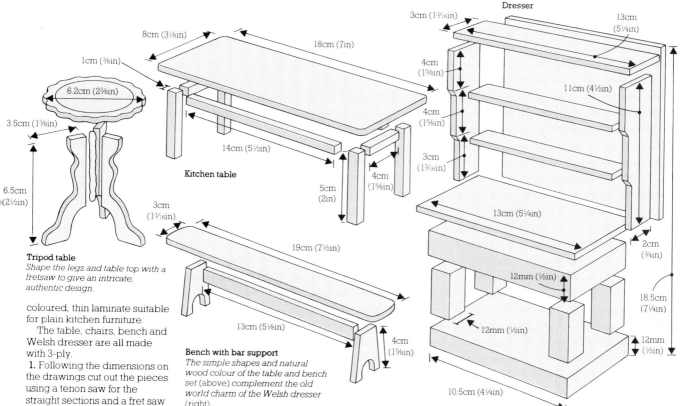

Tripod table
1cm (⅜in)

6.2cm (2⅜in)

3.5cm (1⅜in)

6.5cm (2½in)

8cm (3⅛in)

18cm (7in)

14cm (5½in)

Kitchen table

5cm (2in)

4cm (1⅝in)

3cm (1³⁄₁₆in)

19cm (7½in)

13cm (5⅛in)

4cm (1⅝in)

Bench with bar support

Dresser

3cm (1³⁄₁₆in)

4cm (1⅝in)

4cm (1⅝in)

3cm (1³⁄₁₆in)

13cm (5¼in)

11cm (4½in)

13cm (5¼in)

2cm (¾in)

18.5cm (7¼in)

12mm (½in)

12mm (½in)

12mm (½in)

10.5cm (4¼in)

Tripod table
Shape the legs and table top with a fretsaw to give an intricate, authentic design.

Bench with bar support
The simple shapes and natural wood colour of the table and bench set (above) complement the old world charm of the Welsh dresser (right).

coloured, thin laminate suitable for plain kitchen furniture.

The table, chairs, bench and Welsh dresser are all made with 3-ply.

1. Following the dimensions on the drawings cut out the pieces using a tenon saw for the straight sections and a fret saw for the few curved parts on the chairs and bench.

2. Sand all the parts. They will all be glued with multipurpose glue, so no securing pins are necessary. Leave all the furniture overnight to allow the glue to dry.

Chairs
Place the two side pieces on to a bed of plasticine. This will hold them in position while the seat and back are glued in place.

Table and bench
Place table and bench tops upside-down, this time onto small blobs of plasticine to hold everything in place. These can be removed easily when glue is hard.

Dresser
The top is cut from 3-ply, the base from 12mm (½in) offcuts. Place the top shelf section flat

on the deck so that the sides and shelves can be set in an upright position. Make the bottom section in the upside-down position, as you did with the table, but leave overnight before glueing together.

Tripod table
1. Cut all four parts to size with a fret saw since they are all curved.
2. Fix the three legs in the middle with a thin roll of self-hardening clay covered with multipurpose glue.
3. When the leg section is set, place it upside-down to the underneath centre of the table top.
4. Once the table is set, stain it with dark oakwood stain and finish off with a circle of blue oilcloth 3.5cm (1⅜in) in diameter, or glue on a piece of thin fabric cut to the same size, for a card table look.

Matchbox dresser
1. Glue four matchboxes together with multipurpose glue as shown in the diagram.
2. Cut a strip of card long enough to cover the four-box unit, score fold lines and glue under the base, then cut a piece of card to form the back and mirror 5.7cm (2¼in) in diameter. Paint with emulsion.
3. Remove the drawers before you glue the back on. Punch a hole in each drawer for a brass split pin. Press these down inside.
4. Cut a small semicircle of silver paper and glue to the back for a mirror.

Matchbox dresser
This simple method of making a small dresser can be surprisingly effective.

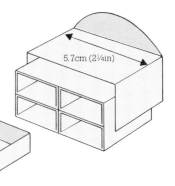

5.7cm (2¼in)

Shelves

There are six shelves, three on each side of the fireplace.
1. Cut six shelves from a piece of 3mm (⅛in) balsa wood 7.7cm (3in) wide and 2.5cm (1in) deep and some small triangular brackets to support them.
2. Paint white and with multipurpose glue fix in place, the middle two each side are level with the mantle shelf, the bottom and top shelves, 3.5cm (1⅜in) above and below.

Single bed

This is made from about eight flat ice lolly sticks.
1. Cut a rectangle from 3-ply to measure 14 x 7.6cm (5½ x 3in). Glue a 1cm square balsa wood frame underneath flush with the edges.

Single bed
Three-ply base on a balsa wood frame with ice lolly stick supports.

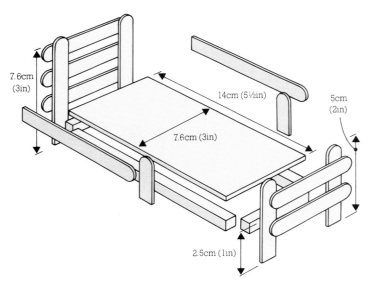

7.6cm (3in)

14cm (5½in)

7.6cm (3in)

5cm (2in)

2.5cm (1in)

2. Place two lolly sticks 7.6cm (3in) each with rounded ends at the top of the bed so there is 2.5cm (1in) of leg below and the remainder above. Repeat at the foot of the bed with shorter sticks of 5cm (2in). Glue into place.
3. Place cross members on bedhead and foot and fix in place. Round both ends on these. Varnish finished bed.

Lavatory seat

Cut this to the size on the diagram from 3-ply with a jig or fret saw. The projecting flange at the end of it is for a panel pin to go through.

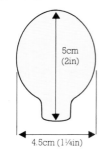

5cm (2in)

4.5cm (1¼in)

The drawing room and bedrooms can be enhanced with small ornaments made from self-hardening clay, also used as the basic bathroom material.

Clay furniture

The material used is nylon reinforced clay, which has the advantage of hardening and keeping its form without being fired. It can be glued when wet and painted either with emulsion, undercoat or gloss paints.

Bathroom

1. Basin Following the measurements on the drawings use the basic modelling method, the pinch pot, where you roll a ball of clay in the palms and push the thumb into it to form a hole. This is then enlarged with the gentle pressure of thumb and forefinger. The basin is just a thumb pot with a flat side.
2. The lavatory is made the same way by pinching it in. Make the waste pipe and pinhole lugs by adding lumps of clay. Smooth, leave to dry, then paint.
3. The pedestal is a roll of clay, drawn out, waisted and one side made flat to fit the wall.

Make a tap from a bent section of coathanger wire and the tap handles with brass split pin heads. When all units are dry, fix with multipurpose glue to the wall.
4. The bath is a mixture of wood and clay. Make a plywood box 15.5 x 7 x 6cm (6 x 2¾ x 2¼in) and brush the inside with multipurpose glue. Line with clay and smooth, making the plug and overflow holes with a nail impression. Put a press stud over the plug hole. The taps and handles are made as for the basin. Paint with white gloss inside and tile the sides and ends with sections cut to size from semi-rigid foam plastic.

Clay ornaments

1. The two jardinières are simply a roll of clay with a small thumb pot on top and scored with decorative lines. Dry and paint with emulsion. Make the plants from green plastic cut into pointed strips and stuck into multipurpose

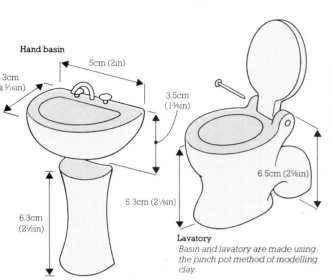

Hand basin

3cm (³⁄₁₆in)

5cm (2in)

3.5cm (1⅜in)

6.3cm (2½in)

5.3cm (2⅛in)

6.5cm (2⅝in)

Lavatory
Basin and lavatory are made using the pinch pot method of modelling clay.

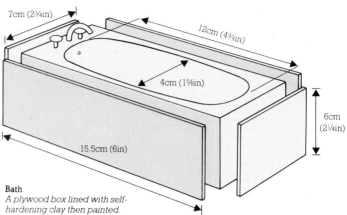

7cm (2¾in)

12cm (4¾in)

4cm (1⅝in)

6cm (2¼in)

15.5cm (6in)

Bath
A plywood box lined with self-hardening clay then painted.

glue mixed with earth or sand.
2. The two dog ornaments are made from a ball of clay the size of a marble. Model two the same and paint the spots on with a panel pin head.
3. Picture Glue a thin sausage of clay around the edge of a picture or photo, then with a match stick, press a pattern. When dry, paint with gold lacquer which will give a gilt frame effect.
4. The mini doll's house. Start with a ball of clay and model a house 5cm (2in) high. Use a kitchen knife to sharpen it up. Make the windows with an end section of wood into which is cut a 'cross' with a saw cut. This will give the window frame pattern when pushed into the clay. Any bits added must be fixed on with multipurpose glue.

Wooden ornaments
The pine kitchen clock, drawing room clock, broom, T.V. and stereo, are all small objects which can be made from the wood left over after

the kitchen units have been made.
1. Pine clock and drawing room clock The pine clock is a hexagonal piece of pine, each side measuring 25mm (1in) and glued onto a 2.3cm (⅞in) square block of pine. The curved-top clock is cut with a fret saw from a 1cm (⅜in) thick block of pine and is 4cm (1½in) wide. Sand after sawing. Cut two clock faces out of a catalogue or magazine, glue them on and then varnish. To make the pendulum for the kitchen clock stick a brass split pin on the front.
2. T.V. and stereo Simply cut two blocks of wood 1cm (⅜in) thick and 4cm (1½in) wide for the T.V., 7cm (2¾in) wide for the stereo. Sand and stain with wood stain. Now cut out a picture of a T.V. and stereo, stick in position and varnish.
3. Broom Cut the head off a toothbrush and round at the ends. Drill a hole in the centre and glue in a 11.5cm (4½in) lolly stick and paint.

MATERIALS

For the oven, hob and sink units:
1 piece of square deal 19cm (7½in) long and 4.5cm (1¾in) square
2 pieces of square deal 17cm (6¾in) long and 4.5cm (1¾in) square
4 buttons without holes
3 silver press studs for sink, basin and bath plug holes
self-hardening (nylon reinforced) clay
aluminium primer
a sheet of thin card
a picture of food cooking from a catalogue
small off-cut piece of thick perspex
undercoat and household gloss paints and gold lacquer paint
varnish, plasticine, multipurpose glue
For the other furniture:
1 sheet 3-ply plywood for the wooden furniture
1 piece of oil cloth 3.5cm (1⅜in) in diameter
pictures of T.V. and stereo, one photo
head of a toothbrush and a lollipop stick for the brush
1 piece 7.7cm x 2.5cm x 3mm (3 x 1 x ⅛in) balsa wood for shelves
1 piece 3-ply plywood 14 x 7.7cm (5½ x 3in) for the bath frame
4 matchboxes, silver paper and card for the matchbox dresser
9 brass split pins for drawer knobs, pendulum and taps
flat lolly sticks for the bed
wood glue
panel pin for lavatory
small piece coathanger wire
semi-rigid foam plastic

TOOLS

Wood chisel, tenon saw, fret saw, cross-cut saw, jigsaw, scissors, small household paint brush, sandpaper, craft knife.

PROJECT **35**

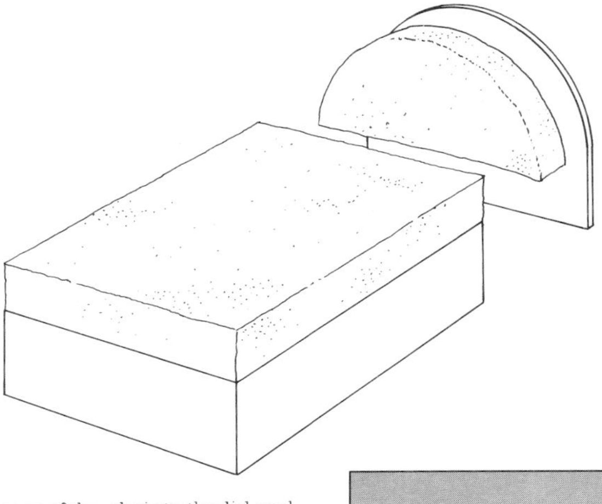

Making the soft furnishings

These are simple to make and include rugs, bed covers, chair covers and curtains. You will be able to ransack your sewing box for most of the materials.

Rugs

For the drawing room, bathroom and bedrooms.
1. Cut a piece of felt 8 x 15cm (3⅛ x 5⅞in) and a piece of iron-on interfacing the same size.
2. Now cut 100 strands of string 3.5cm (1⅜in) long.
3. Place 50 strands at each end of the felt and iron the interfacing on so the strands are sandwiched between felt and interfacing.

Knitted rug

1. Cast on 20 stitches in the yarn of your choice, knit 48 rows in plain stitch and cast off.
2. To make a fringe, cut 24 pieces of yarn into 5cm (2in) lengths. Thread one strand through each stitch along the short sides of the rug and make a knot. Trim the fringe.

Crochet rug

If you can crochet, a round or oval rug looks very good in the bedroom or in front of the fireplace.
1. Round rug For this, make six chains, gather them together, then half-crochet round in a circle until you arrive at the size you want. Change the yarn for the finishing row to give an edging.
2. Oval rug Start with 10 chains and work two rows of crochet, then half-crochet round in the same way until your width is adequate.

Double bed

1. Use a cardboard box or a lid 15½ x 10½cm (6⅛ x 4⅛in).
2. Cut a piece of wadding to fit the box or lid, then glue this on.

3. Now, cut a piece of fabric to fit over the lid and wadding and glue on.
4. Make the back of the bed in the same way as the armchair back but with a diameter of 9cm (3½in).

Duvet

1. Cut two pieces of fabric 13½cm (5¼in) long and 15cm (6in) wide, stitch round three sides with a simple running stitch, then turn to the right side and press.
2. Cut a piece of wadding 5mm (¼in) smaller all round than the fabric, put this inside for filling and stitch the open end with an overcasting stitch.
3. With a running stitch, attach a piece of ribbon or lace round the edges of the duvet as a trim.

Pillow

Cut out two pieces of fabric 11 x 6cm (4⅜ x 2⅜in) and make in the same way as the duvet. Scatter cushions can be made this way too, but vary the sizes.

Single bed

Cut enough fabric and wadding for a mattress, pillow and duvet. Make in the same way as the double bed but leave the lace trim off the duvet because the single bed has side supports.

Armchairs

These are best made with a small print or plain fabric. You will need a box with a lid 7cm (2¾in) wide, 6cm (2⅜ in) deep and 2½cm (1in) high. All the pieces are glued together using a glue stick.
1. Make a pattern from the diagram and cut out all the fabric pieces.
2. Cut a piece of wadding to fit the lid and glue on, then stick the two pieces of fabric for the

seat of the chair to the lid and base of the box. Put the box together to form the base of the chair.
3. To make the back of the chair, cut a piece of cardboard 10mm (⅜in) smaller than the back fabric all round, and a piece of wadding to fit the top half of the cardboard. Glue together. Now, put the back fabric right sides together and stitch, leaving the bottom half open. Turn to the right side and press. Put the card with the wadding on inside the fabric, turn up the fabric at the bottom end to form a neat edge, and glue to close. Glue the back of the chair to the seat, stitch down each side for strength and also along the bottom of the chair.
4. To make the armrests, put wrong sides together and stitch along the dotted line as shown in the diagram, leaving the bottom open. Turn to the right side of the fabric, fill with cotton wool and stitch to the chair.
5. To make the frill, hem the bottom of the length of fabric cut for this purpose. Fold over the fabric at the top and thread a gathering stitch through. Now gather the frill to fit around the seat of the chair, and stitch on.

Make a further chair to match. If a settee is required, make this twice as wide as the armchair.

Curtains

The easiest way to make

curtains for a doll's house is to use felt because it does not require stitching. If you use a different fabric, choose a small print to fit the scale of the doll's house. Thin cotton crochet curtains make a good alternative too, as they have a miniature quality.

Master bedroom

Cut four pieces of fabric 22 x 9cm (8⅝ x 3½in). Stitch the sides either by hand or machine. Now, make a hem at the top and bottom, leaving the top edges open for the curtain rail (a lollipop stick or dowel) to go through.

Small bedroom

Cut a piece of felt 15 x 4½cm (5⅞ x 1¾in) and round off the

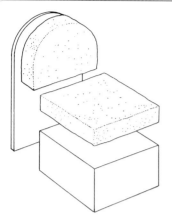

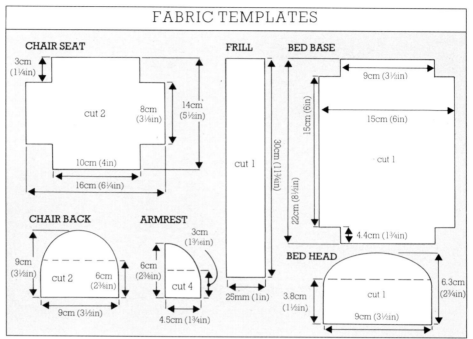

FABRIC TEMPLATES

CHAIR SEAT

3cm (1¼in)

cut 2

8cm (3⅛in)

14cm (5½in)

10cm (4in)

16cm (6¼in)

FRILL

cut 1

30cm (11¾in)

25mm (1in)

BED BASE

9cm (3½in)

15cm (6in)

15cm (6in)

cut 1

22cm (8½in)

4.4cm (1¾in)

CHAIR BACK

9cm (3½in)

cut 2

6cm (2⅜in)

9cm (3½in)

ARMREST

3cm (1³⁄₁₆in)

6cm (2⅜in)

cut 4

4.5cm (1¾in)

BED HEAD

3.8cm (1½in)

cut 1

9cm (3½in)

6.3cm (2¾in)

Drawing room
Make these as for the master bedroom curtains, only a little shorter if you wish.

Kitchen
These are crochet curtains.
1. Make 28 chains.
2. Crochet into the fourth chain from the hook.
3. Work one treble, one chain, miss one chain, into next chain work one treble, one chain, repeat to end. Turn.
4. If you are good at crochet work you can finish off the curtain with a picot edging.
5. Make the second curtain.

Landing
These are crochet curtains.
1. Make 26 chains.
2. Use the same pattern as the kitchen curtains, but crochet 15 rows. Make two curtains.
3. Thread a lollipop stick (or dowel) through the holes at the top of the curtain.

Fitting the curtains
You will need seven pieces of dowel or seven lollipop sticks cut to 11cm (4⅜in) in length and 14 closed eyes (screw attachments with looped ends used to hang net curtains).
1. Put one eye on either side of each window.
2. Thread the lollipop stick or dowel through the top of the curtains and through the eyes.
3. Cut pieces of lace or ribbon to match the colour of the curtains and tie each curtain to the side, then pin down with a matching coloured drawing pin.

corners. Punch eight holes across the top with a paper punch and thread a lollipop stick (or dowel) through.

MATERIALS

For the floor coverings:
1   piece felt 8 x 15cm (3⅛ x 5⅞in)
1   piece iron-on interfacing the same size
    balls of string and yarn
    For the double bed and single bed:
    cardboard box or a lid 15.5 x 10.5cm (6⅛ x 4⅛in)
    glue stick
    wadding
    fabric with a small print – remnants are good
    cotton to match bed fabric
    ribbon or lace
    For the armchair:
    fabric with a small print
    box with a lid measuring 7cm (2¾in) wide, 6cm (2⅜in) deep and 2.5cm (1in) high
    cardboard
    cottonwool
    For the curtains:
    felt or fabric with a small print
7   pieces dowel or 7 lollipop sticks 11cm (4⅜in) long
14   closed eyes

TOOLS

Knitting needles, scissors, crochet hook, paper punch, iron.

DOLL'S HOUSE
FAMILY

Every doll's house needs a family to bring it alive. This one has the great advantage of being both flexible and child-proof. Because they are made out of pipe cleaners, they can be bent whichever way you like to look relaxed in their home, whether sitting in the kitchen, lying in bed or watching the television from an armchair.

The family

The family should be made to the same scale as the doll's house, 1:12 (25mm to 30cm or 1in to 1ft), so the adults will be about 14cm (5½in) high. The size of an adult's head goes seven times into its length.

You will need six 15.2cm (6in) pipe cleaners for each figure and some all-purpose clear adhesive. The heads and feet, made with wooden beads and wood should be more child-proof than clay.

1. Look closely at the instruction layout and make the body armature as shown. Use one pipe cleaner for the head and shoulders, two for the legs, one for the hips and upper leg and two for the arms, crossed over to brace the chest.

2. Bind strips of stretch nylon cut from a pair of tights around the body frame for bulk.

3. To make the head, use a 20mm (¾in) bead for the adults, and a 15mm (⅝in) bead for the children. Glue the end of the head pipe cleaner into the bead hole. Paint the face with enamels in a simple Dutch doll style.

4. Cut two hand-shaped pieces of felt for each hand and glue on either side of the pipe cleaner, sewing to the binding at the wrist.

5. For shoes, drill small holes into a piece of dowel. Then with a fret saw, cut small sections on the slant, about 20mm (¾in) long for the

adults, 15mm (⅝in) long for the children. Now, shape with a blade and sand. Paint with enamels.

6. Glue the end of the leg pipe cleaner into the shoe hole.

Clothes for the family

These are all (with the exception of the boy's crocheted jacket) made by making paper templates to the dimensions shown on the diagram and cutting from dress fabric with a small print, or felt.

Dress

1. Fold the fabric right sides together, stitch sides and

sleeves, then make a hem.

2. Turn to right side and put the dress on the doll then hem the sleeves with a piece of lace.

3. Gather up the sleeves and stitch to the doll. Do the same with the neck then stitch a piece of lace round the neck.

4. To make the belt, fold the fabric in half lengthwise with wrong sides together. Turn in the raw ends and topstitch close to the edge.

5. The underskirt is made from a piece of broderie anglaise 15 x 7cm (6 x 2¾in). Fold in half and stitch the side, then hem the top and bottom. Thread a piece of elastic through the top

hem and stitch a piece of lace to the bottom hem.

The girl's dress is cut to half size and made the same way.

Trousers

1. Cut two pieces of felt, fold each piece with right sides together and stitch each leg.

2. Turn to the right side and sew the centre back and front seams. Put the trousers on the doll and stitch them to the waist.

Felt jacket

Enlarge the boy's jacket template to make this.

1. Fold in half, cut a small hole

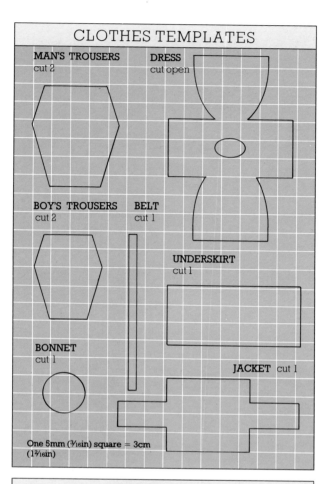

CLOTHES TEMPLATES

MAN'S TROUSERS
cut 2

DRESS
cut open

BOY'S TROUSERS
cut 2

BELT
cut 1

UNDERSKIRT
cut 1

BONNET
cut 1

JACKET cut 1

One 5mm (³/₁₆in) square = 3cm
(1³/₁₆in)

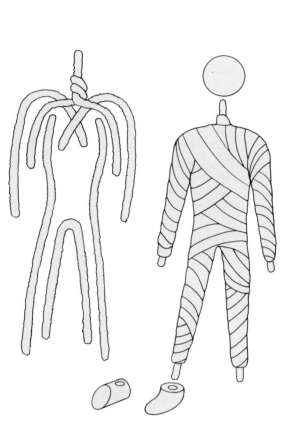

Drill small holes into dowel and cut on the slant.

for the head then stitch sides and sleeves with a simple running stitch.

2. Cut two small pieces of fabric to fit around the bottom sleeves as cuffs. Glue onto the sleeves.

3. Put the jacket on the doll. Cut a small piece of fabric to encircle the neck as a collar and glue onto the jacket.

4. Glue the front opening.

Crocheted jacket

1. Make 12 chains, work six rows of half trebles. Now make nine chains either side for sleeves and work three rows of half trebles. Crochet to the middle. Now crochet front left three rows of half trebles.

2. Decrease nine stitches, so you are left with six stitches. Work six rows of half trebles.

3. Do right side as left. Fold in half. Stitch sides and sleeves together. Turn to right side and put the jacket on the boy. Stitch the front to the doll. For the collar, cut a piece of felt to match the trousers and stitch round the neck.

Bonnet

1. Cut out a circle of fabric 6.3cm (2½in)in diameter. Fold in half, wrong sides together and stitch a piece of ric-rac along the folded edge.

2. Turn bonnet edges in and sew a tiny tacking stitch around the edge, then gather.

MATERIALS

packet pipe cleaners
all-purpose clear adhesive
pair used tights
20mm (¾in) beads for adult heads
15mm (⅝in) beads for children's heads
dowel 30cm (12in) long for shoes
enamel paints or felt-tip pens for painting faces
offcut dress fabric and felt for clothes
15cm (6in) piece of elastic
15cm (6in) piece of lace
15 x 7cm (6 x 2¼in) piece of broderie anglaise
ball of yarn
6.3cm (2½in) piece of ric-rac
cotton to match fabrics used

TOOLS

Hand or power drill, fret saw, a very fine paint brush, craft knife, scissors, crochet hook, needle.

GLOSSARY

Acrylic paint A quick-drying water-based paint, available in a wide range of colours. It is ideal for papier mâché and wood.

Actual size Term referring to the size of wood that has been planed and prepared. Also known as *finished size*.

Awl See *bradawl*

Backstitch Used for strong, handsewn seams.

Balsa The model maker's wood – it is light and can be cut and shaped easily with a craft knife. Joints are made by using balsa cement.

Basting See *tacking*

Batting See *wadding*.

Bias Any diagonal line in relation to the warp and weft threads of a fabric. A true bias is made by folding the selvage at right angles across the fabric.

Bias strip Used for binding raw edges of fabric. The strip will fold over a curved edge smoothly without twisting or pulling.

Blockboard Manufactured sheet material made from rectangular strips of softwood glued together side by side and sandwiched between single or double veneers of wood.

Bracing Technique used to hold splaying legs in close to a soft toy body. Ladder stitch is worked on the surface. Alternatively an optional dart can be made in the wrong side when seaming the skin.

Bradawl Used for making starting (pilot) holes for screws before using a screwdriver. Large screws will need a drilled hole. See *pilot hole*.

Butt joint A simple wooden joint made by nailing or screwing the end of one piece of wood to another.

Buttonhole stitch Embroidered stitch with a rope edge appearance.

Calico A lightweight, plain weave cotton fabric sometimes printed with small floral patterns. A natural colour is used for making doll's bodies.

Chipboard Manufactured board constructed from small wood chips which have been coated with resin and compressed together under high pressure and heat.

Compasses Instrument for drawing circles.

Control Apparatus to which strings of a marionette are attached. The string puppet is manipulated by operating the control.

Coping saw A versatile saw for cutting curves and irregular shapes. Blades are narrow and set with teeth facing the handle. They are adjustable, which makes cutting easier.

Countersink The action of shaping the top of a screwhole so that the head of a flathead screw lies flush with the surface of the wood.

Crown joint Style of jointing soft toys for use with hardboard discs and cotter pins.

Darts Darts are used in sewing to provide fullness at strategic points. They can be curved, straight, single or double pointed.

Dowel or dowelling A hardwood moulding, machined to a round section.

Dowel joint Joint made between two pieces of wood by using short lengths of dowel as pins which are tapped and glued in place.

Dressmaker's graph paper Large sheets of paper covered with a 5cm (2in) grid.

Drill stand Will ensure accuracy for any drilling job and also allow you to drill to predetermined depths by means of fitted stops. Dowelling holes will also be true and square.

Embroidery thread Six-stranded cotton thread used to embroider facial features on the soft toys.

Enamel paint A hard-wearing paint with a high gloss finish, available in small quantities.

Epoxy adhesive A very strong two-part adhesive consisting of a resin and hardener which are mixed in equal parts. The resulting chemical reaction creates a strong, waterproof, durable bond which is set after about 48 hours.

Felt A fabric produced by matting short fibres. Felt does not fray but will tear when damp, consequently it is not advisable to wash felt toys.

Finished size Most wood is sold already planed smooth from nominal size. Thus 25 x 25mm (1 x 1in) nominal size will measure about 22 x 22mm (⅞ x ⅞in) when planed to finished or actual size. Ask for finished size to make the projects in the book.

Forceps Long handled tweezers used to reach narrow extremities inside soft toy skins which would be otherwise difficult to stuff.

Fretsaw This saw has a greater range of cut and more manoeuvrability than a coping saw. It is used for wood, particularly plywood up to about 6mm (¼in) thick and cuts on the downward stroke.

Glasspaper Abrasive material that comes in coarse, medium and fine grades. Always sand the wood in the direction of the grain, and not against it.

Gloss paint Oil based paint used on wooden toys. Paints must be lead-free to meet safety requirements.

Grain The lay of the wood fibres, which is along the length.

Grain line Soft toy patterns are marked with an arrow. The line should run parallel to the selvage which shows the direction of the lengthways grain, or warp, of the fabric.

Halving joint Half the depth of each corresponding piece of wood is removed. Sawn edges are smoothed with a chisel then fixed together with glue and woodscrews.

Hardboard Manufactured board constructed from softwood pulp which has been compressed under high pressure.

Hardwood Comes from deciduous trees such as oak, elm, poplar, mahogany and birch. Generally harder to work than softwood, but it is stronger and longer lasting.

Hemming Handsewn finish to a single edge of fabric.

Holesaw A drill attachment that is a combination of a centre pilot bit and a ring-shaped saw for cutting large diameter holes through wood. Useful for making wheels.

Housing joint Strong joint where end of a cross piece is recessed into the side of an upright. A stopped housing joint is used where appearance is important because the overlap conceals the cut-out.

Interfacing A thin layer of fabric which is sewn or fused to a soft toy skin to add strength.

Invisible thread Nylon thread for making whiskers on soft toys.

Ladder stitch Used for closing openings, attaching parts such as tails and for bracing limbs. It should be worked with a strong thread.

Latex adhesive A natural rubber glue used for bonding fabrics, paper and porous materials. It is white and dries to a translucent film. There is some yellowing with age.

Machine stitches Straight stitch is used for sewing seams, a zig-zag stitch for attaching elastic direct to fabric removing the need for a casing.

Marionette A string puppet.

Measurements Imperial and metric measurements are given. Do not mix them.

Multipurpose glue See *polyvinyl acetate*

Muslin Loose woven cotton fabric similar in appearance to gauze.

Nap The soft, down-like surface of a fabric that is produced by brushing the surface. It has come to describe all fabrics which must be cut with the pattern pieces facing in the same direction.

Needle modelling A soft sculpture technique that provides shaping to a stuffed, fabric object by the placement of stitches which are then pulled tight and fastened off.

Nominal size The size of wood before being planed down. Also referred to as rough sawn.

Optional darts Preparation of the toy skin in place of external bracing stitches.

Overcasting A tacking stitch used to hold two or more fur fabric pieces together prior to seaming.

Padsaw The only saw able to cut a hole in the middle of a large panel. The saw bends easily and is difficult to control.

Panel saw Saw for cross-cutting (across the grain) and ripsawing (along the grain).

Papier mâché Made by soaking strips of paper in wallpaper paste and pressing into a shape. It dries to form a tough, durable material.

Pile In soft toys, a fur-like fabric.

Pilot hole A small starting hole for screws made with a bradawl or a drill. The pilot hole should be slightly smaller than the screw gauge so that the threads of the screw will bite into the wood.

Plasticine Modelling material that may be used over and over again.

Playboard The shelf on which glove puppets perform in a puppet booth.

Plywood Manufactured board constructed from an uneven number of thin layers or veneers which are bonded face to face, with the grain running in alternate directions.

Polyester fibre Good quality, white stuffing material.

Polyurethane varnish Synthetic varnish used to give a clear gloss finish to toys painted with water-based paint. It can also be used directly on unpainted wood to enhance and protect the natural features of the wood.

Polyvinyl acetate (PVA) Strong, multipurpose glue that will bond paper, wood and hardboard. Setting time is about one hour and some projects may need to be clamped while the glue is setting. Remove excess glue.

Power saws 1. Circular saw, for all basic cutting. **2.** Jigsaw, used primarily for cutting curves. The fine blade allows quite intricate work.

Prepared wood See *finished size*.

Primer Used to seal sawn wood preparatory to painting. White emulsion paint is the most popular.

Proscenium Part of puppet theatre where the puppets appear and perform.

Quick unpickit A small tool used for cutting out seams and threads.

Release agent Substance, such as petroleum jelly, that prevents moulding materials from sticking together.

Ric-rac A zig-zag braid used for decorating clothes.

Running stitch A long running stitch is used for tacking. A short running stitch can be used for a seam where strength is not important.

Safety eyes Two-part component consisting of a plastic eye and a metal washer. Once fixed in place they cannot be pulled out of a toy by a child.

Satin stitch Straight stitches worked close together to fill a shape.

Seam allowance A seam allowance of 6mm (¼in) is allowed for on all fabric pattern pieces except for felt pieces which have an allowance of 3mm (⅛in) (and doll's house projects).

Seams The joining of two or more pieces of fabric sewn by machine using a straight stitch or by hand, using backstitch.

Self-hardening clay Modelling material that sets hard on exposure to air. It does not need to be fired in a kiln.

Selvage Edge of a woven cloth.

Slip A mixture of clay and water that is used as an adhesive for joints in clay. It is applied by brush.

Softwood From cone-bearing trees with needle-like leaves such as pine, fir and spruce. It is generally lighter and easier to work than hardwood.

Stab stitch Similar in appearance to a small running stitch, traditionally used on felt.

Standard size See *nominal size*.

Starter hole Hole drilled inside the outline of a shape that is to be cut out of a board or a piece of wood. The blade of a coping saw can then be inserted through the hole and the blade reattached to the saw.

Stem stitch An embroidered outline stitch ideal for facial features.

Strong thread Used for closing stuffing openings and attaching any part of a soft toy to the body. Also used for stringing puppets. Examples are button thread, crochet cotton and upholstery thread.

Tacking A temporary stitch used to hold fabric edges together ready for seaming.

Tenon saw A saw used for all fine cutting and jointing. It is a rigid saw with a strongly braced back to the blade.

Topcoat The final application of a paint or varnish.

Try square Used for working out straight lines and right-angles on wood.

Undercoat Layer of paint applied after the primer has dried. It provides a good base for the top coat. Use the correct primer for the type of paint used.

Vinyl face mask A dollmaking accessory that may be purchased from craft shops and larger handicraft departments.

Wadding Sheet padding used as stuffing in quilting.

Wallpaper paste A proprietary cellulose paste used for bonding layers of newspaper together to make papier mâché.

Warp 1. A twist in wooden boards or sheets that is due to internal or surface tensions. **2.** Fabric threads that lie parallel to the selvage of the cloth.

Winder key A hardboard, plywood or card frame that holds twisted puppet strings in order while puppet is being stored.

Zig-zag stitch A machine stitch used for neatening seams and attaching elastic.

INDEX

Acknowledgements

The authors and publisher would like to thank the following
people and organizations for their kind help in the production
of this book:

Jane, Sam, Katie and Amber Wood; Stanley Tools Ltd,
Sheffield; and the students of the Thamesside Adult Education
Institute and the Tonbridge Adult Education Centre who tried
out many of the soft toys.